The Spanish Frustration

The Spanish Frustration

How a Ruinous Empire Thwarted the Nation-State

Josep M. Colomer

ANTHEM PRESS

Anthem Press
An imprint of Wimbledon Publishing Company
www.anthempress.com

This edition first published in UK and USA 2020
by ANTHEM PRESS
75–76 Blackfriars Road, London SE1 8HA, UK
or PO Box 9779, London SW19 7ZG, UK
and
244 Madison Ave #116, New York, NY 10016, USA

First published in the UK and USA by Anthem Press 2019

British Library Cataloguing-in-Publication Data
A catalogue record for this book is available from the British Library.

Library of Congress Cataloging-in-Publication Data
Library of Congress Control Number: 2020930704

ISBN-13: 978-1-78527-393-3 (Pbk)
ISBN-10: 1-78527-393-0 (Pbk)

This title is also available as an e-book.

COMMENTS ON THE
SPANISH EDITION

"The book is extraordinarily good, even the social criticism, in some ways more important than the politics. Altogether a splendid analysis. The intellectually sturdiest book on Spain some time."

Stanley G. Payne, Professor of History,
University of Wisconsin, USA

"One of the most severe books on Spain that have been published in recent years. *The Spanish Frustration* reviews more than five centuries of Spanish history with an analysis without concessions for optimism. It makes the reader regret having been born into the Peninsula."

El País, Madrid

"Colomer provides a carefully selected empirical information that perfectly illustrates his arguments, and his clear and austere prose, characteristic of all his texts, manuals, monographs and press articles, converts reading into a placid entertainment. He does not resort to his discourse to essences and stereotyped national characters, but he wields serious data and arguments. That's why his book is so stimulating."

Oscar R. Buznego, Professor of Political Science,
University of Oviedo, Spain

PRAISE FOR OTHER BOOKS
BY THE AUTHOR

The Science of Politics

"I don't think that anyone has tried to write something like this before. If one wants to give an overview of political science, then this is about the only book there is!" —James A. Robinson, Harvard University, USA

The European Empire

"Erudite and scholarly, yet accessible and elegantly written. The argument is innovative, yet confident and convincing." —Helen Margetts, Oxford University, UK

How Global Institutions Rule the World

"A thoughtful and thought-provoking book." —Martin Wolf, *Financial Times*

Great Empires, Small Nations

"An original and persuasive book." —Jan Zielonka, Oxford University
"I expect this book to be widely read and greatly admired." —Sidney Weintraub, Center for Strategic and International Studies, USA

Handbook of Electoral System Choice

"A new and highly original theory of electoral change which lays the groundwork for a radical revision of what has become the common wisdom." —Bernard Grofman, University of California, Irvine, USA

CONTENTS

PREFACE

This is an essay of interpretation of several important aspects of present-day Spain in light of its modern history as well as an interpretation of past stories in light of present-day Spain. Old troubles with remote origins persist in current Spain, including huge public debts, extensive corruption, widespread unlawfulness, oligarchical politics, territorial splits and permanent protests and riots. The basic argument in this book is that, in the long term, Spain missed the opportunity to become a consolidated modern nation-state because it was entangled in imperial adventures for several centuries instead of building solid domestic bases for further endeavors. In short, a ruinous empire made a weak state, which built an incomplete nation, which sustains a minority democracy.

The broad overview presented here includes summaries of several original researches by the author and new arguments and elaborations. I have also reviewed all the publications that I thought deserved to be reviewed and quote a selection of supporting observations, narratives or postulates from historians, political scientists, economists, sociologists and literary authors. The greatest intellectual debt, as the reader will observe, is with the always remembered Juan J. Linz, for his knowledge, analysis and insight as well as for the extraordinary bibliographic funds he donated to Georgetown University when I was holding the Prince of Asturias Spanish Chair in that institution. I hope some of my interpretations can motivate revisions of some conventional interpretations, and I wish they may become hypotheses for further research.

I am grateful to Tej P. S. Sood and the editorial team at Anthem Press, to the Spanish editors Jorge Herralde and Silvia Sesé, for support, sources, criticisms or suggestions to Laia Balcells, Ashley Beale, Lluís Bassets, John Carlin, Albert Carreras, Ángel Gil-Ordóñez, Blanca Heredia, Daniel Innerarity, Henry Kamen, Francisco LaRubia-Prado, César Molinas, J. J. Moreso, Leandro Prados de la Escosura, Cristina Sanz, Cynthia Soliman, Rocío De Terán, Joan Maria Thomàs, Enric Ucelay Da-Cal and Jenna Van Stelton, and for public comments on the Spanish edition to Jordi Amat, Óscar R. Buznego, Daniel Fernández, Enrique Gil-Calvo, Luis G. Esteban Manrique, César Martinelli, Javier Nogueira, Stanley G. Payne and the political scientists club *Piedras de papel*. Of course, all responsibility is mine.

Josep M. Colomer

INTRODUCTION: WHEN DID SPAIN SCREW UP?

There has never been anything solid,
there has never been anything stable here.
Spain cannot be a great country because there is no continuity.
The Spaniards survive thanks to a tradition of amnesia,
of forgetting, of living the moment. Carpe diem.

Ian Gibson, writer and Hispanist, 2017[1]

My impression is that we do not know what we want to do with Spain.
It is difficult to identify a project for Spain.
Is there a project for Spain that is truly exciting for the whole of the Spaniards and
attractive to the Catalans as a whole, whether or not they are separatists?
Or is Spain really absent from herself?

Felipe González, former prime minister, 2018[2]

When did Spain screw up? Was it when the recent real estate and banking bubbles exploded? It must have been before, because the impression is that what returned afterward was the eternal Spain, the one of legal and moral laxness, the picaresque and arrogance of both the rulers and the ruled. Was it, thus, when the Civil War and Franco destroyed so many social nets and norms? Or when Primo de Rivera terminated an evolution toward a British-style parliamentary monarchy and provoked the subsequent polarization? Or even before? Perhaps much before.

The initial question is inspired by the obsession of a character of novelist Mario Vargas Llosa: "When did Peru screw up?" Some time ago, I was introduced to a Peruvian politician, Julio Guzmán, who had been controversially eliminated as a candidate for a recent presidential election. After listening to his radical criticism of the country's rulers, I asked him what his answer to that question was. Without hesitation, he said, "In 1513." That is, at the beginning of the conquest by the Spaniards that would destroy the

Inca civilization and impose a centralizing and unproductive system from which the Peruvians have never just recovered (I synthesize, more or less, his words). My response was as follows: "It may be. In fact, I think Spain also screwed up in 1492." The empire made Spain, and the failure and dissolution of the empire unmade Spain.

The Spanish imperial adventure was a disaster for the colonized, the colonists and the people remaining in Spain, from which the country has never completely recuperated. The Spanish monarchy first divided its attention itself between the European Empire, including the Holy Roman and German Empire for a while, and the new American Empire—as it continues faltering now between the European Union and Hispanic America—and squandered its scarce resources on a huge and ruinous double enterprise. Historians have discussed the cost of the empire and the economic consequences of its loss for Spain but much less the opportunity cost of the empire itself: what could have been done if the imperial adventures had not been undertaken so early, so ruthlessly and for so long? It is generally recognized that the silver and gold from America were not major sources of productive investment but rather of inflation, debt and waste. But the worst part was not the meager results themselves but the missed occasion to create an efficient administration of an effective state as well as an integrative culture within the peninsula, just as other European countries were beginning to do at the time.

Spain was born with the empire and broke with it. In 1898, when the Spaniards noticed that there were no colonies left in America, where the United States began to dominate, and that the Pyrenees had left the peninsula outside of Europe, some people realized that they had lost the best opportunities to start building a great modern national state. Then came the intellectual generation of depression and anguish for what could have been and was not. Also, Catalan and Basque movements began the alternative search for nations and states of their own. The desperate counterreaction, rather than nationalist, intended to return to "Through Empire toward God."

Compare the historical experience of the British Empire. In England, first they got rid of the pope, then the Crown was subordinated to the Parliament, a successful industrial and urbanization revolution developed and later the parliamentarians were subject to popular election with broad suffrage. Only then, with a solid and consistent economy and a solid national state, was the British Empire able to expand and consolidate. The previous British imperial conquests in America, parallel to the Spanish ones, did not last long. But those initiated in the nineteenth century left a much more positive legacy and still remain, in a way, with the Commonwealth (up to a point to make many Britons believe that they can survive with it outside the European Empire!).

The premature Spanish Empire, in contrast, relied on weak financial, technical, organizational and military apparatuses, had to resort to the church, and to a large extent to abuses and violence, and disintegrated into a thousand pieces. In fact, the great powers of the world in the period of maximum Spanish expansion, during the sixteenth and seventeenth centuries, were the Ottoman, Persian, Indian and Chinese empires. By the time of what some European historians have called "the age of empire," the late nineteenth and the early twentieth centuries, the Spanish Empire was already dismantled. When, by mid-twentieth century, the United States and Western Europe set the bases of a new global order and culture, Spain was completely isolated. In Britain, as in France, an early state supported a late empire, while in Spain a premature empire deferred and jeopardized a modern state.

The most serious attempt to build a modern national state in Spain began as late as the late twentieth century. Since then, the number of public officers and the collection of taxes have multiplied. But unlike the favorable conditions that would have existed in the past, the project of a nation-state is currently hindered by the insertion in the European Union and in extensive international and global relations as well as by the centrifugal tendencies of territorial decentralization. A large part of the legacy of the imperial failure has been reproduced: an incompetent, corrupt and haughty political class that is not even able to form a majority government and a folkscape hesitating between apathy, cynicism and boisterousness.

As defined by the Oxford Dictionary, "frustration" is a feeling that results from being unable to achieve something. It implies, thus, that something was expected or tried to be achieved. Spain is not a "failed state" in the sense that is applied to some former colonies that lack even the minimal administrative structures and live in permanent violent conflict. For people living in extreme poverty and ignorance in isolated places, there is no "frustration," because nothing is really expected to change or to be achieved—the smarter people rather tend to emigrate in masse. The frustration of Spain derives, in contrast, from having pretended to be the largest and most powerful empire, an efficient modern state, a proud nation and an exemplary democracy and being far away from completely achieving any of these aims.

In the following pages, I argue about four successive, closely interrelated frustrations of Spain:

One: The Empire. A vast, ruthless and long-lasting imperial and colonial adventure over four continents ruined the country and the monarchy. As a consequence, the opportunity of shaping, instead, a modern, civilized Spanish society was lost. Certain imperial legacies still block the development of former colonies, while present-day Spain continues to carry some political and cultural burdens from the imperial past.

Two: The State. Largely as a consequence of the waste of resources in the imperial effort, Spain missed the occasion to build a civil administration, institutions of political representation and the rule of law when it was the right time to do so. For long periods, militarism and clericalism substituted a weak state. As a very latecomer to state building, the effort has resulted in a bubble state submitted to strong European and global constraints.

Three: The Nation. As states create nations, rather than the other way around, the weakness of the Spanish state made the building of a unified cultural nation a frustrated, incomplete endeavor. Catalonia, the Basque Country and other communities remain largely unassimilated to Castilian patterns. All across Spain, the degree of popular allegiance to the nation is about the lowest in Europe.

Four: The Democracy. Lacking the institutional and cultural bases of a solid nation-state, the democratic regime established since the late 1970s has been based on a political party oligarchy that tends to produce minority governments and exclusionary decisions. Centrifugal territorial autonomies also lessen support to the regime and threaten it with splits. People's dissatisfaction and disengagement with the way democracy works are widespread.

In short, a ruinous empire made a weak state, which built an incomplete nation, which sustains a minority democracy. That is, in a nutshell, the political history of modern Spain.

In an integrated Europe and a globalized world, national failure can be a new opportunity. Returning to lost historical moments to try to do now what was not done in due time is an impossible endeavor. Let us hope that a new generation of depressed and distressed intellectuals does not emerge. The potential advantage for the inhabitants of the Land of Rabbits may derive from the possibility to develop their initiative, personal and professional pursuits and innovative creativity with fewer legal, territorial and cultural restrictions than they would suffer under a compact national state. It will be a challenge during the next few decades.

Chapter 1

A RUINOUS EMPIRE

As Poor as Gambia
The American Silver in Genoa Is Buried
The Spanish Fury
A Catholic Monarchy
Elected Kings with the Name of Presidents
The British Alternative
Getting Rid of Ultramaria
Rebuilding Imperial Links

The building of the Spanish Empire, which would have fatal consequences for the frustration of a modern state and nation, was an improvised adventure, without any plan or blueprint.

We could say Spanish empires in plural because the enterprise included several disparate initiatives: First of all, the empire in the Iberian Peninsula, which was never completed because Portugal retained its own institutions separately. Second, the empire formed of scattered territories across Europe, including the Holy Roman and German Empire for a while, as well as Flanders, Milan and Naples, the Free County of Burgundy and other French lands. Third, a few enclaves in Africa, including the Canary Islands, and in Asia with the Philippines. And fourth, the huge North and South American and Caribbean Empire, which was a novelty in world history, as it was separated from Spain by some 70 days' sailing. It was the first sea-born empire.

The whole thing was the haphazard result of arranged marriages, unplanned infertilities, vicious divorces, premature deaths, arbitrary inheritances, assassinations and wars between royal rivals, violent conquests of unknown lands, accidents and mistakes, as can be seen in detail in Box 1.

In total, Spain would claim control over up to 14 million square kilometers of land—about 30 times the size of the territory in the Iberian Peninsula. Both Charles I and Philip II boasted about ruling "an empire on which the sun never sets." This resulted from counting the distances from Naples to California and to the Philippines as if they were located within a single unit.

Box 1
Without Idea or Plan

There were several attempts at uniting the kingdoms of Castile and Leon under a single crown during the period from the eleventh to the thirteenth centuries. They involved the assassination of two kings of Leon for the kings of Castile to be able to marry their bride and sister, respectively; two divisions of the temporarily united kingdoms between several heirs who fought a few wars among themselves; the assassination of a king of Castile by that of Leon; the break of a uniting marriage; and a more peaceful marriage between the King of Leon and the Queen of Castile, who formed the Crown of Castile, also including Galicia, and led to the reign of the Trastamara dynasty from mid-fourteenth century on.

In parallel, the formation of the Crown of Aragon involved the initial assassination of the heirs of two parts of the Kingdom of Navarre by their illegitimate brother in the eleventh century; the marriage of the Queen of Aragon with the Count of Barcelona and leader of the Principality of Catalonia in the following century; the annexation of the kingdoms of Valencia and Majorca, plus conquests in Sicily, Naples, Sardinia as well as other Mediterranean lands for short periods; and the disputed election to the Crown of Aragon of a member of the Trastamara Castilian dynasty in the early fifteenth century.

The grandson of the elected, Ferdinand, married his second cousin Isabella, who had won the inheritance of the Kingdom of Castile by war with his half brother's daughter, and they became the Catholic monarchs. They culminated the Christian Reconquest of the south of the peninsula against the last remnants of the Muslim Empire of Al-Andalus. Later on, widow Ferdinand used "theft, deceit, and bargain"—his words— to annex the Kingdom of Navarre in the north. Finally, the monarch's grandson, Charles I, became the first king of Spain in the early sixteenth century.

The union with Portugal, in contrast, was never consolidated in spite of numerous undeterred attempts. Isabella and Ferdinand married their elder daughter to an heir of Portugal, who died soon, and then to the new Portuguese king, who widowed only to marry her former wife's sister, and when the latter passed away, a niece of his former two wives. One of his daughters married her cousin Charles I of Spain; a Charles's sister married a new Portuguese king, and one of his daughters, a Portuguese prince. But only Charles's son, Philipp II, reached to win the crown of Portugal, not by marriage or inheritance but by war, and leave it to two successors. Yet after less than 60 years, the Iberian Union split and was followed by a succession of conflicts, alternative international alliances, colonial rivalries and wars. While each of the two crowns would engage in hazardous quests in remote and disperse lands, an internal union that would have been most clearly determined by geography was a definite failure.

There was nothing deterministic in the scope and shape of the boundless Spanish Empire. For instance, had Isabella the Catholic lost her war against her half niece, the queen of Castile may not have married a king of Aragon. The latter Crown, in turn, could have kept its independence if one more of the nine representatives who chose a new king at the Compromise of Caspe had voted for a Catalan candidate instead of a Trastamara one. Had Ferdinand the Catholic's son with his second wife not died as a baby, he would have inherited the Crown of Aragon, together with Navarre and the Italian dominions, and there would not have been a king of united Spain.

In turn, Charles might not have won the Holy Roman and German Empire and merged it with the Spanish Crown had his mother Joanna not been declared mad—current research agrees that she was just a nervous person who became the victim of a conspiracy. Had any of the multiple attempts to marry Spanish and Portuguese heirs been successful in producing appropriate offspring, the union of the Peninsula may have consolidated and perhaps the priority for further territorial expansion would have been southward, toward Africa, rather than westward. Or Columbus, after being rejected by potential investors in Portugal, France, England and Italy, might not have been financed either by the Queen of Castile for an adventure that turned out to be a mistake, as everybody knew at the time that the Earth shape was like a sphere and all scholars expected that the trip to the Indies would be longer if taken westward.

One of the empire slogans, as coined on some medals, was "Non Sufficit Orbis," which has been translated as "The World Is Not Enough." It probably did not mean, however, that some visionaries already foresaw the conquest of the space. Possibly, they rather meant that the known world was not enough. The rulers and scholars of the sixteenth century knew that they did not know all the world. The "Orbis Terrarum," that is, the world map, was incomplete;

it was not enough. So, the expanding enterprise needed to be continued endlessly.[1]

Like all empires, the Spanish Empire covered heterogeneous populations and developed asymmetric relations between different territorial units and the center. But the unintentional way the imperial adventures were pursued was a good recipe for overcommitment, chaos and failure. Its enormous territorial dispersion and the weakness of the monarchy's resources made the building of a central political, financial or military administration even more difficult than for other empires. The overblown imperial enterprise proved to be much beyond the capability of a weak government in a poor country such as Spain.

The diagnoses by some political historians have been broadly coincident. Ramon Carande acknowledged that "when we contemplate the magnitude of Spain's hegemony, and compare it with the poverty from which it arose, we should not let ourselves give way to pride." For Fernand Braudel, the Spanish Empire was "a total of weaknesses." John H. Elliott wrote that "Castile—for long the predominant partner in the monarchy that it took its superiority for granted— suddenly discovered that it no longer possessed the strength to impose its will by force." Paul Kennedy concluded that in comparison with the further Dutch, French, British and American empires, "the Habsburg simply had too much to do, too many enemies to fight, too many fronts to defend [...] [it was] one of the greatest examples of strategic overstretch in history."

The determinant repercussions of the imperial adventure on the economy and politics of Spain have also been emphasized. Manuel Fernández Alvarez described the late seventeenth-century Spain, after "the failure of the Spanish hegemony in Europe," as "nothing but ruins, desolation, decay, total prostration." Anthony Marx established that "Spain was born prematurely large as an empire, which presented its own challenges to state and nation consolidation." Henry Kamen observed that "from the mid-16th century the problem of overwhelming financial insufficiencies never ceased to worsen, Spanish imperialism was doomed from the start"; as many agree, "the cost of running this enormous empire crippled Spain." Antonio Miguel Bernal concluded that "for three centuries, Spain, without culminating a unitary national state for the Spanish society as a whole, turned out to be a hostage of its own Empire."[2]

As Poor as Gambia

In 1492, after navigating adrift for 10 weeks, three boats with a few dozen men led by Christopher Columbus landed on a small island in the outskirts of the Caribbean, where "all go naked, men and women, as their mothers bore them," as he wrote in his diary.

At that time, Spain was a very poor country. As poor as today's Gambia or Burkina Faso—in terms of purchasing power of the average person's annual income (at about 1,700 dollars of 2017). France, England, the Netherlands and the North of Italy were at similar level—a little higher, perhaps, like current Uganda or Zimbabwe. It may seem obvious that none of these poor countries could afford the costs of leading transcontinental and transoceanic expansions of imperial proportions. Additionally, Spain was also relatively weaker because its population was scarce: less than 7 million people in the total of all the kingdoms, which was less than half the population of France, its main rival in Europe. Barely one-fifth of the Spaniards were apt for work or militia, according to some estimates.

About 150 years later, by the mid-seventeenth century, when the territorial expansion of the Spanish Empire had reached its peak, the standards of living of the Spaniards had declined in about one-fifth. Then the Spanish Crown lost the Thirty Years' War against the Protestants of Northern Europe, and the empire began to contract. It is not only that the empire was ruinous because Spain was poor. It is also that Spain became even poorer and lost track with other comparable countries in Europe because of the cost of the overambitious, overstretched, ruinous empire. The Spanish economy, then in shambles, would never be able to completely recover from its imperial backlash.

Actually, the inhabitants of the set of the territories that formed Spain had been better off some time before the union of the Spanish Crown and the launching of imperial conquests. They had attained their highest living standards by the mid-fourteenth century, during a long period of peace in which the boundaries between Christian and Muslim lands had remained stable. Those levels of average personal income (in purchasing power) would not be achieved again until the early nineteenth century. No actual economic progress in these terms could, thus, be registered between the beginning and the end of a period of near five hundred years. By then the Spanish economy, by remaining absent from the industrial revolution, would also deepen its relative backwardness relative to most of Western Europe.[3]

In spite of relatively minor differences in their quantitative estimates, economic historians broadly agree on these findings. Jaume Vicens-Vives presented "extremely abundant evidence pointing to a decline in herding, agriculture, industry and trade in the Spain of the seventeenth century." John Elliott summarized that in the Spanish society of the seventeenth century, "one became a student or a monk, a beggar or a bureaucrat. There was nothing else to be." Henry Kamen suggested that "the most useful way in which we can try to understand [early modern Spain's] evolution is to recognize that it was a backward country with poor resources." Carlo M. Cipolla sentenced, "The decline of Spain in the 17th century is not difficult to understand. The fundamental fact is that Spain never developed to begin with." Jan Luiten van Zanden stated that "Spain was one of the poorest and dwindling countries in Europe." Carlos Alvarez-Nogal and Leandro Prados de la Escosura somewhat disagreed, but they provided updated revisions of data that confirm the above-mentioned long-term stagnation of the Spanish economy. They argued that, at the beginning of the imperial period, Spain did not do so bad in relative terms with other European countries. But the authors also registered the "absolute decline" for a few centuries and noted that today's "developing countries [are] not too dissimilar in income per capita from most countries in early modern Europe."[4]

* * *

Political economists have identified several candidates to explain results such as economic failure and persistent underdevelopment in certain countries like early modern Spain. The most recurrent ones are geography, institutions and ideas.[5]

The first candidate, geography, could partially explain the economic failures of Spain. Climate is relatively mild along the Mediterranean coast and maritime and rainy on the Northern Cantabrian coast. But most of the rest of the country is semi-arid, adverse to profitable agriculture and broken up by mountainous chains. Already in the eighteenth century, the French philosopher Montesquieu identified some mechanisms that connect climate, psychology, social norms and politics. They can still be somewhat explanatory of the Spanish case. "The heat of the climate"—he said—reduces vigor and physical strength, and "then the faintness is communicated to the mind: there is no curiosity, no enterprise, no generosity of sentiment; the inclinations are all passive; indolence constitutes the utmost happiness." In the southern parts of Europe—he specified—idleness is subsidized. "In warm climates, despotic power generally prevails."

The second candidate to explain economic stagnation, the role of institutions, has been highlighted in many studies during the last few decades. Many academics, like Nobel laureate economic historian Douglass North, hold that economic institutions such as the protection of property rights, competitive and open markets, the guarantees of contract enforcements and an effective public administration are crucial to permit and incentivize savings, investments, innovation, trade and entrepreneurial spirit. These economic institutions are usually associated with political institutions able to foster mutually beneficial exchanges between the ruling few and the subject many, including separation of powers and the independence of the judiciary. The Spanish monarchy was an example of all the opposite: concentration of power, scarcity of public resources, arbitrariness in decision making and bureaucratic ineffectiveness.

Finally, the third candidate, "ideas," means both technological inventions and habits of mind and heart favorable to innovation and progress. Yet, for several centuries, religious dogmatism prevailed over liberal, rationalist and enlightened inspirations in Catholic Spain.

Already in the sixteenth century, Rodrigo Manrique, the son of the inquisitor general and brother of another inquisitor, wrote from Paris to his master, the scholar Lluís Vives:

> You say very well: our country is a land of envy and pride; and you can add: barbarism. In fact, it is increasingly evident that no one can cultivate fairly the good letters in Spain without the discovery of a heresy, of errors, of Jewish tares. So it is this, that silence has been imposed on the learned; and those who ran to the call of erudition, have felt, as you say, a huge terror.

The further enduring reluctance to promote or adopt novelties among Spaniards is inveterate and may not need much documentation. Let us just read a brief dialogue reproduced by writer Maríano-José de Larra in the nineteenth century, which reflected old, deeply rooted attitudes and may still ring resounding bells in current Spain. A Spanish bureaucrat dismisses an innovation brought up by a foreign visitor:

> "It might harm those who have done in a different way the very things the foreign gentleman wants to do."
> "Those who have done them differently? By that you mean they have done them less efficiently?"
> "Yes, but at least they got them done!"
> "What a pity it would be if things stopped being done badly!"

Similar observations were still relevant during the twentieth century. Neurologist Santiago Ramon y Cajal, the only Spanish Nobel laureate in science, famously complained that "doing research in Spain is crying"; he also established that "the main problem of our University system is not independence, but the radical and definitive transformation of the aptness and the ideas of the teaching community."

This aptness and these ideas were well represented by philosopher and novelist Miguel de Unamuno, rector of the University of Salamanca, who, in discussion with José Ortega y Gasset about the need to open Spain to European influences, shouted, "Let them be the ones to invent!"[6]

The previously mentioned explanatory factors of diverse paths toward either economic development or stagnating poverty are interrelated. The first two, favorable natural conditions and socially efficient institutions, shape the conditions for the third, the emergence of entrepreneurship and technological innovation. Further on, neither institutions nor technology can be effective in triggering economic growth without a favorable public opinion created with ideas of mental openness and the wish of improvement.

In Spain, both the lack of socially efficient institutions and the scientific and technological isolation were part of the costs inflicted by the imperial enterprise. The overreach of its extent ruined the public finances, weakened the government and made the church its inescapable support and guide, which brought about an ideological dominance of traditional beliefs and the neglect and rejection of new modern ideas. The poor imperialist Spaniards had to rely on Portuguese navigation, Italian weaponry, Dutch soldiers and Genoese and other Northern financial know-how. The opportunities for learning from large-scale communications and great voyages were missed, as the imperial escapades involved strenuous, desperate efforts at exerting control by violent means and ruinous extraction of scarce resources from the potentially productive population.

The most consequential development is that, in the long term, even if external conditions change, certain traditional institutions and habits can remain and become even more inefficient than when they emerged. Social inertia can give long life to obsolete rules and practices through intentional transmission across generations, by copy, imitation of popular mistakes and by deterring change due to the high costs of facing and modifying established norms.

It is understandable that if people invest time and develop skills to learn how to behave within existing institutional and cultural contexts, they wish to obtain compensation for such investments, which consolidate the traditions. Seen from the other side, playing against the established rules and norms broadly followed by other people, even if it is in favor of efficiency and decency, can be painful and a source of frustration, resentment and permanent stress. Thus, idleness and wastefulness become contagious and reproduce themselves.[7]

This is how we can observe some long-term historical continuities with roots in the remote imperial period in Spain: low proportions of working population, low technological skills, love of traditions and reluctance to foreign novelties, small group privileges, parasitic bureaucracies, widespread corruption among both private actors and public servants and forever protracted judicial administration. As we will see, other developments that have also marked the collective life of Spaniards in the first decades of the twenty-first century can find distant precedents and continuities; they include financial bubbles, gigantic government debts and defaults and bankruptcies charged on small savers and taxpayers' backs.

The American Silver in Genoa Is Buried

Trying to sustain the imperial military effort was the primordial cause of Spain's financial ruin. Public spending multiplied by about 2.5 between 1500 and 1640. The primary sources of revenue to finance such spending were domestic taxes, American silver and European loans.

Domestic taxes were particularly unfair, extractive and painful for the private economy. The nobles, the clergy and anybody enjoying a special jurisdiction or royal mercy were exempted from paying taxes, as were the hidalgos, that is, those who could prove their "purity of blood"—Christians not having mixed with Jews or Muslims or not having converted. The nobles were allowed to collect taxes themselves in their dominions. There was not a central tax collector or, for that matter, a real fiscal policy or unity of criteria across the several territories of Spain.

The taxpayers were known as *pecheros*, that is, commoners or plebeians. The verb *pechar* came to mean charging with an obligation or paying consequences for one's action—such as, for example, "pechar" with the dishonor of one's family or with a penalty of prison. So did the *pecheros* with taxes. The vast majority of tax revenue was collected by a trade tax called "alcalaba," similar to the current value-added tax. Further increases were attained by charging the clergy and the colonists in the Americas and by introducing poll and wealth taxes, which provoked resistance and hostility.

The second source of public revenue was the precious metal arriving from America. American gold and silver was the coveted treasure that strongly motivated the dreams and the ambitions of most conquerors. How it became a primary source of financial ruin of Spain is, perhaps, the weirdest story of the empire. Very rich mines were exploited in New Spain (current Mexico) and Peru. The silver was transported in bullions or bars, in the north from Zacatecas to the port of Veracruz in the Gulf of Mexico and in the south from Potosi to the port of Portobelo in the Caribbean Sea; both routes converged into Havana, Cuba, and from there the bullions led to Seville, which was granted the royal monopoly on such a trade. The king took 20 percent of the silver as a tax and many illegal seizures from private merchants. Yet, as was vastly documented by economic historians Earl J. Hamilton and Pierre Chaunu and summarized by John H. Elliott,

> In spite of the prohibition on the export of precious metals from Spain, the silver did not stay in the country, its registration at Seville was often a mere formality before its owners sent it abroad at the earliest possible opportunity.

The receivers were banks in Genoa, Milan, Flanders and German lands, where the bullions were transformed into coinage—as Spain lacked the most rudimentary technology for that—and resent to Spain in the form of bank loans to the government. There was not a central bank in Spain able to support the government finances and manage the public debt and its repay. In fact, even the king's portion of the bullion imports tended to be mortgaged in advance to foreign bankers who transferred it abroad at once, without in its way touching the Spanish economy.

As it was versified by troublemaker member of the Royal Court and satirical writer Francisco de Quevedo (and sung more than three hundred years later by protest troubadour Paco Ibáñez),

> Mighty Lord
> is Mr. Money.
> In the Indies he is born honest,
> While the world stands around;
> He comes to die in Spain,
> And is in Genoa buried.

It was as if the Spaniards sold trinkets to the Indians in exchange for silver, and then they sold the silver to European bankers in exchange for ruinous loans. The typical interest rate on foreign short-term loans was higher than 20 percent, but as they were continuously refinanced, especially through long-term debt to the cities, it reached up to 50 percent or 65 percent. The Spanish Crown debt created a perfect instance of a financial bubble. As much as three-fourths of all government expenditures were devoted to war or debt repayments from previous wars. This required still more taxes, selling public assets, and so on.

Of course, all these resources were diverted away from private production and trade, provoking enormous inflation, blocking potential economic growth and spiraling down the entire Spanish economy. Like the real estate and financial bubbles of the early twenty-first century, the sixteenth-century financial bubble triggered higher concentration of property and wealth and a huge reduction of people's salaries—up to 50 percent in real terms.

The trap of increasing public debt and its consequences for the economy have been carefully studied by current economists, especially after the financial crisis of 2008. By analyzing government defaults on international and domestic debts in 66 countries during eight centuries, Carmen Reinhart and Kenneth Rogoff found that poor countries experience deep crises when they accumulate relatively low proportions of debt, as low as 15 to 20 percent of domestic income (also known as GDP). The explanation of such vulnerability is the weak fiscal structures and financial systems of poor countries. Also, once a default occurs, the next one is more likely because the economy declines, the fiscal basis shrinks and revenue decreases. Massive inflation and debt make a poor country more prone to repeat defaults. For some countries, serial defaults can become a way of life—as it was the case of imperial Spain.

Note the similarities and the differences with current states in developed countries that can control much larger portions of domestic income. On the one hand, they are also, indeed, heavily constrained in the allocation of resources in their budgets, as most expenditure is committed—like in the historical case here reviewed—to military programs, debt repayments and, nowadays, also social security and other transfers. But, on the other hand, the crucial difference is that in early modern countries, like Spain, as in current poor states, the domestic income was very low and the proportion of public spending out of domestic income was also very low—about 5 to 10 percent.

The key to evaluating the financial unviability of the Spanish Empire and its permanent wars does not lie in comparing the country's average income per person or the proportion of public spending out of domestic income relative to other countries of the time. The point is that the absolute values of those two variables—in all countries—were extremely low.

With the data and estimates available, we can calculate that during the seventeenth century, the Spanish government's annual expenditure per inhabitant, in current purchasing power, was about one hundred times lower than in the early twenty-first century (in constant 2015 US dollars, about 90 to 180 dollars at the time, depending on the estimate of the country's income, and about 13,000 in 2015). If the spending is so low and most of it must be allocated to war and debt repayments, the remaining resources for public services are so meager that they do not permit the government to provide almost anything to its subjects.

As a consequence of the imperial endeavor, the poor Spanish Crown defaulted its debt seven times in 90 years (between 1557 and 1647). The Spanish Treasury collapsed, and in 1700 Spain was the only European country that collected lower taxes per inhabitant than it did one hundred years before. During the eighteenth century, the Crowns of France and the newly United Kingdom multiplied their revenues by about 5 and 10, respectively, and became financially much more powerful than the exhausted and declining Spanish Crown, then headed by the Bourbons. Both the building of the Spanish Empire and its dissolution during the nineteenth century provoked, again, higher numbers of financial defaults than any other country at comparable periods.[8]

The Spanish Fury

King Charles the Emperor did not have a real army. The conquerors of America were, in fact, a small handful of adventurers with no military competence. The hidalgo Hernán Cortés conquered the Aztec Empire of 25 million people with less than six hundred men by using a few scary horses, iron arms and gunpowder, harquebuses and spreading unknown diseases among the indigenous population; Cortés had to burn the ships to prevent his crew from reasonably choosing to retreat. The illiterate laborer Francisco Pizarro faced the Inca Empire of 12 million people with less than two hundred men by using similar weapons. Most conquests were private enterprises, not royal endeavors. They were based on such rudimentary technologies as sailing ships, horses, gunpowder and swords. To increase its effectiveness, by the mid-sixteenth century the royal army began to be organized in corps called *tercios* (thirds) composed of pikemen, swordsmen and arquebusiers. It also began to recruit foreign mercenaries by means of external contractors. But the government was frequently unable to pay its troops and faced frequent mutinies.

During the near two-hundred-year reign by the Habsburg dynasty, Spain was at war virtually every single year. Major conflicts included the conquests of the indigenous peoples of the Americas, including the Aztecs (1519–21), the Mayas (from 1523 on), the Incas (1532–72) and the Mapuches (from 1536 on) as well as the wars with England, like the Eighty Years' War (1568–1648); against the Protestants in Europe, including the Thirty Years' War (1618–48); with France in the follow up until 1659 and again in the Nine Years' War (1688–97); and the Succession War (1701–14).

Recruitment was then massive. By the end of the sixteenth century, the army encompassed about 160,000 men—about three times the size of the French or the English armies of the time. It reached its peak of 300,000 men by the 1620s. Yet, the Crown and the country did not have the capacity to finance such a machine, which was also technically backward.

Military competence was often substituted with brutality. The famous "Spanish Fury" was openly exhibited in the late sixteenth century against the Dutch Revolt. Both underpaid mutinous troops under regular commands and abandoned soldierly sacked, slaughtered, raped and pillaged several cities on looting expeditions. As Philip II's captain-general Fernando Álvarez de Toledo, Grand Duke of Alba, reported after one of those feats, "No nail was left on the wall." The imperial spirit of the Spanish Fury would become the motto for the Spanish national football team.

One of the most famous episodes of war in Europe also exposed these drawbacks. Philip II had tried to associate with England by marrying her queen, but he was soon widowed without descendants. Eventually, he decided to invade England by force. The Spanish Great and Most Fortunate Navy, which English historians would scornfully name "Invincible," was superior in numbers but inferior in technology—as England disposed of modern, less heavy and more mobile vessels and cannons of bronze (instead of steel). The Spanish Army was scattered by English fireship attacks, forced to circumnavigate the British Isles and was disrupted during severe storms. Only one-half of the vessels and one-third of the men returned to Spain. A large subsidy granted by the pope was canceled. The classical Spanish version tells that, once defeated, King Philip complained, "I sent my vessels to fight against men, not against tempests." Yet, this may seem to suggest that the storms were biased and anti-Spanish, as if they could not have affected the English side. It seems more sensible to find an explanation of the asymmetry in management and technology gaps.

The Crown of Spain tried to substitute a weak state with a strong government. But for several centuries, the rulers of Spain misidentified strong government with harsh centralization and concentration of power, which was the best recipe for state weakness. The Spanish Crown of the early modern times not only was very weak in financial and technological terms, as we have seen. The Spanish "absolutist" monarchy was also feeble in administrative resources and in social and cultural cohesion and remained very far away from exerting "absolute" control over the population of its territories.

During the imperial years, the kings were tough on their weaker subjects and weak regarding the powers that be. On the one hand, the kings stopped pledging loyalty to the *Cortes* or advisory parliament and called their meetings with decreasing frequency. The *Cortes* of Castile were reduced to procurators from 18 cities; the cities were put under control of a Crown's agent called "Corregidor" and had to pay taxes directly to the king, not through the *Cortes*. From the eighteenth century on, the control of the peninsular territories from Madrid was organized analogously to the administration of the overseas colonies, around a captain-general and a royal audience in each territory.

On the other hand, both the nobility and the clergy were exempted from paying taxes, as mentioned; they kept their properties, fortresses and private armies and maintained their exclusive jurisdictions and domains where the king could not rule. In the Americas, the king, also unable to rule directly, entrusted his powers into Spanish conquerors and colonists in the form of an institution called "Encomienda," or entrustment, which collected its own taxes from the indigenous subjects and often derived into a private system of near-slavery.

The personal managing styles of the kings varied between imperiousness and absenteeism. Charles I, who traveled incessantly for four decades (and slept in 3,200 different beds), tired, ill and prematurely aged, quit his posts of emperor and king and retired to an austere monastery. Philip II was also a workaholic ruler. He was known for his insistence on trying to do everything himself; he read every paper, studied the dispatches, drafted the orders, carefully supervised the labors of his secretaries and pretended to be in central command of every action, even of military operations, from his palace in El Escorial. On the contrary, Philip III the Pious was a good specimen of the absent ruler, surpassed only by Charles II the Bewitched, a man vastly deprived of any physical, intellectual or emotional ability who died childless and heirless.

The latter managerial style fits the Spanish saying, "he who embraces too much holds on too little." Or, no one could hold onto that much of an empire—especially if the country is utterly poor and the empire is down and out. Regarding the other style, the overbusy, we could apply a reversed version, he who holds on too much embraces too little. It tends to happen to excessively controlling managers. Either way, the results were bureaucratic delays, incompetence, last-minute improvisations and reckless decisions. An alternative model based on division of labor, institutional counterweights and consensus building would have required much larger amounts of human, organizational, technical and financial resources than those available to the Spanish monarchy.

All in all, the shortsighted, unenlightened project of trying to make the Crown strong by making it concentrated backfired. As is well known, a rigid stick is not strong but easily breakable. A flexible cane will always be more resilient.

A Catholic Monarchy

The weakness of the Crown can explain its tight closeness to the church. When, after the first conflicts between Catholics and Protestants, the Holy Roman Empire established that "Cuius regio, eius religio," that is, that for each kingdom there should be one religion, the Spanish kings had already been moving in that direction for several decades. In contrast to similar institutions that the pope controlled in other countries, the Spanish Inquisition had been placed under control of the kings. The pope had granted them the titles of Catholic monarchs, first, and Catholic king, later on.

The Kingdom of Spain, like the other larger kingdoms of Europe, England and France, routinely interfered with the election of popes in the conclave by producing lists of acceptable and nonacceptable candidates and sometimes even moving troops and galleys to the frontier of the papal states to pressure the locked-in cardinals. The main Spanish success on this field was the election of two popes from the Valencian aristocratic, powerful and libertine Borgia family, who took the names of Callixtus III and Alexander VI. The latter arbitrated between the crowns of Spain and Portugal regarding the areas along the two sides of the Atlantic Ocean on which each of them would have priority of conquest—one would say, rather biased in favor of Spain.

Several Spanish theologians and prelates, especially Jesuits, Dominicans and Augustinians, were also highly influential in the church's Council of Trent, the embodiment of the Catholic Counter-Reformation. Then the Spanish Crown embraced the ideological monopoly of the Catholic Church as it was promoted by the council. As an exchange, papal bulls conferred in perpetuity on the rulers of the Spanish territories the right to select their bishops and abbots, against the previous traditions of elections by the faithful. The archbishop of Toledo, Primate of Spain, became the second authority in the country after the king. Every Spanish king had the opportunity to appoint dozens of canons, deans, priors and chaplains; they controlled promotions and salaries and exiled dissident clerics. The king also appointed all members of the Council of the Inquisition, including the inquisitor general.

The church provided substantial administrative resources to the feeble Crown and took charge of essential services such as children's instruction, charity and registers of births, marriages and deaths. The missionaries in the Americas did a great job at taming and subjecting the indigenous population and at building numerous, fairly impressive churches and convents. But all was at the service of the Spanish Crown because no cleric could go there without royal permission and the Spanish clergy did not have direct contact with the pope.

In short, the Crown gave the church the monopoly of ideology and the church gave the Crown legitimation and material support. The medieval theory of Saint Thomas Aquinas held that the church was the sun and the Crown was the moon, which derives its light from the sun.[9] But the absolutist Spanish kings exerted control and censorship even over Roman Catholic dogma. They ordered the adaptation of the Council of Trent's decrees and controlled their implementation in Spain by the bishops without the pope's

approval. By an *Exequatur*, the kings granted themselves the right to suppress
any papal initiative that they disapproved. The Spanish Crown published its
official, amended version of the Roman catechism in Latin after Trent and
in Spanish two hundred years later. As the saying goes, the Spanish kings
were "more Catholics than the Pope." In fact, they acted like little local popes
themselves.

Had the Spanish kings intended to save the Universal Christianity, they
would have followed the Roman pope instead of so forcefully trying to control
the Spanish church. In fact, they vastly used the Catholic Church and faith as
an aid to save their own Spanish Empire, as the Crown's resources were clearly
insufficient for such a grandiose endeavor.

In spite of the further emergence of new liberal ideas and movements, the
ideological fusion between empire and Catholicism would remain central in
the rhetoric of Spanish nationalism until the late twentieth century. Some of
its legacies are still alive, as we will review later on.

Elected Kings with the Name of Presidents

The dissolution of the Spanish Empire began by the mid-seventeenth century.
The Thirty Years' War between Catholics and Protestants was lost by the
Catholics, that is, mainly by the pope and the Kingdom of Spain. The Treaties
of Westphalia in 1648, by which the sovereignty of a number of political units
in Europe was asserted and recognized, marked the beginning of the end of
Spain's imperial adventures. Even the internal union was challenged, as the
peoples of the peninsula lost the imperial common cause that had brought
and somehow had held them together. By mid-century, Portugal achieved its
independence, which also implied the loss for Spain of the Portuguese colonies
in Africa and Asia, while the Catalans fought for it, and a series of revolts
arose in Aragon, Andalusia, Naples and Sicily.

One after another, most colonial possessions were lost. The Dutch United
Provinces were legitimized as an independent unit by the principal powers
of Europe. The Roussillon and the French County passed to France. Naples,
Sicily and Sardinia went their own ways. Louisiana and Florida joined the
United States.

In the rest of the Americas, the Spanish colonists and the Creoles had been
asking for the formation of autonomous local assemblies to be represented
before the Crown, as had been the case with the old medieval kingdoms at the
beginning of the Habsburg reigns. But the Bourbon dynasty that had been
established in Spain since the early eighteenth century had suppressed most of
the traditional territorial institutions and aimed at intensifying centralization
and concentration of power. By the late eighteenth or early nineteenth

centuries, it was too late for the American communities to obtain consensual pluralistic representation within the Spanish Crown.

Then, when Spain was invaded by the French troops of Emperor Napoleon and the absolutist monarchy collapsed, the elites in the colonies rose up to create new independent republics. The *cabildos* or municipal councils, which had largely escaped the ambition of centralized control from the metropolis, led the insurrections, even trying to mobilize indigenous populations. Soon, the four viceroyalties in which the Spanish Empire had been organized in America—New Spain, New Grenada, Peru and River of Silver—dispersed into 15 countries of disparate sizes and consistencies to which a few more would add soon. By 1826, the Spanish Empire had lost more than 90 percent of its area and population.

The Spanish colonial legacy in the Americas was not particularly enjoyable. The colonial government had organized or created old-style social and economic structures without effective administrations or clearly defined and enforceable property rights. Social life was structured in a number of cities, but also in many small-scale farming communities, including the so-called "Indian republics," under the influence of local churches.

The leaders of American independence were not able to rely on previously existing governmental resources or on their own organizational or institutional capacity to structure a stable political system. Largely as a result of the fragile and outdated colonial legacy, the new independent republics were very weak states. Somewhat like the previous Spanish Crown that had ruled over them, they attained very low levels of tax collection and public expenditure, very rudimentary administrative structures, little law enforcement and ineffective armies. Rebellions in the countryside further increased the ruralization of social life and territorial fragmentation. Competition for power among elites developed by means of coups and preventive countercoups that spread civil wars across the continent. The liberation of colonial rule meant, in the short and medium term, social disorder, political chaos and economic disaster. As the leader of the Andean region's independence, Simón Bolívar, soon recognized in a dramatic confession that his grandiose initial project had failed: "America is ungovernable [...] Independence is the only good we have acquired at the expense of all the others."

In large spaces with low population density and little administrative and technical capacity—such as the recently created republics of Mexico, Colombia or Argentina—the new rulers were unable to control vast territories and to incorporate varied and dispersed ethnic groups into a single institutional framework. At the same time, several of the new small states and closed societies proved to be unviable and did not reach minimum levels of institutionalization and social and political stability for many years.

Over weak administrative apparatuses, backward economies, fragmented territories and scattered ethnic groups, independence led to the adoption of new political institutions prone to instability. They were unable to channel conflicts and even contributed to provoking political hazard and frequent social shocks. Like the ineffective Spanish monarchs of the sixteenth and seventeenth centuries, political leaders of the American independence in the nineteenth century sought to replace weak states with strong governments. There were several attempts to name new emperors in Mexico (as well as in Haiti and Brazil). But as the formation of new monarchies was generally discarded, the design of concentrating powers in the hands of a single individual in a republic led to the form of regime usually called "presidentialism." Bolivar's constitutional project for a Greater Colombia included "a life-appointed president, with the right to choose his successor"; in other words, "an elected king with the name of president." His design would be resumed by the so-called Bolivarian republics of the Andean region in the early twenty-first century.

The typical concentration of presidential power in Hispanic America creates small, weak and contentious governments. Especially in societies with low levels of income, large economic inequalities and ethnic heterogeneity, presidentialist governments tend to be alienated from society, belligerent, vulnerable and unstable. In countries with ancient regime social structures, precarious state resources and small size and isolation, any minor social conflict, protest or rebellion tends to become a general political crisis, which provokes reactions and counterreactions that challenge the foundations of the community. As a result, political instability, long-term economic stagnation and continued emigration—mostly to the United States—have been hallmarks of most countries in the region.

In contrast with Britain's colonial legacy in North America and the Caribbean, the levels of compliance with the rule of law, orderly governance and economic and social prosperity in the rest of the continent have long suffered the consequences of the ill-fated colonial legacy of the Spanish Empire.[10]

The British Alternative

All this does not mean that the Spanish Habsburgs and Bourbons failed to do what other kingdoms could have achieved at about the same time. During the fifteenth to eighteenth centuries, all European governments, including the Dutch, the English, the French or the Portuguese, were under severe strain by the constant drain of financial resources for military enterprises; all experienced mutinies of troops and lacked the resources and the techniques to mobilize their subjects for imperial conquests and to sustain wars efficiently. Yet the failure of Spain was pretty unique.

The most outstanding comparison is with England. By the early sixteenth century, England shared some important characteristics with Spain: a small population and a low average income of its inhabitants, a traditional absolutist monarchy and a location open to the Atlantic, which moved the two kingdoms to explore and try to colonize the Americas. Like the huge Spanish Empire all along the continent, the small British Empire on the east coast of North America proved fragile and vulnerable. It ended by the late eighteenth century—precisely from a revolt initiated as a protest against new taxes imposed by the penurious Crown. Yet, about one hundred years later, Britain began to build a new worldwide empire that was much more successful, both in terms of profitability for the metropolis and the legacy to the former colonized.

Some important differences can explain the different results of the alternative paths followed by the Spanish and the British imperial endeavors. First, technology: The Spanish Empire of the sixteenth century was made, as we saw, of caravels, horses and infantry soldiers with blades and gunpowder firearms. In the late nineteenth century, the British Empire relied upon steam-propelled, ironclad armored vessels, railways, the telegraph and heavy artillery using dynamite.

Second, instead of becoming a Catholic monarchy by tying itself to the church, the British Crown got rid of the pope by the late sixteenth century and established the Church of England, also called the Anglican Church, under the chairmanship of the Crown. By not being dependent on help from the Catholic Church, the British monarchy would be more able to develop its own way.

Third, instead of maintaining absolutist rule, the king of England was subordinate to Parliament. Since the early eighteenth century, the British House of Commons affirmed its supremacy by exerting its powers of summoning and ruling itself, legislating and sharing guidance on national policy, enquiring into Crown and rulers' abuses and appointing the prime minister and his cabinet on the basis of electoral results.*

Fourth, instead of fiscal deficits, massive debts and monetary bubbles, the British government developed a tax system that implied a pact with its constituents: economic contributions in exchange for limited government and respect for private property rights. Created in the late seventeenth

---

* The last time a British king vetoed a parliament law was in 1707, while the prime minister, supported by parliament, has appointed the ministers and become the actual chief executive since 1730.

century, the Bank of England was the world's first central bank in charge of dealing with the government debt and monetary stability—it achieved success almost one hundred years before the creation of the Bank of Spain, which still needed another hundred years to establish a single common currency, the peseta.

Fifth, political stability was provided by a gradual enlargement of suffrage rights during the nineteenth century, which made the British monarchy, first a consensual mixed system, and then an early democracy, in contrast to permanent instability and oligarchical rule in Spain.

All of these political and economic institutions favored the advancement of scientific and technological novelties, which fostered economic development and made the British Royal Navy the most powerful one in the world. The development of agriculture permitted increases in population and, through the formation of a new middle class, gave way to industrialization. By 1850, a majority of the population in Britain lived in urban areas, for less than one-fourth in Spain, and the income of the average British person was two and a half times higher than that of the Spaniard. Britain had goods to sell and was able to explore new markets overseas. Also, for 100 years, from the Napoleonic Wars around 1815 to World War I in 1914, Britain was able to keep its military expenditure modest. Some major imperial enterprises were organized by private companies, not directly by the Crown. Although public spending remained relatively low—at around 10 percent of domestic income—the much higher absolute levels of income and the low military expenditures made the imperial enterprise affordable.

By the mid-eighteenth century, British dominions had already begun to expand in India and Canada. During the nineteenth century, they were extended to most of Africa, large parts of Asia and Australia. The British Empire peaked between World War I and II with an area of around 35 million square kilometers—two and a half times larger than the largest area of the Spanish Empire in the mid-seventeenth century and more than 150 times larger than the British Islands.

The legacy of the former British colonies was favored by a few factors that we have discussed above as crucial for sustained development. First, climate. It is not usually noted that, in their initial expansion across the Atlantic, both the Spanish and the British empires expanded not only westward but also southward. Canada is at the same latitude as the British Islands and the United States is south of it, both at relatively mild climate areas. In contrast, the Spanish dominions were all south of Spain: present-day Mexico is at the same latitude as the Sahara Desert; most lands from there to Bolivia suffer the harshness of the equatorial climate. It is not by chance that the countries along the equator, including Ecuador, Equatorial Guinea (both former Spanish colonies), the Congos and others in Eastern Africa, are among the lowest in standards of living in the world.

The British colonial institutions also favored decentralized rule in different territories in the name of the Crown without the pretension to keep tight control of them from London. Somehow, the British rulers learned the hard way the lesson from the failure in North America. The colonists tended to elevate the status of some local leaders and make them partners in rule. In contrast to the Spanish Catholic fanaticism, the British expeditionaries did not bring their own missionaries trying to impose a religion. They did not try to push an English cultural agenda of ways of living, such as food (thank goodness!). Or to eliminate the native languages; on the contrary, they promoted the study of local cultures and the history of the societies of the ancient Asian empires.

A more qualified management of the riches of the colonies produced positive balances of payments for Britain, even allowing for an early resumption of trade with the United States. Substantial income was reinvested overseas by building durable infrastructures. All in all, the empire made Britain ever wealthier and gave material stimulus to global trade and communication.

The British Empire was dismantled during the second half of the twentieth century amid a mood of depression. But the independence of the British colonies did not provoke a national trauma as distressing as those set-in in Spain both in the late seventeenth and in the early twentieth centuries. In fact, the imperial experience and the edulcorated memory of it became a substantial element of British nationalism. Britain remained a great world power and became a founding member of the United Nations Security Council. Later on, it was also a founding member of the Group of Seven, which is the closest thing to a world government that has ever existed.

Nowadays, former British colonies such as the United States, Canada, Australia, New Zealand and others have higher levels of compliance with the rule of law, of democracy and of good governance than most former colonies of other European countries, certainly including Spain. An institutional reflection of their common colonial legacy is the Commonwealth of Nations, headed by the Queen of England: it is formed by 52 former territories of the British Empire in five continents and encompasses one-third of the world population. The member states are committed to "the development of free and democratic societies and the promotion of peace and prosperity to improve the lives of all peoples of the Commonwealth," according to its charter. Sixteen of the countries share the Queen of England as their head of state. In the United Kingdom, every citizen of the Commonwealth enjoys the same civic rights as British citizens, including the right to vote in elections, to run for a seat in Parliament and to be eligible for public office.

As is summarized by two economic historians, Mauricio Drelichman and Hans-Joachim Voth,

> There can be no doubt that by 1800, in the European concert of powers, Spain had "failed" where England succeeded [...] Two of the great empires during the early modern period ended up on radically different trajectories. Spain under the Habsburgs, in the 16th and 17th centuries, is today a byword for poor governance, profligacy, economic stagnation, and military decline, from which Spain even now has not fully recovered. 18th- and 19th-century Britain serves as a paragon of good institutions, fiscal probity, economic growth, and military prowess.

And as is concluded by historian Antonio Miguel Bernal,

> The verdict of history, by comparison with the "other" colonialism of North America and its metropolis, is unappealable: after three centuries of empire, the metropolis and the former Spanish colonies, for wealth and material and political progress, have figured, and in part continue some of them, in the platoon of the backward nations of the Western world.

Basically, the Spanish imperial ventures overseas failed because they were undertaken too early, when no government had the human, technical and financial resources to make such a giant enterprise a success, the political regime was both extremely centralized and overstretched and the rulers never learned from that experience. When some Spanish rulers tried to replicate it much later, even as late as the third decade of the twentieth century—when more favorable conditions existed—the country was still marred by the costs and fatal consequences of the previous endeavor; the same ruthless ways of conquest and dominion leading to failure were repeated.[11]

Getting Rid of Ultramaria

It is not that no voices were raised against the ruinous imperial journeys in early modern Spain. For example, already in Charles I's time, the *Cortes* of Castile warned that "the remedy to the royal needs can be obtained only by putting an end to the wars that it maintains in Europe." Some years later, the *Cortes* challenged Philip II by complaining, "If God had placed Your Majesty under an obligation to remedy all the troubles of the world, He would have given you the money and the strength to do so."

Most famously, the Dominican bishop Fra Bartolome de las Casas wrote a detailed account of the destruction of the Indies, which in its English version wore the subtitle: "A faithful narrative of the horrid and unexampled massacres, butcheries, and all manner of cruelties, that Hell and malice could invent, committed by the Popish Spanish Party on the inhabitants of West-India, together with the devastations of several kingdoms in America by fire and sword." Las Casas not only condemned the slaughters committed against the indigenous peoples and their forced depopulation. He explicitly asked the king to withdraw. He begged, "Most inopportunely, that Your Majesty not concede such license nor allow those terrible things that the tyrants did invent, pursue, and have committed against those peaceable, humble, and meek Indian peoples [...] and prevent any repetition of the atrocities which go under the name of 'conquests.'"

Shortly after Philip II's death, his ambassador in Rome, Duke of Sessa, noted, "No empire, however great, has been able to sustain many wars in different areas for long [...] I doubt—he added—we can sustain an empire as scattered as ours."[12]

After losing all of the American continental empire in the 1820s, Spain maintained rather hostile relations with the new independent republics. In the 1860s, the Dominican Republic temporarily reversed its status to Spanish colony; Spain invaded Mexico at the Yucatan peninsula; it fought against Cuban rebels; and it fought a war in the Pacific against Peru and Chile. It also fought several wars in Morocco and joined France in sending expeditionaries to the Cochin China. The Spanish Crown maintained the fiction of remaining a great imperial power, although at the time it retained basically a few islands that encompassed less than 10 percent of its previous colonial possessions.

For almost every politician and for many intellectuals, the loss of the last shreds of the empire at the end of the nineteenth century was a traumatic shock. When a serious rebellion for independence began to arise again in Cuba in the early 1890s, the official reaction was one of denial and despair. The two parties that were alternating in government by turns under the monarchy, the Conservatives and the Liberals, made a very united front. For the former, Prime Minister Antonio Cánovas del Castillo had warned, a few years before, that they "would use, if necessary, the last man and the last peso [sic]" to maintain control of Cuba. Then, by 1895, Liberal prime minister Práxedes Mateo Sagasta proclaimed in the Senate that "the Spanish Nation is ready to sacrifice until the last peseta of its Treasury and spilling until the last drop of blood of the last Spaniard, rather than consenting to anybody snatching even not a bit of its sacred territory!" ("Very good, very good," cheered the senators). Following the usual turn, Sagasta was replaced with Cánovas a few days later, and before a month passed the new incumbent repeated almost literally the same words in Congress (also to standing applause by their lordships).

"Spilling the last drop of blood" was a typical Spanish medieval formula of loyalty to the king that had become part of the pledge to the flag recited by the new conscripts of the army. Both the conservative and the liberal prime ministers tried, apparently, to make it valid not only for enlisted soldiers but also to "the last Spaniard." The expression reflected the despair of the speakers, fearful of losing everything, as they probably felt that it was already too late for settling on autonomous or federalizing arrangements with the rebels. It survived as a lemma for intolerance, together with others such as "negotiating is giving in" or "the more you give them, the more they want," which revealed the weakness of the state.

When the United States government, goaded by some belligerent tycoons, decided to intervene, the Spanish Armada in the port of Santiago de Cuba was destroyed in a few hours. Its commander, Admiral Pascual Cervera y Topete, reflected the general mood in official circles when he wept, "We have lost everything." The Regent Queen, Mary Christine, called the episode "the Disaster," which would become the reference label for many years.

The loss of the Cuban, Puerto Rican and Philippines colonies in 1898 did not have direct catastrophic consequences for the Spanish economy. During the most intense colonial times, nearly half of the Crown's fiscal resources were extracted from the Americas, but they were depleted in military expenditures in the region to try to keep control of it, as we reviewed. So, ridding themselves of Ultramaria, as English utilitarian liberal Jeremy Bentham had advised the Spanish rulers to do, could have allowed a greater liberalization and efficiency of the economy. But the occasion was not taken, rather the opposite. After getting rid of the colonies, Spain also withdrew from international markets through the adoption of high commercial tariffs and other protectionist, isolating measures, which produced disastrous economic consequences.[13]

Still, the Spanish imperialists tried to replace the missing American Empire with a very late attempt at actual conquest of other peoples and lands. The few old coastal enclaves in Africa, including the Canary Islands, a Western strip of the Sahara Desert and a small outpost in the Gulf of Guinea, were expanded with the cession of a tiny part of the French protectorate in Morocco by the early twentieth century. Maintaining control, however, was a very costly and bloody endeavor that prolonged through the decade of the 1920s.

Captain General Miguel Primo de Rivera, who had fought in the colonial wars in Cuba, the Philippines and Morocco, and was also the nephew of the last governor of the Philippines and brother of one of the military commanders in Morocco, led a military coup and was appointed prime minister by King Alphonse XIII. After suspending the Constitution, dissolving the Parliament and beginning to persecute dissidents, he went to Africa to help lead the troops in person. His defeat and fall, however, precipitated the fall of the monarchy.

General Francisco Franco also developed most of his military career in Africa. He led, first, the shock troops against the resistance in Morocco, then the foreign legion, which he also used to repress a miner's strike in Asturias in Northern Spain, and finally led the uprising of the army in Africa in 1936. The two dictatorships of the twentieth century had, thus, deep roots in the late imperialistic wars in Africa.

At the beginning of World War II, Caudillo Franco met Fuhrer Adolf Hitler and asked to enter the war with the aim of occupying Gibraltar, French Morocco and part of French Algeria and attaching French Cameroon to the Spanish colony of Guinea. His demands, however, were vaguely dismissed.

Franco's propagandists used the slogan "Through Empire toward God." Yet, they must rather have gone toward the Devil in Hell if the fate of the empire was taken into account in their résumés. The little enclave of Ifni was occupied by Morocco shortly after the country regained independence from France in the mid-1950s, not without some military confrontation with Spanish troops. Western Sahara was subject to a decolonization process by the United Nations, but it was taken by Morocco in the mid-1970s and has never achieved an internationally recognized status. Equatorial Guinea, which became independent in the late 1960s, is the only African state with Spanish as an official language; it is ranked among the "worst of the worst" dictatorships in the world and has enjoyed the Africa's longest dictator.[14]

But we may never know. All documents and diplomatic archives about the Spanish governments' actions regarding Morocco, Ifni, Sahara, the Spanish enclaves of Ceuta and Melilla in Northern Africa and the British enclave of Gibraltar in the Spanish Peninsula are still classified and forbidden to the researchers on the basis of a Law of Official Secrets established by Franco in 1968.

Rebuilding Imperial Links

By the mid-twentieth century, Spain had been left completely isolated. The three great powers that had designed the new world order and institutions at the end of World War II were all alienated from Spain: Great Britain had been its major imperial rival and a much more successful one, the United States had eliminated the last remnants of the Spanish Empire in the Americas and the Soviet Union had been the main international enemy of the existing political regime.

Slowly, by presenting itself as an anti-communist stronghold and taking sides in the Cold War, the dictatorship began to be accepted in some international organizations. Spain became a member of the United Nations 10 years after its creation, as Franco's dictatorship was considered an accomplice of the defeated Nazi and Fascist losers of World War II. Likewise, Spain did not enter the World Bank and the International Monetary Fund until 13 years after they were founded. Only after the democratization of the country was Spain accepted in the North Atlantic Treaty Organization or NATO, 32 years after the alliance had been created. It joined the European Community as a member state 29 years after its foundation.

For many years, Spain also lost political connections with almost all members of its former empire. In the Americas, a series of International Conferences of American States that were held since the late nineteenth century under broad promotion by the United States led to the formation of the Organization of American States (OAS), headquartered in Washington, in 1948. Its members are the 35 states of the Americas, that is, all the countries that emerged from both the British and the Spanish colonial empires, not including Spain. Among the OAS' notable achievements are the creation of the Inter-American Development Bank, the Inter-American Court of Human Rights and several initiatives in favor of peace and security, free trade and democracy in the whole Western hemisphere.

Spain began to develop some initiatives to reach back to the American republics more than 40 years later, once in democracy, around the time of the celebrations for the 500th anniversary of the discovery of the New World. The Ibero-American Summits of chiefs of state and government were gathered together since 1991 with attendance of Spain, Portugal, 18 Spanish-speaking American republics, Brazil—and a little later also Andorra. Other former Spanish colonies have also participated as associates, including Puerto Rico, the Philippines and Equatorial Guinea (the latter two not exactly Ibero-Americans, as far as can be seen). Imperial fantasies have led summit leaders to invite even other countries currently containing parts of what was the seventeenth-century Spanish Empire, including France (for the Burgundy and the French County), the Low Countries and Belgium (for Flanders), Italy (for Milan, Naples and Sicily) and Morocco (for parts of it).

Every summit meeting tries to issue a declaration on some topic. But, in fact, the Ibero-American Summit is mostly a photo opportunity, with all the presidents sitting around the two representatives of Spain, the president of government and the king, the latter chairing the meeting as the successor of the former imperial kings, the only nonelected person there, and the tallest of all. Attendance was declining, with up to 11 absent members of the 22 formal members, which moved the organizers to phase down the summit meetings to biennial gatherings since 2014.

A reaction has developed among some countries to increase their coordination and common action without Spain or the United States. The Community of Latin American and Caribbean States (CELAC in Spanish) was formed by 33 countries, that is, all of the OAS except the United States and Canada, in 2011. The summit of heads of state and government gets together every year and aims at monitoring the process of unity and integration of the region. It takes leverage from previous free-trade agreements between several subsets of countries, such as Mercosur and the Union of South-American Nations (USAN or UNASUR in Spanish), which have launched programs for developing an increasingly integrated economy, communication infrastructures, energy and to facilitate the mobility of workers across the countries.

The Ibero-American Summits led by Spain face, thus, strong challenges from more institutionalized alternatives: the OAS centered in Washington, on one side, and the Latin American and Caribbean states coordinating among themselves, on the other. The prospect that Spain could regain a leading influence on its former colonies comparable to that of Britain in the Commonwealth looks highly problematic, to put it mildly.[15]

Chapter 2

A WEAK STATE

The Breakdown of Public Finances
A Pretorian Army
A Ruling Church
From Picaresque to Corruption
Primitive Rebels
Derailment from the European Track
A Bubble State

When Spain had lost almost all of its empire at the end of the nineteenth century, many Spaniards realized that they did not have a true state or a true nation either—not even a unified national market. Spain had wasted its human and financial resources in the imperial adventure and had missed the opportunity to follow the paths of Britain, France and, more recently, even Germany or Italy, in building modern legal, political, economic and administrative structures of governance.

Some unacquainted people use the word "state" to categorize disparate political communities, including, for example, the Visigothic kingdoms, the Renaissance city-republics or the Aztec Empire. This is incorrect and confusing. In these and all the other political forms that existed everywhere in the world until, at least, the European late Middle Ages, there was no unity of power, which is the typical feature of the form "state." There were empires covering fragmented territories without formal borders; princes subject to multiple feudal allegiances, special jurisdictions of estates, guilds, towns, bishoprics and monasteries; multiple currencies, weights and measures; and a variety of rules, local customs and usages.

The "state" is a specific form of political organization based, in contrast, on the monopoly of taxation, law and force by a single authority over the population of an encircled territory with clearly defined borders. As such, the state is usually branded with the attribute of "sovereignty." Building states was a modern project mostly centered on Western Europe—and later on, tried to be replicated in some former European colonies. On this endeavor,

Spain, which had been entangled in the imperial adventure, was very late and attained rather poor results.

Building a modern state may require a new pact between "the ruling few" and "the subject many," as they said in England. At some moment when the complexity of public issues increases, it may be not enough for the traditional Crown to summon some aristocratic or intermediate body periodically to negotiate financial contributions or a new war. With the new pact, the subject may be convened to pay regular taxes, to serve in the military and to comply with the laws. The rulers, in turn, can commit themselves to grant and respect some rights of their subjects, which transform them into citizens, to set a system of representation to share collective decision making and to provide public goods.[1]

None of these exchanges was successfully achieved in Spain, as we will review in this chapter. The public finances of the Spanish state for most of the nineteenth and twentieth centuries remained broke and insolvent, like those of the previous empire; the traditional imperial bodies, the army and the church, maintained their autonomous jurisdictions and a prominent role in the governance of the country; the people's weak compliance with innovative rules of law transformed the classical picaresque into widespread corruption; a fraudulent system of political representation was established, but recurrent revolts and insurrections pervaded the country. Permanent conflicts and political instability postponed once and again the project of building a modern state to replace traditional structures and habits inherited from the imperial monarchy.

Only by the late twentieth and early twenty-first centuries more comprehensive state structures were built and were able to survive for a few generations. Yet, the effort was fatally marred by strong constraints imposed by new European-wide and global developments and challenged by centrifugal processes of decentralization. The state's meager effectiveness in providing public goods, rule of law, inclusive representation and rulers' accountability was disappointing. Under the new legal framework, many of the old features of traditionally backward Spain revived and persisted, including huge public debts, extensive corruption, widespread unlawfulness, ineffective justice, oligarchical politics, permanent protests and riots.

The Breakdown of Public Finances

When it was the moment to begin building a modern state, by the early nineteenth century, the existing economic institutions in Spain were unapt for constructing its new financial bases. The empire had left fiscal privileges to the nobility and the clergy, which collected their own "rents," the powers of the *Cortes* and the cities had been curbed, the bureaucracy was prebendal and corruptible, the government held the monopoly on foreign trade and the internal markets were fragmented by regional and local tariff barriers. At the same time, there was not a single centralized tax collector or tax tribunal, no central bank and no common currency (even money coinage had to be outsourced).

The empire's early start, its absolutist rule and its long duration have been largely identified as responsible for the persistent backwardness of the Spanish economy and the appalling weakness of the Crown's finances. Historian Josep Fontana published a seminal study on the bankruptcy of the absolute monarchy that was later included in a longer appraisal of the "bankruptcy" (or collapse, as they can be synonyms in Spanish) "of the Spanish Empire." In his view,

> The bankruptcy of the Crown's finances was due to a political system which, thanks to the income from its American empire, had been able to afford to act as a great power during three centuries without the need to face serious internal reforms (like those that came with the English revolution of the 17th century or the French one of the late 18th century), [and] arrived at the beginning of the 19th century in bankruptcy, having accumulated some defaults in its last periods of international wars that it was not able to pay.[2]

Indeed, after the loss of most of its colonies, Spain, like in its imperial times, continued to be a serial defaulter. The Spanish Crown increased public spending from about 4 percent of the country's income in the eighteenth century to about 10 percent in the nineteenth and most of the twentieth centuries. But lacking an efficient tax system, the bulk of the spending was financed by debt, which could rarely be repaid. A series of formal defaults ensued, which were eventually replaced with debt "rescheduling" or "restructuring," as well as with purposive inflation to reduce the value of bonds and provoke their repudiation, and with government actions forcing private banks to invest in the government and in state-owned firms. The bad financial reputation of Spain made the country more vulnerable to further crises and reboots.

The Spanish public finances remained weak as a consequence of the frustration of modern economic development. There is no modern state without sufficient revenue, and no state can collect significant amounts of revenue if, after losing the colonies, the country's economy remains poor and destitute. The backwardness of the Spanish economy in the nineteenth and most of the twentieth centuries is, thus, a crucial factor to explain the enduring financial weakness of the Spanish state.

A number of economic historians have excelled in quantifying and ana-lyzing the economic backwardness of Spain. Nicolas Sánchez Albornoz unforgettably portrayed nineteenth-century Spain as "a dual economy." On the one hand, there was a traditional, stagnated subsistence agriculture most of whose production was consumed by the great rural mass. On the other hand, there was an immature capitalist industry, mostly based on textiles and railroads, which was concentrated in the periphery of the country. This suggests that there were real attempts at "taking equal strides like the more advanced countries," but the most primitive economy subordinated the development of the capitalist sector and produced "an underdeveloped economy *avant la lettre*," which for most of the modern period was comparable to the poor countries of nowadays.

The failure of industrialization was thoroughly studied by economic historian Jordi Nadal. He took the leading experience of Great Britain as the main comparative reference and concluded that Spain failed in "replacing the agrarian basis of traditional societies with a new one, of industrial mark." For Nadal, the Spanish case was not one of a "late joiner," such as Italy, Japan, Australia, China, India or several Latin American countries, which industrialized late, by the late nineteenth or the early twentieth centuries, most of them without a previous imperial experience. As the first industrial enterprises began to be installed in Spain in the 1830s and 1840s, "it rather was an attempt, largely aborted, to appear among the first comers," like Britain, the United States, Switzerland, France, Germany or Sweden—that is, it was the story of an early frustration.

Economic historian Albert Carreras confirmed Nadal's interpretation, expanded the analysis to a longer period until the late-twentieth century and emphasized proximate causes of the backward Spanish industrialization such as little technology and low productivity. He referred to the classical model of successive stages of economic development fashioned by economist W. W. Rostow, who, in an invited study, estimated that Spain had been near the fulfillment of some crucial conditions between 1840 and 1870, but it failed to "take-off." The main failures included lack of modernization of agriculture (especially due to the frustrating effects of the expropriations and privatizations of nobiliary and clerical properties), insufficient international openness and bad political impacts.

Economist César Molinas and historian Leandro Prados de la Escosura also contrasted Spanish backwardness with a "typical" European development. They found that, indeed, "Spain was different" and experienced a widening gap with most of Europe. "The differential of absolute levels of per capita income between Spain with the Northwestern European countries became larger and larger," they observed. The authors also noted the lack of public concern about education, which they identified as a crucial factor of economic development, as it could be measured by the slow growth of schooling rates below those of population and of per capita income.

Throughout the nineteenth century, Spain "as a whole remained traditional, agrarian, and backward in comparison with Europe," in the partly concurrent words of economist and historian Gabriel Tortella. His and other authors' data show that, regarding its levels of per capita income, the gap between Spain and Great Britain, France and the newly created Germany and Italy widened during the nineteenth century.

Regarding the fatal consequences of Spanish economic backwardness for the failures in building a modern state, Carreras and Xavier Tafunell's verdict was as follows: "Since 1808, the Spanish public finances struggled in a situation of manifest insolvency and extreme hardship." As a consequence of subsequent spending cuts, "the State failed to provide the pure public goods indispensable for its own legitimation and political survival."

As a consequence of the Great Depression of the 1930s, the Civil War, the subsequent isolation and an autarchic economic policy, the levels of per capita income in Spain did not reach any increase during 25 years. In contrast, the large countries that participated in World War II, Britain, France, Germany and Italy, recovered their previous highest levels in about 10 years.[3]

As is well known, the actual jump of the Spanish economy into the prevalence of industry and services took place as late as in the 1960s and early 1970s. When economic development finally arrived, it was really too late for building a more successful empire (had the idea come back by then to the mind of some of its rulers, which it actually did). By building the empire before the state, Spain had put the cart before the horse. And building a modern state was still a pending endeavor. To achieve financial and adminis-trative public structures able to deliver public goods efficiently, Spain lacked some long-overdue structural transformations. The first significant fiscal reform in modern history was introduced as late as 1977 by, for the first time ever, making direct charges like income and corporate taxes more effective in collecting revenue than indirect ones.

In 1986, Spain joined the European Union as a late, relatively poor and in need-of-protection partner that became a net recipient of benefits rather than a contributor, similar to the smaller countries of Greece and Portugal at about the same time. For about 20 years, the Spanish economy obtained great benefits from European tourism, consumption and investments. It also received massive amounts of financial aid from "regional", "cohesion" and "structural" funds of the European Union in "the greatest solidarity operation in history" for a total of 118 billion euros, as calculated by economists José Luis González and Miguel Ángel Benedicto for the European Commission.

The EU's aid to Spain was equivalent to three times (in purchasing power parity) the amount of the Marshall plan implemented by the United States at the end of World War II to rebuild Western Europe (from which Spain was excluded). This means that the average Spaniard received two times more money from the EU every year during 20 years than the average West European had received from the United States annually during only three years (always in purchasing power parity).

All these aids were issued against the expectation to foster genuine prosperity and well-being. But the crisis initiated in 2008 showed that much of the public and private expenditure had been widely wasted. Further European aid to rescue the Spanish economy amounted to 55 billion euros, from which more than 90 percent were never returned.

From the historical perspective summarized above, Spain was an aborted early comer and a tremendously late joiner. Sanchez Albornoz observed that when he was writing, in the late 1960s, the Spanish economy was still as "dual" as it had been a hundred years before. Fifty more years later, well into the twenty-first century, Spain again looks like a dual economy, split between services and tourism areas in the capital and the periphery and vast interior regions plagued with unemployment, precariousness and poverty.

According to several international reports of the World Economic Forum, Spain is at the bottom in the ranking of European countries and many others in the world in human capital and in taking advantage of new technologies (especially due to the low quality of education) as well as in judicial independence, legal dispute resolution system and protection of intellectual property and, as a result, in the productivity of the economy (also due to debt and the weight of government regulations). The Spanish government expects that the per capita income and the number of employees in the country that had been achieved before the Great Recession will not be recovered for 15 years. The differences with other countries of Europe have widened again.[4]

A Pretorian Army

A major consequence of the weakness of a modern Spanish state was the long-living prevalence of the military in politics and public life. Of course, the military themselves also resisted some modernizing transformations of the country and were, thus, a factor of the country's backwardness, but their power to do so was more a consequence of the failures of reforms of imperial structures than a primary cause of them.

The members of the military enjoyed special jurisdictions that left them outside the control of civil law, while they subjected civilians to their own military rules and judgments. As military officers lived in social seclusion and professional endogamy, they developed their own networks and values, which reinforced their rhetorical, imperialistic patriotism and anti-civilian disposition. The army was also in charge of the bodies to control the public order, that is the police and the Civil Guard. The Spanish Army not only fought continuous colonial wars, as we reviewed in the previous chapter. It also launched a series of coups d'état and other political initiatives that made outstanding generals and other high officers main political actors and direct rulers for most of the nineteenth and twentieth centuries.

The only thing that the Spanish Army has never done is the only thing an army is expected to do: to defend the country from foreign attacks. Spain was invaded twice during the nineteenth century, in 1808 and 1823, in both cases by France, and in both cases the Spanish Army immediately collapsed. The Spanish Army, defeated inside by foreign invaders and outside in the colonies, focused on controlling and persecuting its own people.

The historical role of the Spanish military is the opposite of the one an army is supposed to play in a civilized society with a modern state. Analogously to what one can expect, for example, from firefighters, postal carriers or state-school teachers, the soldiers must be good professionals and pursue the aims determined by the civil authority. But "where public attachment to civilian institutions is weak or non-existent, military intervention in politics will find wide scope—both in manner and substance," as put by political scientist Samuel Finer in a seminal work on the subject.

In a more ambitious design of modernizing processes, political scientist Samuel Huntington also remarked that "the most important causes of military intervention in politics are not military but political and reflect not the social and organizational characteristics of the military establishment but the political and institutional structure of the society [...] The extent to which military institutions and individuals become politicized"—he continues—"is a function of the weakness of civilian political organizations and the inability of civilian political leaders to deal with the principal policy problems facing the country." In this type of situation, it is said that the military, rather than being "professionals," become "praetorians," an expression taken from the Imperial Praetorian Guard that, in ancient Rome, campaigned with the emperor and served as political police.

Regarding the effect of imperial experiences, political scientist Charles Tilly noted, "To the extent that war making went on with relatively little [fiscal] extraction and state making, military forces ended up playing a larger and more autonomous part in national politics. Spain is perhaps the best European example."[5]

This approach is, indeed, brightly illuminating for the Spanish case. In the analysis by historian Stanley Payne, it was due to "the institutional weakness of modern Spain" that the army "became a central factor in politics, not necessarily because the military was ambitious or greedy, but because the Spanish political society had broken down [...] Elements of the Spanish military felt called upon to supplement an inadequate government." In concurrent words, historian Raymond Carr stated, "In Spain it was the structure of politics that was decisive in fostering a race of political generals [...] It was the poverty of the Spanish State that was at the root of the military problem." We should add that, in turn, the central role of the military in politics hindered the development of civil institutions and confirmed the weakness of the state, a vicious circle from which it was difficult to escape.

Defeated abroad, the Spanish military fervently focused on intensive and extensive interventions inside the country to try to substitute many weak administrative structures and functions of the state. According to the usual organicist metaphors, the army conceived itself not as the "armed arm" of the state but as "the spine of the Fatherland." The military style of dealing with public affairs was not by the rule of law but by a "command and control" mindset.

The captain-generals heading the military regions, together with the provincial military governors, prevailed over the civil governors, controlled all the territory of the country and were able to easily mobilize the troops for political purposes. "Militarism was encouraged by the civil element, which has been historically incapable to present its own alternative of effective organization of the State," as eloquently explained by administrativist Manuel Ballbé. "The militarization of political life, the coups d'état and the military *pronunciamientos* [proclamations] always had their origin in the intervention of the army in affairs of public order, by decision of civil rulers," he holds.

Since the liberal Constitution of 1812, the military kept its own special jurisdiction, alien to regular law and justice. A law of 1821 gave the military the competence to judge civil persons for political actions, a power that was confirmed and expanded by successive laws in the 1860s and 1870s, until the Law of Jurisdictions of 1906, which submitted all criticisms or attacks to the army by civilians to military tribunals. During the monarchical period 1875–1931, there were suspensions of constitutional guarantees for 45 percent of the time and declarations of "state of war" during 26 percent of total time. Not only during dictatorships but for most of the nineteenth and twentieth centuries, protesters, journalists, students and strikers were often subject to trials by military tribunals, known as Councils of War.

The early-nineteenth-century liberals had not created a civil police corps but had relied upon the National Militia formed by volunteers at the local level. By mid-nineteenth century, the moderates had created the Civil

Guard, which, in spite of its name, was a militarized institute dependent on the Ministry of War. In the twentieth century, the Second Republic gave birth to the Assault Guard. And Franco's dictatorship widely used the Civil Guard, together with the new armed police, and militarized all municipal and auxiliary police corps.

As the imperial armies were led by aristocrats, the state armies tend to be managed by career officers. In Spain, the main organizational problem was the army's macrocephaly. Every colonial war, every *pronunciamiento*, was followed by a cataract of promotions; the top of the structure became superpopulated. From the mid-nineteenth century to the late twentieth century, there was one officer for every five or six men, "the most grotesque disproportion in any European armed forces," in Stanley Payne's words, as France, Britain and Germany had proportions of one officer for every 20 or 25 men.

Military and security expenses amounted to a long-term average of about one-third of the state budget (with significant ups and downs). But the proportion of military expenses in personnel was always between two-thirds and four-fifths. Very little money was spent on equipment and training.

Regarding the army at the beginning of the nineteenth century, a Royal Commission of Military Chiefs reported, "In May 1808 [the time of Napoleon's invasion], nor did we have ships or armies or weapons or treasure or credit or borders or governments or political existence."

One hundred years later, by the early twentieth century, conservative prime minister Francisco Silvela still described the desolated panorama of the military barracks this way:

We do not have to pretend arsenals and shipyards where there are only buildings and staffs that keep nothing and build nothing; we must not suppose squads that do not maneuver or fire, or cite as armies the new additions of conscripts, or strive to preserve more than we can manage without disastrous fictions, nor to lavish rewards and deduce heroism from them.

Even in Franco's times, the Spanish industry could produce little more than light artillery and submachine guns to chase guerrilla bands. Only after the first military agreements with the United States in 1953, the Spanish Army received its first jet fighter and a few heavy tanks, which were United States residues from World War II and the Korean War.

"Structurally, the army was a far from healthy element. It was a sedentary, bureaucratic monstrosity rather than a fighting machine," in the words of Raymond Carr. Commander and historian Gabriel Cardona has summarized the context:

The problem was not exclusively Spanish, but it corresponded to a question typical of the liberal states of the time. Adapting military institutions with a traditional mentality was a difficult task, not only for the Third French Republic, but for the British governments [...] But while in Western Europe the State imposed its criteria, the weak system of the [Spanish] Restoration failed, as it had failed on so many other things.[6]

* * *

The different forms of direct political interventions of the Spanish military for nearly two centuries can be ranked by the degree of violence they imply: *pronunciamientos*, coups and civil wars. In all cases, the expected effect of the military action is a change of government or of political regime, but the degree of conflict varies.

Actually, a *pronunciamiento* is nothing but a coup threat: a general makes a statement against the incumbent government and either the latter surrenders because it has no means to resist the force of the rebels and prefers to avoid an onslaught or the rebels do not obtain sufficient support from the rest of the army and they are fusilladed by their own comrades or escape into exile. The actual coup involves more explicit displays of military force, typically occupying government buildings and the streets.

Counting all *pronunciamientos* and coups of contemporary Spain together, at least 56 major movements have been clearly identified, an average of one every three years. Of these, 14 were immediately successful.

In turn, a civil war may follow a failed *pronunciamiento* or a resisted coup d'état and provoke a bloodshed. In the international academic literature, a civil war is usually categorized as a conflict producing at least 1,000 deaths or, as a major category, 1,000 deaths per year. For any of these criteria, at least seven Spanish episodes qualify.

Regarding foreign wars, the Spanish Army did not participate in the mostly European two World Wars of the twentieth century that shaped international relations. The former great imperial power of Spain was left weakened and greatly isolated from the modern world. However, the number of Spanish deaths caused in the colonial battlefields was not lower than those suffered by the countries involved in the World Wars. You can look at Box 2 for a list of episodes and estimates of mortal victims.

As a result of the diverse forms of political interventionism of the military, the Spanish chief of government was a general during almost exactly half the time from the first post-absolutist government in 1834 to the death of Franco in 1975 (during 70 of 141 years). During the so-called regime of the Generals of Isabel II, in the second third of the nineteenth century, more

Box 2
Coups and Wars

Successful military *pronunciamientos* without major violence in Spain produced the restoration of the absolutist monarchy of Ferdinand VII in 1814, a number of liberal and moderate constitutional changes at the beginning of the regency of Mary Christine in 1834–37, the coronation of Isabel II in 1843, a liberal government in 1854, the overthrown of the First Republic in 1874, the restoration of the Bourbon monarchy the same year and the establishment of a dictatorship in 1923.

The list of relatively minor civil wars includes the liberal insurrection of 1820, the reactionary French invasion of 1823, the Second (1847–49) and the Third (1872–76) Carlist Wars and the so-called Glorious Revolution against the Bourbon monarchy in 1868, which ended with a few thousand deaths each. At higher levels of conflict, the War of the French or of Independence (1808–14), the First Carlist War (1833–40) and the insurrection against the Second Republic (1936–39) produced a toll of a few hundred thousand mortal casualties each.

To estimate the number of Spanish deaths caused in the colonial battlefields, let us leave behind the wars for independence of the colonies in America during the first half of the nineteenth century, especially in Mexico and the Grand Colombia, which produced several hundred thousand deaths, and let us focus only on the closer conflicts to the time of the major European wars. During the Ten Years' War and the War of Independence in Cuba, about 144,000 Spaniards died; in the Rif Wars in Northern Africa, about 29,000; and in the Philippines, about 3,000. A total of near 200,000 deaths was a little more than 1 percent of the country's population, which compares favorably with some rates of victims in World War I, in particular near 2 percent of the population of Britain and 3.5 percent of France.

The Spanish Civil War, however, turned the counting down: about 500,000 deaths or 2 percent of the population contrasts with less than 1 percent in Britain and 1.4 percent in France during World War II. All in all, for the first half of the twentieth century, Spain got the deaths and the pain but not the benefits of fighting and winning international wars.

than 40 percent of the ministers were members of the military, as were the leaders of the main political parties; later on, they were also chief executives on several occasions under Alphonse XII and Alphonse XIII, who were given the imperial title of "Soldier King"; and, of course, they were the chiefs of the further Primo's and Franco's dictatorships. See a list in Box 3.[7]

* * *

As a matter of fact, the Spanish Army was never integrated into the new democratic regime that was built from 1977 on. It rather had to be, on the contrary, disintegrated to make democracy viable. The first effort took about 25 years, from the creation of the Ministry of Defense in 1976 to the abolition of the compulsory military service in 2002. A second period of dismantling the Spanish Armed Forces is currently ongoing; it is partly a consequence of the general reduction of the size of the public administration after the Great Recession initiated in 2008.

Some reforms aimed at putting the military under civil control were initiated by minister of defense, General Manuel Gutierrez Mellado, under Prime Minister Adolfo Suárez, in 1976. Five years later, Prime Minister Calvo Sotelo appointed a civil minister for the office, Alberto Oliart, in the first Spanish cabinet in many decades (probably ever) that did not include a single member of the military.

The size of the armed forces has shrunk enormously since then. A first paramount concern was to get rid of the generals who had fought on Franco's side during the Civil War and still completely dominated the top structure of the armed forces in the early 1980s. Those others who had supported or have shown themselves acquainted with the failed coup d'état in 1981 were also pushed aside.

During the period of Minister Narcís Serra, under Prime Minister Felipe González, the purge was gradual and relatively smooth. It was implemented by the introduction of voluntary passes to the Reserve, punishments for airing critical views on political or defense issues, the decrease of the retirement age, reduction of positions on each grade and devaluation of seniority as the exclusive criterion for promotion.

On the other hand, none of the members of the Democratic Military Union, a group of officers that was organized to prevent the army from intervening against the democratic opposition, ever returned to active service. Its leaders had been imprisoned during the last months of Franco's dictatorship, and while they were liberated by the general amnesty a couple of years later, they were not reintegrated into their jobs and only eventually passed to the Reserve.

During the following few decades, the number of generals was reduced from 824 at the peak of the Franco era in 1970 to 200 in the current plan for the period 2017–21. It is planned that, in this period, the total number

Box 3
Praetorian Military

Main instances of political intervention of the Spanish military include the following: the leadership of General Baldomero Espartero for the Progressive Party (who was three times president of the council of ministers and once regent for a total of five years), General Ramon Narvaez for the Moderate Party (president of the council of ministers five times for a total of nearly nine years), General Leopoldo O'Donnell for the Liberal Party (in the same office three times for a total of six years), General Francisco Serrano for the Liberal Party (four times for a total of 16 months), General Juan Prim for the Progressive Party (for one year and a half), somehow also Manuel Ruiz Zorrilla for the Radical Party (for six months, before creating the Republican Military Association), General Miguel Primo de Rivera (dictator for six years), General Damaso Berenguer (for one year), Admiral Juan B. Aznar (for four months), General Francisco Franco (self-proclaimed chief of the state for more than 37 years and chief of government for 35 years), Admiral Luis Carrero Blanco (chief of government for one year and a half) plus about one dozen more uniformed men for shorter periods.

Once and again, military *pronunciamientos*, coups and dictatorships were led by former chiefs of the police or the Civil Guard previously involved in internal repression. For instance, the leaders of the two coups of 1874, to overthrow the Republic and to restore the monarchy, Generals Pavia and Martinez Campos, respectively, had been appointed chiefs of police by the governments of the Republic for the repression of social agitations in Andalusia and Cartagena. The *pronunciamiento* against the Second Republic in 1936 was led by defeated Africanists, as mentioned, but also by Generals Queipo de Llano, who was director of the Carabiners Corps; Munoz Grandes, chief of the republican police known as the Assault Guard; Cabanellas and Sanjurjo, former directors-generals of the Civil Guard; Mola, former director-general of security; and Franco, who had also participated in the repression of strikes.

During Franco's rule, more than one-third of the ministers were members of the military (40 out of 114), including the two vice presidents of the government, General Agustín Munoz Grandes and Carrero; the three ministers of the army, the navy and the aviation; most ministers of public order or governance; and a number of generals in charge of foreign affairs, finances, industry and commerce, public works and the movement (the fascist party). There were always between four and eight members of the military in Franco's governments. Also, in the fake parliament named like the medieval Cortes, near 1,000 of the about 4,000 procurators in

25 years were members of the military. As was acknowledged later by the chief of Falange, several times minister and Franco's cuñadissimo, Ramon Serrano Suñer, "In the end, the center of gravity, the support of the regime (despite the [fascist] appearances that we foolishly tried to exaggerate), was and would continue to be the army."

Likewise, the coup of 1981 was mostly executed by members of the Civil Guard, including its would-be leader, General Armada, who had fought the anti-Franco guerrillas in the 1940s; its main operator, Lt.-Colonel Tejero; and numerous members of the secret police for the so-called anti-subversive war, which was the origin of their politicization: Lt.-Colonel Sanmartin, majors Cortina and Pardo Zancada and Captains Alba and Sanchez Valiente.

of military personnel will be reduced to about 100,000 individuals, which is about half the size it was in 1930 and less than one-third the size it was in 1970—that is, a proportion of the country's total population about four times smaller than in many decades (and 15 times smaller than at the peak of the empire in the seventeenth century).

Crucial for such a dwarfing was a gradual reduction of the length of the military service and the lessening of the quotas of young men recruited, which culminated with the suppression of the draft. In fact, the actual number of soldiers and marines may be significantly lower than planned due to lack of volunteers. The current armed forces are, in fact, a small mix of professional mercenaries, temporary soldiers and foreign recruits, which may evoke prestate formulas from before the nineteenth century.

Some remnants of the past praetorian army still exist. In the Constitution of 1978, the armed forces are included in the preliminary title that deals with the basic elements of the state and the nation. They are assigned, among other missions, the "defense of the territorial integrity" of Spain. This is in contrast to most democratic constitutions, which naturally place the army in a title dealing with the government and the administration elements and circumscribe its tasks to the external defense of the country.

The Royal Ordinances of the armed forces establish the following: "The members of the Armed Forces will feel to be heirs and depositaries of the Spanish military tradition," which, as we have seen, in its vast majority was formed by colonial wars, *pronunciamientos*, coups, civil wars and dictatorships. Still on the Day of the Fallen for the Fatherland of 2017, General Fernando Alejandre, chief of staff of the defense, that is, the highest military authority, proclaimed, "Our history is full of examples where the Spanish military put their love of Spain before any other consideration, contributing to that today, proud of our past, we are a great Nation," and confirmed that "the same spirit of the Spaniards that so many glorious pages have written is still alive today in our Armed Forces."

While the military jurisdiction does not deal with crimes committed by civilians anymore, it includes sanctions for the military for conduct unrelated to crimes in the penal code, and it remains largely independent (except for the possibility to appeal its sentences to the Supreme Court).

Also, the Civil Guard continues to be a military organ, in spite of its name. It is subject to the Royal Ordinances of the Armed Forces, it is entrusted with military missions, even abroad, and one-third of its members continue to live in socially secluded barrack houses. During 15 of the 20 years after 1996, the director general of the Civil Guard was a general or a high officer of the army.

The main technical modernization of the Spanish armed forces was the consequence of successive cooperation agreements with the United States since 1953 and of joining NATO in 1981 and its military structure in 1999. As such, a few hundred Spanish soldiers and civil guards have participated in multiple missions abroad, especially in Lebanon under a mandate of the United Nations, Afghanistan within the NATO structure and in Bosnia under European Union command.

After the housing and financial bubbles burst in the early twenty-first century, the government expanded public spending and approved Special Programs of Armament to purchase frigates, airplanes and drones, which eventually produced enormous debts, a financial crisis and operational paralysis. Like in the extra spending in reaction to the other bubbles, grandiosity and incompetence bloomed. A telling anecdote is that one of the star gadgets of the programs, the battle tank Leopard, which weighs 66 tons, cannot be transported by air because the maximum load of a military aircraft is 40 tons.

In an austerity reaction, since 2012 successive cuts of military spending have been implemented in the annual budgets, which have severely reduced the army's operationality. While NATO members hold the commitment to spend 2 percent of their GDP in military resources, the Spanish contribution is below 1 percent and gives no sign that it is going to imitate the increases in the larger European countries.

The reduced military budget continues to be almost entirely spent on personnel at the expense of equipment and materiel. During the second decade of the century, fuel for aerial and navigation practices has been drastically reduced. Military maneuvers have been virtually canceled. Some experts have described the current inoperative armament of the Spanish Army as "wrapped in bubble paper." In fact, only a fraction of the officially enrolled officers and soldiers are active and very few are permanent. The old words of a prime minister, above quoted, could be repeated without loss of accuracy: "We do not have to pretend arsenals and shipyards where there are only buildings and staffs that keep nothing and build nothing."

As a consequence of its small size and the scarcity of operational resources, the Spanish Army continues to be unable to defend the country from foreign attacks. This has been the case during the last 200 years, but it is even more so now, when the army is a miniature copy of what it had been. As the territorial regions under control by a few captain generals were disbanded, the army would not be able to display an internal occupation of the country either. The current Spanish Army appears to be a shrunken version of what the institution was during the previous two centuries: "a sedentary, bureaucratic" carcass, as it was branded by historian Raymond Carr. A weak state that tried to surrender almost all its tasks to the army has been replaced with a weak state that cannot even count with sufficient armed forces to defend the country.[8]

A Ruling Church

The other crutch of the Spanish state in early modern times, next to the army, was, like in the imperial age, the church. The sword and the altar were the main supporters, actually the indispensable substitutions of a precarious modern state.

The influence of the Catholic Church proved even more resilient and perdurable than the traditional Spanish militarism. Still today, in the twenty-first century, the church keeps its special jurisdiction away from the laws and courts that rule over all the other citizens of the country. It receives financial aid from the state, and it enjoys other privileges in education and the media. Most reverends in Spain conceive the church activities as a substitute for, or sometimes as a rival alternative to, the pretended monopoly of legislation by the state.

Since the early nineteenth century, the weak Spanish state continued to be dependent on the church, which fatally hindered its possible strengthening. The Spanish rulers did not share the universal ambition that gives the church its mission and is implicit in the meaning of the word "Catholic." On the contrary, every king, queen, regent, military or civil chief executive tried to retain the imperial privilege to appoint the bishops, thus chocking the connection between the dioceses and the pope. Then all durable conservative, moderate, liberal or progressive governments of modern Spain deferred to the ideological and secular powers of the Spanish Church.

The Constitution approved in Cadiz in 1812, which Raymond Carr saw as "the classical liberal constitution in Latin Europe in the early 19th century," was proclaimed, in fact, "In the name of Almighty God, Father, Son, and

Holy Spirit, author and *supreme legislator* of society." In its articles, it specified the following monopoly: "The religion of the Spanish Nation is and will perpetually be the Catholic, Apostolic, Roman, the only one true. The Nation protects it by wise and just laws and prohibits the exercise of any other." Only those professing the Catholic religion could be, thus, Spaniards. The bishops were devolved jurisdiction to censor books, which they would exert for more than 150 years.

The second most durable constitution of the period, approved in 1845, confirmed the main design: "The Religion of the Spanish Nation Is the Roman, Catholic, Apostolic"; the ensuing concordat with the Holy See added: "to the exclusion of any other cult." During the following Moderate period, the church retained its own jurisdiction over its members as well as the capacity for censorship. After the bitter experience of having seen many of the church's possessions expropriated without compensation by liberal and progressive governments and sold in the market, the church now obtained "the right to acquire by any legitimate title, and [that] its property and all that it has now or will acquire from now on will be solemnly respected."

This fusion or collusion between civil-military government and the church was kind of unique in Europe. The separation between the state and the church was firm not only in Britain and other majority-Protestant countries where the local churches were independent of the pope and the Catholic dogma but also in countries with a majority Catholic population, especially Belgium and France, most stably since the 1830s.

Even more consequential, since the mid-nineteenth century it was established in Spain that the "instruction in universities, colleges, seminaries, and public or private schools of any kind will be in all respects consistent with the doctrine of the same Catholic religion."

The most fundamental tool for keeping such a mission was the catechism; all Spanish children learned it by memory from thousands of editions during nearly four hundred years. The two most popular catechisms or summaries of what a Catholic should know and fulfill in order to be saved were named after their authors, "the Ripalda" and "the Astete." Both were largely overlapping on the basis of the doctrine established by the Counter-Reform Council of Trent. They postulated, for instance, that "the enemies of the Soul are three: The World, the Devil, and the Flesh." The Astete specified that "the flesh is the greatest enemy," because we can run away from the world and the devil, but the flesh "cannot be thrown out of us."*

---

* The book *El Catecismo explicado* (The Catechism Explained) was printed annually for many decades to guide the priests and teachers in their catechesis; specifically, it clarified that this doctrine about the flesh came from Saint Augustine, who held that when people

After the Vatican Council I, in 1870, the Astete itemized that "the principal errors condemned by the Church are fourteen, namely: Materialism, Darwinism, Atheism, Pantheism, Deism, Rationalism, Protestantism, Socialism, Communism, Syndicalism, Liberalism, Modernism, Secularism, and Freemasonry." It did not include, unfortunately, militarism or clericalism, which were, indeed, much more powerful in Spain than any of the other -isms mentioned, even than all of them combined.[9]

The most durable Spanish constitution ever, the one established in 1876, proclaimed Alphonse XII king by the grace of God and stated again that "the Catholic, Apostolic, Roman religion is that of the State." It softened the prohibition of other cults, as it settled that "no one shall be molested in Spanish territory for their religious opinions or for the exercise of their respective worship." But it confirmed that "no other ceremonies or public manifestations will be permitted than those of the State religion."

Franco's dictatorship resumed and exacerbated all those traditions. The concordat with the Vatican in 1953 consecrated the religious monopoly and the prohibition of other cults to manifest publicly. The church was assured legal immunity, it was given tax exemptions, the state generously defrayed the expenses of its activities and the priests and seminarians were released from the military service. The Catholic Church regained its competence in matrimonial causes, the control of teaching—focusing again on the ill-fated catechisms— and the censorship on books, songs and movies. Traditional processions, peregrinations, pilgrimages, congregations and liturgic displays proliferated all across Spain. A priest in the role of chaplain was appointed in every school, military barrack, youth recreational group, prison or hospital. In exchange, Generalissimo Franco recuperated the traditional imperial kings' power to appoint the bishops and the support and adoration of the church, which made the dictator march under a canopy and consecrated him as Caudillo of Spain by the grace of God.

The Spanish Church received some influence from the doctrinal renovation of the Catholic Church in the 1960s and early 1970s, the years around and after the Vatican Council II (including the replacement of the centenary catechisms). Some Catholic militants joined anti-Franco movements that took benefit from the legal immunity of churches and convents.

lived in paradise before the original sin, "Rather than being excited by lust, the men's genital organs moved at the will's command, as the other members are," or like "some people can move their ears or produce at will such musical sounds from their backside that they seem to be singing from that part." He suggested that women had similar powers, but he did not elaborate. After losing that power of will on the genital organs, the humans fell victims of "concupiscence, of their disordered passions and appetites," which they ought to fight.

This facilitated that a new democratic Constitution approved in 1978 declared that "no religion shall have a state character." It was the first time for such a declaration in the history of Spain. Yet, at the time, a new concordat had already been negotiated and was signed immediately thereafter. It guarantees the Catholic Church "the free and public exercise of its own activities, especially those of worship, jurisdiction, and magisterium," large public funding, the right to acquire new properties and a tax exemption regime. Most new presidents of government and ministers continued to be sworn into office on copies of the Bible and the Constitution and in front of a crucifix.

From Picaresque to Corruption

If there is no state, there cannot be rule of law. As we saw, the peak of the Spanish Empire, in the sixteenth and seventeenth centuries, was years of glory and also of ruins and desolation. The arts and literature reflected the duality: the "Golden Century" of famous literates ran in parallel to the picaresque, the genre depicting the lives of those who made it by their wits, that is, in a society without law or state.

The picaros have been described as petty criminals skipping rules in a corrupt society. "They all steal, they all lie, they all cheat; none complies with their duties, and the worst thing is that they take pride in it," it is said in the novel *Guzmán de Alfarache*. But the picaros can also be understood as clever and inventive folks making their lives in a poor and lawless society. If "all" steal, lie and cheat, that is, if nobody complies, if "all live in stalking each other," as also summarized by Guzmán, it must be because there is no such thing as law and civilized social norms where they live. The picaros characters are presented in the literature as dishonest but appealing; if they take pride in their behavior, it must be because their demeanor responds to prevalent codes and norms.

Actually, the picaro is a mostly positive counterfigure to the military hero and the religious saint, the byproduct of a society dominated by militarism and clericalism. The picaresque is a way of life in a society in which one could make one's way by cleverness and roguery rather than by legal compliance and honest work. The readers who see the idle soldier, the vicious cleric, the venal judge, the ignorant doctor, the pedantic wiseacre, parading in the picaresque tales, are seeing the society of the time.[10]

Modern corruption is just a continuation of the picaresque way of life. The word "corruption" literally implies the decomposition of something that was pure or correct, such as a corrupted fruit or a degenerate boy that was pure but mingled with bad companies. But that is not the case of political corruption.

Traditional picaresque practices are not a degeneration of anything that was pure or correct before. It has been the normal way to do things. The picaresque becomes something morally condemnable and the occasion of scandal only when some innovative legislation or regulation is introduced. The introduction of standards for contracts, laws affecting commerce, new taxes, regulations of political party finances, regular procedures to hire public personnel and to make public decisions clash with arrangements that were traditionally not submitted to formal restraints. In this sense, it is the law that makes the corrupt, as the latter is nothing but the traditional picaro, just living now in a different legal and institutional context.

After all, making deals with relatives, neighbors, protégés, clientele, previous business partners, friends, casual acquaintances or passersby is simple and primitive, one could say almost "natural" forms of economic and political exchanges. In contrast, to treat everybody on equal basis, attending only to merit and the rule of law, requires high levels of learning and training and of institutional development that some countries, including Spain, have not gotten to achieve on a highly visible degree.

"Corruption is one measure of the absence of effective political institutionalization […] also symptomatic of the weakness of political institutions," as put by political scientist Samuel Huntington. "Corruption in a modernizing society is thus in part not so much the result of the deviance of behavior from accepted norms as it is the deviance of norms from the established patterns of behavior," he insightfully elaborates. That is the source of scandal: "New standards and criteria of what is right and wrong lead to a condemnation of at least some traditional behavior patterns as corrupt."

In Spain, the deviance between norms and conduct can be traced back to imperial times, when the colonists in the New Indies followed the lemma: "The law is acquiesced but not enforced." A "cultural habit with strong historical continuity" was then formed and persists to our days, in the view of sociologist Enrique Gil-Calvo. It is "the apparent compliance in public with the official regulations while in the private sphere they are breached in practice. Such a cultural and moral ambivalence, reproduced by the picaresque and the tolerance with corruption, is at the origin of the little respect for the law that continues to persist in Spain to this day [2016], where informal practices often contradict constitutional legality."

The critical point, in which Spain sank in early modern times, is when the innovative, modernizing norms are strong enough to call into question old standards but not sufficiently strong to prevail in social uses. Then, the legitimacy of all standards, of all norms, old and new, is undermined.

This kind of normative vacuum was brightly reflected in the Argentinian tango *Cambalache* (pejorative for *Swaping*), which complains,

Today it turns out that it is the same
Be right that traitor! [...]
Ignorant, wise or crook,
Generous or scammer!
Everything is the same! Nothing is better!
Same a donkey that a great professor!
There are neither fails nor promotions.
The immoral ones have leveled us.
If one lives in the imposture
And another steals in his ambition,
It does not matter whether it is a cleric,
slacker, king of wands,
conman or stowaway.
What a lack of respect! what outrage to reason!
Anyone is a gentleman!
Anyone is a thief!

This type of situation makes some individuals feel that they have open opportunities to act in ways that are not justified any longer by traditional norms—the picaros are not as admired as they were—but not strongly condemned by the new ones either, as their implementation is so loose. The weakly enforced innovative rules of law transform the traditional, pervaded picaresque into widespread, systemic corruption at relatively low cost for those involved in that kind of transactions and cheats.

In turn, corruption tends to perpetuate the weakness of the rule of law or to weaken it even more. If the state administrative, legal and judicial resources devoted to monitoring illegal activities are feeble, the probability of detecting such behavior may be low, which can encourage more individuals to engage in illegal affairs. For every individual, the moral cost of feeling guilt for committing illegal actions may be lower the higher the number of people around doing the same. Socially, even if a social norm exists that stigmatizes corruption, the loss of reputation may be relatively moderate when corruption is widespread.

The peculiar point about Spain is that, as in some other fields of social activity, some modernization of laws and regulations has been, indeed, tried, but most attempts have been scarcely successful. It is not that everybody has always been content with perpetuating the picaresque. If business had been kept as usual, people would not be unhappy but rather ignorant and resigned— as occurs elsewhere, in very poor, isolated places. But in Spain, most civilizing attempts have either stopped midway, failed or even backfired all along, which is the source of broad frustration.

Well into the twenty-first century, it has been estimated that the amount of illegal or "black market" economy that lies outside regulation and taxation amounts to up to one-fourth of Spain's production and prevents the state from collecting more than one-fourth of its potential revenue. Another hint about the relative volume of corruption in the private sector comes from the estimate that 20 percent of the 500euro bills are in Spain, while the Spanish GDP is only about 7 percent of the eurozone.

In the public sector, it is estimated that thanks to the lack of competition and transparency, outsourced contracts are overpriced up to one-fourth of their real cost, in order to make private companies able to pay bribes and fees to public officers, political parties and brokers. Of course, tax evasion on the one hand and overcost of public projects on the other make the ruin of public finances. To be able to fund planned public budgets, regulators have imposed on honest taxpayers relatively high fiscal pressure, in European comparative terms—naturally, at the expense of availability of resources for legal private economic activity.[11]

* * *

With the approach just presented, we can realize that the succession of scandals is not a good measure of actual corruption. The occurrence of scandal depends only on the strength of innovative legal rules clashing with traditional behavior and on the efficacy of fiscal, police, judiciary and public opinion mechanisms to detect the clashes and publicize them.

In modern Spain, the first sound scandals of corruption began to detonate in the 1830s and 1840s, when liberal reforms began to be attempted. The Regent Mary Christine, the widow of King Ferdinand VII, was sent into exile twice after being accused of mingling in railway, salt and slave traffic businesses, together with her second husband (a sergeant of her bodyguard) and her prime minister Narvaez. Every further attempt at introducing more transparency in public affairs was followed by the emergence of new scandals when traditional practices were uncovered and agitated in public.

In the Restoration period, two main party leaders and alternating presidents of government, Canovas and Sagasta, held shares in banks and companies that had been given monopoly positions by the government for building railways, even while they each held the office of executive chief. During the Second Republic in the 1930s, a scandal exploded when a center-right minister was accused of being involved in a fraudulent roulette business, with the major consequence that the government resigned and the subsequent snap election opened the door to the left government of the Popular Front.

The regime of General Franco made corruption an instrument of government. Covered by secrecy, intimidation and fear, public officers at all levels took over and appropriated private companies, trafficked with imports and exports licenses, provoked fraudulent bankruptcies and speculated with urban planning and with the construction of lodging in the surroundings of large cities in what was called vertical barracks. Listing the ministers and other officials or accomplices involved in this type of activity would require the volume of a telephone list. But only a few scandals came to light, such as when an apartment building collapsed, fraudulent products poisoned hundreds of customers or a Ponzi scheme fell apart.

There is no evidence that there is more corruption in the current democracy than in the previous dictatorship. Probably there is less in relative terms to population and the number of public officers but more in absolute terms because the volume of private and public resources has expanded so much. What there is certainly much more is scandals, again produced by the clash between traditional practices and new regulations and norms conceived to favor transparency, efficiency and the rule of law. Since 1990, about 1,700 denouncements (an average of more than one per week during 27 years) have provoked about 500 investigations or allegations.

Pervading irregular exchanges that have been potential subjects of scandals include mismanagement of private companies, the looting of public offices or publicly subsidized companies and contractual and financial exchanges between the private and the public sectors, the latter including the coffers of political parties.

In the private sector, it is not unusual to see managers and executives accused of having led a large company to ruin while plundering its funds or concealing assets. Famous examples include Rumasa, owned by the Ruiz-Mateos family; Banca Catalana, managed by Jordi Pujol, who had become president of Catalonia when he was accused; Spanish Credit Bank or Banesto, managed by Mario Conde; several successive presidents of the General Society of Authors and Publishers in charge of managing intellectual property rights; or Marsans Travels, led by Gerardo Díaz Ferrán, who was also the president of the Spanish employers' organization (CEOE or Spanish Confederation of Entrepreneur Organizations). Most often, private company managers may self-allocate mammoth bonuses or retirement pensions in their own benefit. Sports celebrities and stars of show business are prosecuted for tax evasion.

In the public sector, some officers have just taken money from public coffers by forging receipts for expenses, setting fraudulent preretirement pensions or grabbing personal bonuses from reserve funds officially allocated to persecute crime, terrorism or other secret missions. Traditional "reptile funds," which were used to pay rascal informers, infiltrators and whistle-blowers, have passed directly to the pockets of politicians and their appointees. Minister of Interior José Barrionuevo, chief of the Civil Guard Luis Roldán and some of their accomplices were imprisoned for these and other crimes.

Some financial subsidies from the European Union or certain ministries have also been allocated to different recipients than those officially entitled, such as a textile industry, humanitarian aid or professional training for the unemployed. Minister of Agriculture Loyola de Palacio and Minister of Public Works José Blanco, among others, were accused of such things.

Much more generalized has been the selling of public contracts not put up for tender, zoning requalification, permits and licenses of activities and the irregular hiring of personnel, in exchange for kickbacks from private companies, especially those involved in construction and the real estate business. A number of big construction companies, in particular, were suspected of participating in those kinds of exchanges, including Agromán, Copisa, Cubiertas y MZOV, Dragados y Construcciones, Entrecanales y Távora, Ferrovial, OHL and many others. Naturally, the subsequent projects were overpriced for the additional cost.

Members of governments of all 17 autonomous communities have been involved in this type of scandal, together with mayors or local councilors from 39 of the 50 province capitals. Several regional presidents, including from Andalusia, Asturias, Balearic Islands, Cantabria, Madrid, Murcia, Navarre and Valencia, as well as a few dozen town mayors, especially from coastal and touristic zones, have been formally indicted and arrested or have resigned from their jobs.

The president of Catalonia, Artur Mas, acknowledged in 2014 that he "would not put [his] hand in the fire for anyone." The deputy secretary of the Popular Party, Javier Maroto, declared in 2016, "There have been large numbers of people accused and even charged for corruption that have not been substantiated. Some are ministers today. If we had acted as Torquemadas [and removed them from office] with each case that appears, today there would be no councilman working in any city, no deputy, no senator, no member of any government."

Political parties were initially the main beneficiaries of the money illegally collected through their members' positions in the central, regional or local governments. The scandals have revealed that the usual fees paid by real estate and construction companies amount to a fixed percentage of the public works budget, whether 5 percent (to be split between 3 percent to the party and 2 percent to the broker), 4 percent (split 2.5 percent and 1.5 percent) or just 3 percent if the broker is directly a member of the party in place. The Gürtel scandal has shown that, at least in the case of the Popular Party led by Mariano Rajoy and Dolores de Cospedal, the same bribe for the party's finances has also been used to pay secret bonuses to senior officials.

Most denouncements of corruption against members of political parties in public office have originated in accusations from members of rival parties. While past harsh confrontation on major public policies tended to wane, corruption was becoming an expedient issue in political party competition. When Jordi Pujol was summoned to the Parliament of Catalonia to render explanations about his and some family members' covered business, he warned the parliamentarians of the diverse parties that "if a branch of the tree were bent, all would fall." His organicist metaphor meant, obviously, that persecuting one party could provoke reprisals against other parties and end in the destruction of the entire political party system. In fact, the tree has been shaken again and again. All in all, 44 percent of the scandals have implicated members of the PP, 31 percent of the Socialist Party (PSOE) and 25 percent of regional and local parties and candidacies.

Other scandals involving a mix of public and private arrangements include forging public contracts or using publicly subsidized bank funds for personal benefit. Modern picaros of this sort include, among many others, Iñaki Urdangarin, the husband of Infanta Cristina; Rodrigo Rato, former vice president of PP's government; Narcís Serra, former vice president of PSOE's government; banker Miguel Blesa; and Angel María Villar, president of the Spanish Football Federation.

The scandals have also touched the top of the judiciary: Carlos Dívar, president of the General Council of Judicial Power and of the Supreme Court, resigned from his posts under the accusation of using public resources for private expenses, and even Manuel Moix, the anti-corruption attorney himself, did it for evading taxes. This implies that the introduction of administrative and legal measures against corruption was fatally marred by the sleaze of some of the magistrates who were supposed to guarantee compliance with the anti-corruption measures.

Perhaps the most picturesque and closest case to the classical petty picaresque, in both style and substance, was the one featuring the Association of Users of Bank Services (Ausbanc) and an alleged trade union of public employees called Clean Hands. Ausbanc was supposed to defend the rights of bank customers regarding loans, mortgages, insurance and other financial services; it presented a Universal Declaration of the Rights of Users of Bank and Finance Services in Salamanca, which included access to credit without racial, religious or other discrimination and similar points. Clean Hands took its name from an Italian judicial investigation that had led to the overthrow of a few Italian governments and the dismantlement of the party system in the 1990s. Yet, it turned out that the leaders of Ausbanc and Clean Hands acted in collaboration to extort company executives, politicians and members of the royal family against whom they had lodged legal complaints. The two chumps that led the two mentioned gangs coordinated to demand large sums of money for one of them in exchange for the other to withdraw the complaint.

Thus, not only some top members of the judiciary in charge of prosecuting and condemning corruption turned out to be practitioners of the same type of crimes. In what could be a typical mischievous tale of the Golden Century, the anti-corruption popular campaigns by two saviors of the motherland were nothing but gross blackmail.

With this approach, one can understand that the more administrative and legal measures to monitor and prosecute corruption are adopted, the more scandals arise. It seems a paradox, but it just reflects the underlying, broadly pervasive practices that are gradually unveiled. An index of citizens' perception of corruption (not of corruption itself), which is published annually by Transparency International, shows that most Spaniards surveyed think that the levels of corruption are increasing year after year, corruption in Spain is more widespread than in most European countries and it will keep increasing in the foreseeable future. This does not mean, however, that there is increasing corruption. The increasing perception of corruption means that, as prosecution advances, more and more people are becoming aware of the extension and magnitude of traditional practices—which had been just a-legal for a long while.

Even under modern regulations, the subject may consent to some degree of corruption if the ruling few provide public goods and public policies improving security and well-being that are sufficiently satisfying. Let us take the example of some of the highest public expenses in democratic times: the massive public works and transportation ways that were set up for the Olympic Games in Barcelona and the Universal Expo in Seville in 1992. In retrospect, it is not easy to believe that so much public spending did not involve covered private businesses. But at that time many citizens who still remembered the systemic corruption and miserable performance of the previous dictatorship had the perception that the new authorities were delivering more. In those international events, even being Spanish was not necessarily a dishonor—an unusual feeling. Why, then, spoil the party with inopportune suspicions?

Yet, about 15 years later, the public sector entered a major crisis, much public spending was cut and a lot of public work projects were canceled. Condoning theft did not bring about sufficient compensation anymore. So, scandals and protests have surged. A vast, generalized panorama of irregular, unconstrained and illegal activities for private benefit has been uncovered. One after another, many branches have been falling from the entire tree.[12]

Primitive Rebels

A primitive, weak state also has primitive, wild rebels. Low institutionalization of social relations and low compliance with the rule of law favor protests, riots and rebellions rather than organized demands, ordered judicial processes and successful negotiations.

The typical Spanish riot is unorganized, confrontational and deprived of clear objectives, as it was already identified by Golden Century's playwright Lope de Vega in the town of Fuenteovejuna in the fifteenth century. In the fictionalized story based on real facts, the whole town, anonymously, and without leaders, rises against the tax, expropriation and abuse of women by the commander, occupy his palace and throw him out the window. The most active troublemaker encourages the others by shouting, "Knock them down, tear them down, smash, destroy, burn, sear them!"

As a sketch, the revolt profiles distinctive characteristics of protests and rebellions in Spain during the following centuries up to the present: secret conspiracy, violent assault, occupation of public buildings, personal attack, loitering and pillage, absence of concrete demands, failing to parley with the authorities, no alternative authority promoted, sheer defeat, codes of silence and refusal to give evidence to law enforcement agents.

There is "direct action" and no intermediaries, which displays the blatant weakness and refusal of institutions and law. Unsurprisingly, this course of action is self-reinforcing: it blooms from the destitute and the excluded, and their attacks provoke the rich's fear and the rulers' repression, thus excluding the rebels even more and jeopardizing the opportunities for building institutions with social consent.

Further notorious real episodes with similar styles include the "mutinies of the hungry" in Cordoba in the seventeenth century, the protests against Minister Esquilache for banning the wearing of long capes and broad-brimmed hats in Madrid and the riots against the recruitment of soldiers and the commotions for the price of bread in Barcelona, both in the eighteenth century. The *bullangas* of the nineteenth century, full of hustle and bustle, disturbance and merrymaking, added the burning of churches, convents and monasteries; the killing of monks; the rape of nuns; the assault of prisons, storage facilities and factories; tearing down statues; and fighting the army by violent means—each time producing hundreds of deaths.

Historian Eric Hobsbawm studied several variants of those "primitive rebellions." He paid attention, in particular, to the figure of the social bandit or bandit rebel: they are "robbers and outlaws who are not regarded by public opinion as simple criminals but rather as champions of social justice, as avengers or as primitive resistance fighters." Writer and Hispanist Gerald Brenan had anticipated the type: "The bandit had always been a feature of Andalusian life and for centuries had acted as a safety-valve for popular discontent. In the eyes of the country-people, he was a hero, the friend of the poor and its champion against the oppressors."

Hobsbawm saw those and other primitive forms of collective action as originated in the Middle Ages but also happening in the nineteenth and twentieth centuries in a number of backward regions in Europe. In Southern Spain, "villages had run themselves, both economically and politically, in their primitive way with a minimum of actual organization for administration, government and coercion," he noted. And in the context of such a weak state, "it seemed reasonable to assume that authority and the State were unnecessary intrusions"—that they could easily be eliminated. In short, the weakness of the state induced simple, primitive rebellions, which, in turn, served to weaken the state even more.

Historian Pierre Vilar also observed "those collective outbursts of passion which shook the Spanish people again and again during the 19th and 20th centuries, alternating with periods of depression and indifference, and always catching the government by surprise." He also noted that "they retained from the Middle Ages a taste for the spectacular and the macabre, a tendency to mass hysteria."[13]

Notary public Juan Diaz del Moral wrote a highly remarkable history of a series of rebellions in agrarian Andalusia, including a number of major ones provoked by periodic famines. He described those peasants' movements as "simple," "primitive," "infantile," "without any complication," as corresponding to "an imaginative and enthusiastic, totally uncultivated people," ready to follow any instruction or utopia, mixed with "groups of criminals."

Numerous episodes of direct action and unorganized revolt took place all across Spain. A defining characteristic of those agitations was their alienation from politics, that is, from parties, elections, representation and institutions. In Diaz del Moral's words,

> There was then in Andalusia, as in all Spain, an extensive current of opinion, common to all social classes, which considered politics as an amoral, lower order activity, whose themes and motives were used by its professionals to thrive, to create a position for themselves and to justify all sorts of excesses and deceits.

All students of the workers' movements in Spain have remarked its relatively weak intellectual component. Both the socialist parties, according to their first international leader, the German Karl Kautsky, and the communist parties, according to the Russian Vladimir Lenin, were formed by the merger of workers' syndicalism with ideas imported by intellectuals. The second component lacking in Spain, the workers' participation in regular politics, was always marred and bent toward anti-politics and anti-state instances. For historian Murray Bookchin, Spanish social movements, largely dominated by anarchism and anarcho-syndicalism, must be understood "as an expression of plebeian Spanish society itself rather than as a body of exotic libertarian doctrines."

The anarchist movements, "which dominated the workers' world in Catalonia from 1868 to 1939," according to historian Josep Termes, developed many of those traits. As he cites from anarchist journalist and writer Jacinto Toryho,

> In Spanish anarchism, they have come together the mystic and the criminal, the good man and the common delinquent, the sober labor leader and the vulgar demagogue. Alongside exemplary human behavior, we find tortuous individuals, confidants, gunmen, agents provocateurs, robbers, misfits.

In other words, a genuine representation of the wrecked Spanish society of the time.

Strikes, demonstrations, personal aggressions and assaults eventually led to terrorist attacks by bombs, first, and by gun and rifle shots and grenade explosions later on. Bombs were thrown, since the late 1870s, twice against King Alphonse XII in Madrid, against the captain general, the Opera Theater and the procession of Corpus Christi in Barcelona and twice against King Alphonse XIII in Paris and on his wedding day in Madrid as well as on other several dozen targets. A number of prime ministers were effectively assassinated: progressive Juan Prim in 1869, conservative Antonio Cánovas in 1897, liberal José Canalejas in 1912, conservative Eduardo Dato in 1921, as would also be the case of fascist Carrero Blanco in 1973.

From about 1914, it became increasingly usual to parallel every workers' mass strike with targeted armed attacks against employers, managers, policemen and squirrels, which were responded to by employers' counterterrorism against syndicalist leaders, lawyers and activists. More than one death every five days occurred for about 10 years. During the 1930s, assassinations for political motives skyrocketed, up to about three per week.

One of the anarchist leaders, Juan García Oliver, solemnly proclaimed, after he had become minister of justice of the Republic, that his anarchist group was "what I am not ashamed to say, what I am proud to confess: the kings of the workers' pistol of Barcelona! [...] the best terrorists of the working class."

During the Civil War and its immediate aftermath, up to about 80,000 landowners, bourgeois, priests, monks and nuns, on one side, and leftist politicians, intellectuals, syndicalists and anarchists, on the other side, were assassinated separately from the fights on the front and the tranches or the aerial bombardments. Some rural and urban guerrillas continued the resistance against the dictatorship until the 1950s.

Syndicalist Ángel Pestaña, who had been expelled from the anarchist union for his opposition to violence, wrote in his memoirs,

> We must recognize, with pain and shame [...] [that] almost all the robbers, those of Barcelona as those of other provinces, all come from the ranks of syndicalism and anarchism, and almost all have been good militants.

Assaults, political banditry or terrorism were not conceived, nevertheless, as a sufficiently strong weapon to change the social system or the political regime. They were just "revolutionary gymnastics," as put by García Oliver—a kind of training. It was widely assumed that the way to get the real thing would be the general strike, a mass action that would magically stop everything and would make people wake up in a different world. The myth was successively embraced by syndicalists, anarchists, socialists and communists.

The first general strike in Spain was initiated in Barcelona in 1855, and it was followed by numerous town and city strikes in places such as Alcoy, Jerez, Moron and on the first May Day in 1890. A most notable riot exploded during the so-called Tragic Week in Barcelona in 1909. Initially a revolt against military recruitment for the wars in Africa, it immediately became a chaos of demonstrations and barricades, assassinations, burning of churches, assaults on police stations and attacks on tramways, the results of which were about one hundred deaths, two thousand people subjected to military trials, and two thousand more moving into exile.

Since the foundation of the Work National Confederation (CNT) under anarchist inspiration in 1910, there was a general strike in Barcelona almost every year. Diaz del Moral also remarked the importance of the "general strike, the driving myth of all workers' movement," for the agitations in Andalusia.

The Socialist Party and its Workers' General Union (UGT) promptly joined the salvific myth. In 1917, the two unions, the anarchist CNT and the socialist UGT, called together a "general strike, without a defined deadline," which paralyzed the country for a week and produced several dozen deaths in clashes with the police. Such actions became more frequent in the 1930s, when repression receded and public policy did not deliver any substantial improvement, including in Madrid, Seville and the industrial towns of the Upper Llobregat in Catalonia. The socialists also participated in calling a general strike to be turned into an armed revolutionary insurrection against the rightist government of the Republic in 1934. The initiative mostly failed, except in Asturias, where for a few weeks the movement involved assaults to military barracks, public offices, mines and factories and numerous assassinations. There were about 1,500 deaths. Since then the socialists adopted the salute of raising the left fist, as the right arm was busy with holding the rifle.

In the late 1940s, the communists abandoned guerrilla tactics and also embraced the vintage myth of a general strike as a "weapon to put an end to the Franco's regime." After mostly unorganized boycotts of the tramways of Barcelona burst in 1951 and 1957 and some students' protests initiated in Madrid and Barcelona, the Communist Party tried to call a "Political General Strike," or HGP for its acronym in Spanish, focused on workers, which should provoke a "Peaceful National Strike" or HNP of the general population. Since the late 1950s, some communist activists tirelessly tried to call the Aitch En Gee and the Aitch En Pee as a major way to provoke a regime change. Strikes of miners in Asturias in 1962 raised some hopes. Still in the early 1970s, after some workers' strikes whose repression by the police resulted in deaths in Granada, Erandio (in Biscay), the SEAT factory in Barcelona and Ferrol, the Communist Party presented "the concept of National Strike as going further ahead than the one of Political General Strike." In the words of the communist leader in exile, Santiago Carrillo,

It is not only a question of paralyzing work, but of organizing the workers of each company, the neighbors of each neighborhood, each of the participating sectors, to intervene massively in the street [...] to institute organs of struggle and power at all possible levels [...] a modern form of the popular and national uprising.

During the first four years after Franco's death, the number of workers' strikes surged, largely motivated by a new economic depression and huge unemployment rates and facilitated by the easing of repression. Subsequently, there were a few calls for political strikes: against the military coup of 1981, against the war in Iraq in 2003 and even for the independence of Catalonia in 2017, but with few results. Other calls focused on specific union demands, especially regarding the labor market, the unemployment subsidy and retirement pensions, some of European scope. But the general strike was never substantiated as an effective weapon of general political change.[14]

* * *

Well into the twenty-first century, Spain is the country of Europe with the lowest rates of political association and the highest rates of public demonstrations, political violence and illegal protests.

The bottom place is granted to Spain for voluntary membership in political parties, labor unions, professional associations, community action groups and organizations concerned with the environment, human rights, women, peace or animal rights, which gather only between 1 percent and 3 percent of the population. The comparative low evaluation is valid for peoples of all ages, levels of education, levels of income and especially for women's participation. The levels of associational membership of Spaniards are between 5 and 10 times lower than those in Central and Nordic Europe and North America. Far from decreasing, cross-national differences are increasing over time.

At the same time, Spain is number one regarding protests that involve violence against persons or property, and it is very near the top on other confrontational direct mobilizations, such as sit-ins and boycotts—all according to survey data provided for eighteen Western democracies by political scientist Laura Morales.

The fact that the two features, low association and frequent protests, go together is not a special curiosity. In general, sociologists argue that, in current democracies, the frequency of protests is inversely related to the levels of political association membership. The countries where more intense protest is frequent are also those where the traditional socioeconomic, religious or territorial issues of conflict have not been pacified and institutionalized. This historical legacy of permanent disobedience and revolt acts as a deterrent to participate in better-established and more stable political structures and organizations. In Spain, long periods with authoritarian rule have also left many people with a permanent propensity to protest.

Again, there is a self-reinforcing circle: the persistence of old conflicts stimulates old forms of protest and riots, which in turn postpone the institutionalization of social struggles and leave the country behind others with more successful developments. In the words of sociologist Ruut Koopmans, social movements and political regimes "coevolve" or change together as the result of mutual adaptation. "The development and characteristics of protest are shaped by the available political opportunities for mobilization"—and vice versa, one could add.

The most outstanding recent contribution from Spain to shaping the profiles of social protest was the movement of the "Indignados," which followed a typical social movement cycle between 2011 and 2015. Visible connections with old Spanish traditions of protests and riots include the prominence of "the people" as a single mythical entity opposed to the privileged and corrupt elites, its anti-politics tone, the abundance of hustle and bustle, disturbance and merrymaking and a repertoire of forms of action largely centered on demonstrations, marches, assaults and "escraches." The latter word, which seems to be related to the Italian *scaracchio*—spit—means a concentration outside the house or workplace of public figures to shame them and draw attention to their crimes; it can be compared to very old traditional forms of protests above reported, from Fuenteovejuna on.

The peak of the Indignados movement was the concentration, sit-in, assembly and camping in the Puerta del Sol of Madrid from March 15 of 2011 on, promptly followed by similar actions in the Catalunya Square in Barcelona and in other several dozen cities, from which the movement was also known as "15-M." On the truck at the head of the demonstration in Madrid that very first day, the loudspeaker was foully chanting against the established political parties and labor unions:

> "Pesoé, Pepé [the two larger parties], it's the same shit."
> "Where are they, they cannot be seen, Commissions and Ugeté
> [the two larger workers' unions]."

The most popular slogans during the sit-in the following weeks were addressed against parliaments and governments and all kinds of formal institutions. The protesters chanted,

> "They do not represent us,"
> "It's called democracy but it is not."

The movement emphatically refused to have any leaders. It praised an undefined "direct democracy" and preached civil and political disobedience. Major forms of violence included the attempts to assault the Congress of Deputies in Madrid and the Parliament of Catalonia in Barcelona.

The typical dynamics of a noninstitutionalized protest movement such as this is as follows: its "power arises quickly, reaches a peak and soon evaporates or gives way to repression and routine," according to the analysis of major cases mainly drawn from Britain, France and the United States by political scientist Sidney Tarrow. "Because structures of opportunity change so rapidly, these successes are usually brief and their outcome sometimes tragic," he observes. For centuries, collective action arose among a variety of social groups without producing sustained interaction with authorities or elites. "Today, as well"—notes Tarrow—"violent, passionate collective action often erupts, only to be followed by dispersion and disillusionment."

Some of the sectoral movements that developed under the triggering influence of the 15-M were called "Tides," which may be an apt metaphor for a quick rise and fall. According to Tarrow and his disciples, a protest movement tends to rise like a tide and then split between those who choose to follow an institutionalized path and those who keep using forms of direct action, radicalize and may entangle themselves into a loop of sectarian involution.

Beyond these general characteristics, the specificity of the recent Spanish Indignados may lie in the massive use of the internet and its social networks, which accelerated the cycle: extremely quick rise and sudden disappearance when new political elections were held in the country. Political scientists Helen Margetts and Peter John observed in a broad comparative perspective that "social media can produce fast-growing but volatile grassroots movements. It is much easier to pull off a large protest than it used to be. But most mobilizations fail."

As analyzed by sociologist Sandra González-Bailón, "Decentralized networks facilitate mobilizations of unprecedented reach and speed, but are actually not very good at maintaining momentum, or creating particularly stable structures in comparison with traditional organizations."

For sociologist Zeynep Tufekci, "These networked movements would often devise initial innovative tactics and pull off a spectacular action, but they were unable to sustain and organize in the long term in a manner proportional to the energy that had been able to attract initially and the legitimacy they enjoyed in their demands."[15]

Derailment from the European Track

During the nineteenth and for most of the twentieth centuries, there were recurrent attempts in Spain to build new political and administrative structures appropriate for modern states. An agrarian reform, an industrial revolution, a professional army, public laicity, civil laws and labor regulations were indeed tried to be introduced —as we discussed—but the resistance against innovations frustrated the efforts, and the reaction prevailed.

As was insightfully summarized by political scientist Juan J. Linz,

> The 19th century saw a period of sudden break with tradition through political means that provoked reactionary rather than, strictly speaking, conservative responses and that was largely unaccompanied by other processes of modernization.

As a consequence of frequent political breaks and cultural and social discontinuities, "traditional legitimacy weakened without any successful modernization taking place," he concluded.[16]

This was different from the historical paths of England or France, each of which had built the bases of a modern state during the eighteenth and the early nineteenth centuries and only embarked themselves into new imperial enterprises after their states were solid enough. Also, the new state of Germany largely relied upon previously existing Prussia's administrative and military structures, while the new Italian state was initially created from the core of the older Piedmont Kingdom. These two latter countries suffered harsh although short-lived dictatorships and the destruction of World War II, but they were able to resume and improve their structures of governance from 1945 on and soon thereafter within a helpful European common framework. Spain experienced comparable calamities but upon weaker foundations and for longer periods, it remained gloomily isolated for decades, and only much later did it seriously begin to try to build a modern state. Meanwhile, the European and world contexts had already begun to change into a new era of broad interdependence and openness, which has partly frustrated the effort in an innovative way.

A crucial moment for the ultimate deviation of Spain from the European pattern may have been 1923, when Captain General Miguel Primo de Rivera staged a coup d'état after his *pronunciamiento* for "the salvation of the Motherland." This was the first of a series of five dramatic swings during the following 16 years that led to the definite derailment of Spain from the European track.[17]

Let us see, first, the initial moment. The initially excluded republicans, socialists and Catalan regionalists had been pushing to enter political competition within the existing institutional framework of the restored Bourbon monarchy. With that aim, they had set in motion an uprising against the regime in 1917, paralleled by a strike led by the anarchists. The subsequent monarchical governments responded by drafting some integrative and modernizing institutional reforms. In particular, the liberal prime minister Manuel García Prieto presented in December 1922 a broad program of reforms of taxes, religious cults, parliamentary rights, citizens' guarantees, the electoral system, agrarian property and labor arbitrage. The minister of grace and justice, Count of Romanones, would remember that they "believed that it was still time to consolidate the Monarchy as long as it was on a foundation of broad democracy, and we set forth a complete program affirming the supremacy of the civil power" over military and ecclesiastical powers.

It was "a transition from oligarchy to democracy," in Raymond Carr's words. "A catalog of reforms that, taken together, amounted to a radical democratization" of the regime, in the view of historian Carolyn Boyd. The government "embarked indeed upon a process of democratization and reform alarming vested interests," according to Shlomo Ben-Ami. García Prieto's was "an ambitious program which aimed at transforming in a democratic direction the constitutional monarchy to give it viability in the long term," as estimated by historians Ramon Villares and Javier Moreno Luzon. And then the Primo de Rivera's coup was motivated "by the need to stop García Prieto's program and his reformist-regenerationist agenda," for historian

Joan M. Thomàs. Because the government had announced that it would seek responsibilities for the defeat in the colonial war in Africa, the military reacted and the king conceded, thus supporting Primo de Rivera's *pronunciamiento* a few months later. This was the first coup.

It was followed by a republican countermove. The dictatorship was met with insurrectional and general strike conspiracies and a spurious electoral victory of a coalition of republicans and socialists. In the municipal elections of 1931, the latter obtained less than a minority of votes nationwide but most of the local councilors in the larger cities, which led them to proclaim the republic and to provoke the exile of the king.

The counter-counter-coup came soon, again in the form of a military uprising led by General Sanjurjo in 1932, and another spurious electoral victory, this time of the conservative right. In the second election of the Republic in 1933, a center-right republican split reached pre-electoral agreements with a new rightist party, the CEDA, formed by Catholics and agrarians. As the electoral system gave high premiums to the larger candidacies, both the coalesced center-right and right were supported by fewer voters but were given more seats than, this time, the more separated center-left republicans and left socialists if the latter are counted together. This was the third move.

The political left and the anarchists soon counter-counter-counter-reacted, again with a strike and armed insurrection in 1934, already mentioned, and a new spurious electoral victory in 1936. The center-left republicans and the left socialists and communists now ran together in a Popular Front, while the center-right was weakened and the right ran in a more extreme National Front formed by Catholics, agrarians and monarchists. This time it was the Popular Front that received support from fewer voters but was given more seats than the less unified center-right and right parties if the latter are counted together. (See Appendix with data on votes and seats in the Notes section at the end of the book.)[18]

The fifth counter-counter-counter-counter reaction did not take long to arrive. Just five months after the election, a military insurrection provoked a three-year carnage usually labeled "civil" war. In the two previous sweeps, 1932–33 to the right and 1934–36 to the left, violent uprising was both a form of protest against the previous equivocal electoral results and also the beginning of a pre-electoral campaign for the next occasion. Somehow, the insurrectionists were both pushing for a new, snap election and calling the electorally defeated groups to get together in the following contest. After two alternations in government, however, the military insurrection in July 1936 did not pretend to prepare any further election, neither spurious nor fine.

In short, the story was as follows:

1923—rightist coup and dictatorship.
1931—leftist spurious electoral victory and revolution.
1932–33—rightist coup and spurious electoral victory.
1934–36—leftist revolution and spurious electoral victory.
1936—rightist coup, civil war and dictatorship.

At the end of the Civil War, whatever elements of a state had existed had been destroyed. That is how the winners asserted the beginning of a "New State." Yet, immediately thereafter, Spain returned to a slightly revised version of its old political tradition: an absolutist military Caudillo by divine right ruling through a paltry, inept bureaucracy, now with the complements of firing squads, a fascist party and a political police and tribunals, serving a clique of landowners and a few bankers, over an ocean of unlawful and corrupt practices. In total, from the derailment by the coup of Primo to the late years of the Franco regime and the further transition, the project to build a modern, democratic national state was postponed for near 60 years.

A Bubble State

By the time Spain entered the European Community, by the mid-1980s, the still feeble Spanish state had begun to get rid of its two traditional crutches, the army and the church. The army was being dissolved as a political actor and was becoming a shrunken, sedentary bureaucracy, as we reviewed, while the church had also dwindled and was seeing its public influence significantly diminished.

Better able to walk on its own, without annoying crutches, the state began to inflate. Its financial and administrative resources expanded during the course of a couple of decades. Much of this inflation, however, would turn out to be a massive bubble prone to deflate. The illusion that, finally, after a very long historical delay, Spain had reached the status of a modern European state would be largely disappointed after the Great Recession.

Let us examine the changes with some data. In the last year of Franco's life, 1975, Spanish public spending had already increased a little but amounted to only about 25 percent of the gross domestic product (GDP). This was in contrast to the ratios of most West European countries of the time, which were at about 40 percent. In the following period, the Spanish public spending would almost double in relative terms, up to a peak of 48 percent of the GDP in 2012.

Yet, the central government was in control of just a little more than half of that spending (53 percent in 2016), while the rest was now in the hands of the autonomous communities and the local governments. This made the central government's spending as small in relative terms as it was about 40 years before (.48 × .53 = .25 percent).

Still, the relative robustness of the central government is an optical illusion—a kind of artistic trompe-l'oeil that it is perceived as something voluminous but turns out to be flat. Three-fourths of the central public spending is devoted, first, to payments automatically regulated by the Social Security system, especially elderly pensions and unemployment benefits; second, to payments of interests and repayments of public debt, which amounts to about 100 percent of the GDP and is—as typically in the history of Spain—impossible to be repaid but erodes public finances without pause; and, third, other transfers out of decision-making power by the government in place. Similarly, the autonomous communities spend the vast majority of their budgets on wages for health and school employees and on debt repayments.

It can be estimated that a central government that hypothetically pretended to modify the allocation of all expenses of the entire state budget would actually be able to reallocate less than 4 percent of the GDP. In practice, the government's discretionary spending is even lower, as it is constrained not only by entitlement programs with mandatory funding but also by long-term programs and other commitments.

The magnitude of absolute and relative public spending has been decreasing further since the rescue of the Spanish private and public finances by the European Union in 2012, which came together with a specific program to reduce public deficits and the subsequent accumulated debt. According to the plans of the Ministry of Economy, the total public spending of the Spanish state should drop to about 38 percent of the GDP in the early 2020s, which implies a cut of one-fifth of its previous size in 10 years. This will make the central government expense significantly smaller, in relative terms to the economy, than it was at the end of Franco's dictatorship—as it would land at around 20 percent of GDP.

A major consequence is the collapse of public investment. Spain is placed at the bottom of the European countries in infrastructure, health, education, research and development and other investments able to promote growth, at less than 2 percent of GDP. This is less than what would be needed for the maintenance of the existing installations. The consumption-oriented public spending cancels any potential effect on the recovery of the economy and rules out economic and social returns in the mid or long term. These types of drastic spending cuts have been introduced for years not only on the central government but also in the regional and local ones.

A similar evolution can be observed regarding public employment. In 1975, there were nearly 700,000 public employees in Spain, about 90 percent of them in the central government. Since then, the public staff has multiplied, up to nearly 3 million people—the vast majority of them being life-appointed civil servants. Yet, more than 80 percent of current public employees now work in the autonomous communities, the local governments or the universities. The absolute number of public officers in the central administration of the state, including Social Security and the armed forces, was in 2017, at 522,000 people, much lower than in 1975, and their relative number is, obviously, very much lower regarding the increased population.

That is not all. In fact, the most important constraint on the capability of the Spanish state to rule on its own derives from its membership to the European Union (EU). Like in most European countries, much of the Spanish legislation enacted every year is derived from the EU. During the four years 2012–2015, the institutions of the European Union, that is, the Parliament, the council and the commission, approved an annual average of 22 directives to be transformed into state law or administrative acts by the member states. During the same period, when the Spanish single-party government had a majority of seats in the Congress of Deputies, the latter approved an annual average of 63 legislative initiatives, counting organic laws, laws, decree-laws and legislative decrees. This means that 35 percent of all Spanish legislation was derived from European directives. The proportion nears 50 percent regarding legislation with significant economic impact.

During the last two decades, the EU has approved about 2,000 directives that have been transformed into state legislation or administrative acts, with similar effects on the legislative activity of state parliaments, in addition to some 12,000 regulations that are directly binding on all European citizens without going through state institutions. Thus, the vast majority of recent legislation to be enforced over the citizens comes either directly or indirectly from the EU.

The absence of government in Spain during 2016, when two elections took place in six months, and the minority status of the governments that followed them, further reduced the legislative production of the Spanish Parliament. The Parliament limited itself to ratifying European Union directives, updating and extending the budgets of the previous period and calling the next election, while the government routinely resorted to governing by decree. Most of the autonomous communities, more than ever before, did not approve their budgets on time either.

In short, the Spanish central state is, in both financial and administrative resources, relatively smaller than it was more than 40 years ago. The growth of the population and the economy during that period has accompanied the growth or the creation of local and regional governments and the decrease of the relative size of the central government, which has transferred decision powers on many issues to the new decentralized bodies. Since the explosion of the Great Recession, the state has been consistently thinning. Also, the Spanish state's capacity of decision making is now strongly constrained on important issues by the principles, directives and guidelines of the European Union, which jeopardizes the notion of sovereignty traditionally associated to the essence of the state.

The current Spanish central state is neither what it was nor it will be what it could have been. The state relies upon a big financial and administrative bubble. The state bubble is not likely to suddenly burst, like the real estate or the banking bubbles did. But it has been pricked and, like an erratic balloon leaking air, it may keep deflating for a while.[19]

Chapter 3

AN INCOMPLETE NATION

Local Patriotisms
The Imperial Burden
The Damned "Mili"
Parochial-Catholicism
Multiple Languages
Tribes with Flags and Chants
National-Footballism
Not Very Spanish, After All

Some nationalists hold that "nations" exist from time immemorial and that they have always been the basis for sovereign national states. This approach to the question, which is called "essentialist" or "primordialist," has been challenged during the last several decades, as the emphasis in the analysis has moved to the importance that diverse economic and political processes have for initially creating and constructing "nations" where there were not.

The "constructivist" approach has become dominant in current social studies. Several decades ago, political scientist Karl Deutsch had already remarked that "the idea of nationality became compelling to people only in the modern period as a result of economic and attendant social changes," especially regarding education and the construction of areas of social communication. Historian Ernest Gellner observed that "nationalism, which sometimes takes pre-existing cultures and turns them into nations, sometimes invent them, and often obliterates pre-existing cultures." Historian Eric Hobsbawm sternly stated, "Nationalism comes before nations. Nations do not make states and nationalisms but the other way around."

More recently, political scientist David Laitin has observed that, still, "people often believe, mistakenly, that certain social categories are natural, inevitable, and unchanging facts about the social world. They believe that particular social categories are fixed by human nature rather than by social convention and practice." Contrariwise—he holds—it was the "English,

French, and Spanish kings [that] sought to emphasize a common 'national' culture to help bring coherence and efficiency to state rule."

A modern nation exists as long as people who do not know each another on a face-to-face basis imagine that they form a unified community. The basic shared references in people's imagination are a territory, a race, a religion, a language and other cultural elements. A typical process may start, first, with nationalist movements and state rulers selecting and activating some previously existing cultural traits of the population, such as those just mentioned, making people believe that they form a single community with others that share the same traits and trying to make them the unifying standard for all.

Then, the drawing of borders and boundaries depends on political developments, including empires, states and rebellions' victories or defeats in wars, partisan fights and diplomatic arrangements. It is, thus, the nationalists that may design cultural nations and create political communities, such as modern states, which in turn can establish borders and actually try to build and complete culturally unified nations. The nation is not the main explanatory factor of political developments but rather one of its results, whether successful or frustrated. As put by the "constructivist" approach, the building of nations and homogeneous ethnic communities is "endogenous" to political and economic changes.

The relevant point regarding Spain derives from the fact that, generally speaking, a weak state cannot build a robust modern nation. And that is why the weak Spanish state—which had been marred by imperial adventures during several centuries—has never been able to complete the construction of a unified Spanish nation. Many people in Spain imagine that they belong to a unified community called Spanish nation. Many other people do not; large groups have resisted Spanish cultural assimilation and some imagine, instead, that they belong to alternative nations.

The building of large nation-states in Western Europe in modern times was made feasible by new transport technologies that changed the scale of human relations and the size of viable political communities, especially railways in the nineteenth century and roads in the twentieth century. Although many individuals living in the same state territory did still not know each other face-to-face, they could travel, trade and relate to hypothetical compatriots farther away than before when the local arena was paramount.

The states tried to inspire a common language, common patriotic values and new symbols and myths by modern means of persuasion, coercion and repression. They include compulsory instruction by state schools, the military service and the expansion of messages by mass communication media, particularly newspapers in the nineteenth century and public radio and television in the twentieth century.

In all these endeavors, the success of the Spanish state was limited, and the building of a culturally unified nation remained incomplete. In comparison to other, more successful attempts to build modern nation-states, Spain has remained highly fragmented inside, where localisms prevail, and rather isolated outside, which does not help to imbue a sentiment of national unity in rivalry with neighbors or against foreign enemies either.

Political scientist Stein Rokkan noted that in medieval and modern Europe "there was nowhere a complete fit between the 'state' and the 'nation.'" Even in the case of France, which is usually conceived as the most successful one in achieving a culturally unified nation, the aim was not significantly fulfilled until very late. Just to mention some data: During the Revolution and the First Republic, in the late eighteenth century, only 20 percent of the population spoke French and 40 percent were able to follow a conversation in that language. Before the establishment of the Third French Republic in 1871, "many did not speak French, but a wealth of tongues, or know (let alone use) the metric system, *pistoles* and écus were better known than francs, roads were few and markets distant," as extensively studied by historian Eugen Weber. He saw, in general, "the nation not as a given reality but as a work-in-progress, a model of something at once to be built and to be treated for political reasons as already in existence"—as has happened in all other cases, including Spain.

Rokkan suggested that in the "model" case of France, state building indeed preceded and drove nation building, but in other cases, such as Italy and Germany, it was a process of nation building, both economic and cultural, that supported late processes of state building. However, it has been noted that, even in Italy and Germany, some forms of state building historically preceded nation building because it was the existence of core states, Piedmont and Prussia, respectively, that made the building of modern nations possible.

In the case of Italy, in particular, at the time of the unification of the peninsula under the Savoian Crown in 1870, less than 3 percent of the inhabitants spoke the variant of Tuscan that would be adopted as the national language. The vast majority spoke Sicilian, Lombard, Venetian and other tongues (including the Savoyards themselves, whose habitual languages were Piedmontese and French). When the Republic was established after World War II, in spite of the previous efforts of the fascist government to impose a homogeneous language, less than 20 percent of the population spoke standardized Italian. State school, radio and television eventually made the biggest difference.

Regarding the Spanish experience, political scientist Juan J. Linz, who extensively studied the case, concluded that Spain achieved "limited success in state-building and failure in nation-building." During the final years of Franco's dictatorship, he observed,

The Spanish state never achieved what French kings and ultimately the Revolution did: to create the fully unified state and a nation-state with its linguistic-cultural and emotional integration [...] The ultimate outcome of the Spanish state-building process was not like the French, Portuguese, or even Italian or German, nor was it like the British [...] It did not fully succeed in building a nation-state [...] Castilian-speaking Spain was not strong enough to assimilate the periphery to the degree France was capable of doing with Brittany and its small Catalan minorities. Spain, born in the era of state-building, could not undergo the deep emotional process of democratic nation-building that the Italians underwent and Germany experienced since political unification.

More than 30 years later, Linz and Alfred Stepan confirmed, "In the Spanish case, like that of quite a few other countries, would-be nation-builders who sought to create a unique sense of identity based on language, history and culture following the French model, ultimately failed."

In the context of a new democracy and European integration, Linz saw the project of completing the building of a Spanish nation-state as unviable: "From today's perspective those endeavors of modern states appear as far from formidable and represent a cost that many of us would not like to pay." Specifically, "an educational and cultural policy like that of the French Third Republic is difficult to conceive," since it included oppressive and discriminatory policies that now would probably turn to authoritarianism.[1]

The following pages review some of the limited, frustrated and failed attempts to build a culturally unified Spanish nation in modern times. After a brief overview of the historical dynamics, we will focus on the main elements of the frustrated nation: the burden of the imperial legacy, the counter-effective military service, the superficial and localist traditions of the Catholic religion, the incomplete dominance of the Castilian language and the divisiveness of national symbols. The result of the weakness of these processes is, as we will see, that the Spaniards' allegiance to the nation is the lowest of all democratic states in Europe, they are divided about the contents of the national identity and large parts of them do not consider themselves Spanish nationals.

Local Patriotisms

The resistance against the invasion of the Iberian Peninsula by Napoleon's French troops in 1808 has often been taken as the origin of a modern Spanish nation. To sustain this, however, the focus has been put on the beliefs, speeches and plans of those members of the Parliament (*Cortes*) who took refuge in Cadiz who called themselves "liberals" and produced the Constitution of 1812.

The Spanish liberals did not consider the possibility of designing a federation of diverse political and territorial units as had been done in Switzerland or the United States but rather tried to follow the French model of political and administrative unification of the large territory. In the absence of the sovereign king and his heirs, who had been kidnapped by Napoleon, the Parliament transferred the sovereignty to "the nation," which is why they have been considered modern nation founding fathers.

However, the 1812 Constitution defined the Spanish nation as "the gathering of all the Spaniards of both hemispheres." It included, thus, the colonies in the Americas whose colonists were represented in the Parliament (in contrast to the British colonists in North America, whose lack of representation in the British House of Commons had triggered their movement for independence about three decades before). The Constitution of Cadiz was, thus, an imperial constitution, rather than a national one. The most basic element of a modern nation, territorial unity, was not fulfilled for both the exclusion of Portugal and the inclusion of the transatlantic empire.

Also, as we have mentioned, the Constitution was strongly confessional. It was proclaimed on behalf of "Almighty God, Father, Son and Holy Spirit," who was appointed the "author and supreme legislator of the society." The Catholic Empire was still a sturdy foundation of the constituents' endeavor.

In parallel, the popular uprisings against the French troops that developed across the peninsula were rather varied in their inspirations and aims but, generally speaking, not very liberal at all. Local patriotisms predominated over national unity. The number one heroine of the resistance—who would become one of the myths of the Spanish patriots later on—was Agustina Zaragoza or Agustina of Aragon. Her folks and followers famously sang:

> The Virgin of the Pillar says
> That She does not want to be French,
> That She does want to be captain
> Of the Aragonese troops.

Note that Spain was not even mentioned. The most popular slogans of the fighters against the French and Napoleon, who were pinpointed as atheists and sacrilegious, were for the religion, the church, the virgin and God as well as for the absolutist king Ferdinand VII. For most participants, rather than a nationalist uprising, it was a holy war, a new religious crusade.

In Catalonia, "nation is not part of the vocabulary of the spontaneous popular resistance [...] Homeland (patria) dominates over nation in an overwhelming way and has no precise political content (perhaps not even territorial)," according to the documents compiled by historian Pierre Vilar.

In other places, the war's discourse "sometimes it is pure xenophobic emotion; in others, it responds to a liberal ideological discourse [...] the local juntas are plagued with patriotic content very different from the triumphant one" in the Cadiz Parliament. Even in the speeches of many members of the latter, "the nation was the land, the blood, the inheritance, the mother," a medieval notion alien to the modern liberal concept of citizenship and shared law, according to historian Ricardo García Cárcel.

Historian Ronald Fraser reviewed hundreds of pamphlets from local juntas from all across Spain looking for "the voices and actions of common people" and concluded, "Popular sovereignty, like the modern nation, was an abstract notion to those, like villagers, brought up to believe in monarchy and Church, a novelty which was vigorously combatted by absolutists—and the many priests among them—as yet another French revolutionary import."

Karl Marx said that, in anti-Napoleon Spain, the Parliament thought without acting and the guerrillas acted without thinking. The breach between the liberals in Parliament and the people's sentiments was demonstrated by the fact that while Napoleon's invasion, which was widely seen as derived from the Revolution, found virulent resistance, the prompt restoration of the absolutist monarchy and the dissolution of the Parliament were broadly celebrated. A further French reactionary invasion to abolish the reestablished Constitution of Cadiz in 1823 did not face opposition from the people, but it was rather welcomed with chants of "Up with the chains," that is, in favor of submission and slavery. "The masses of 'black Spain' triumphed over the enlightened minority," in Pierre Vilar's words.

The divorce between some liberal political initiatives and the popular resistance would become a long-lasting legacy. "The Peninsular War gave birth to the violence and popular antagonism that, along with military intervention in politics, were to be nineteenth-century Spain's most pronounced characteristics," concludes historian Charles Esdaile.

A modern Spanish nation was barely built, neither as a juridical-civic community nor as a cultural one. The liberal politician Antonio Alcala-Galiano is frequently cited as having said, in 1839, once most absolutist mechanisms had been legally abolished, that the task ahead for the liberals was "to make of the Spanish nation, a nation, which is not, nor has it been, up to now." This is similar to the claim of Italian politician Massimo d'Azeglio, who wrote at the unification of the country in 1860, "We have made Italy. Now we must make Italians."

Building a nation after having begun to centralize political power was a common challenge in modern times. But the fragmentation of the Spanish territory was much more durable. For historian Juan Pablo Fusi, "The Spain of the 19th century was a country of legal centralism, but real localism [...]

The Spanish nationalism of the 19th century was too weak as a force of social integration, the Spain of that century was a social network of poorly integrated counties, defined, in addition, by the strong social and economic fragmentation of its territory."

The standard traveler guide for foreigners visiting Spain by the early twentieth century, "the Baedeker," offers an insightful point of view from outside. In 1908, barely any element of Spain-wide national unity could be perceived, except the peseta and the Guardia Civil (while "it is seldom advisable to call in the help of the ordinary police"). The outside borders were weaker than the internal frontiers and the customs controls across cities and regions. On the one hand, "passports are not essential in either Spain and Portugal" and "the custom-house examination on the inland frontiers is generally lenient." On the other hand, the visitor must mind about the examination by the officers of the "octroi" tax at the exit of the railway station or at the gate of the city, while it is also advisable to bring identification documents "in excursions in the less-frequented regions of the interior." The official Spanish time is "gradually introduced, but, as a rule, local time is still generally authoritative."

The general description shows a country with generalized poverty: "The trains are very slow and uncomfortable"; motor cars cannot be recommended "chiefly on account of the inferiority of the roads"; "it is impossible to apply the standard prevailing in more advanced countries to the hotels in Spain," where posadas and ventas "are miserable taverns"; "ordinary Spanish beer is almost certain to produce diarrhea"; and "begging is a national pest in Spain."

The country continued to be territorially fragmented, as explained to the visitors. In "the Basque Provinces, the Basque language (*Euskera*, Span. *El Vascuence*), which still survives throughout Spain in numerous geographical names, is wholly unintelligible to the modern Spaniard." "The universal activity, diligence, and comfort find their only parallel on Spanish soil in Catalonia." Its language is also spoken "in the greater part of Valencia, the Balearic Islands, and to the N. as far as Andorra and Roussillon [...] All that lies beyond the frontier of his native province is foreign land to the Catalan, and not least 'España Uniforme', with its centralization, and the 'Corte' of Madrid, with its superficial polish [...] To this day the natural affiliations of the Catalans attract them towards the S. provinces of France; and they are always ready to revolt."

About one decade later, José Ortega y Gasset saw Spain as "invertebrate." "Spanish social life offers in our days an extreme example of atrocious particularism," he said. "Today is Spain, rather than a nation, a series of watertight compartments."

The first president of the council of ministers of the Second Republic, Manuel Azaña, pretended, "The union of the Spaniards under a common State, which is what we have to found, maintain and defend, has nothing to do with what has been called Spanish historical unity under the Monarchy [...] the Spanish unity, the union of the Spaniards under a common State, we are going to do it ourselves and probably for the first time; because the Catholic Monarchs have not made the Spanish unity." Likewise, the socialist leader Indalecio Prieto openly spoke about the pending, never completed task. In a speech that was later titled "The Interior Conquest of Spain," given at a mass meeting on May Day, 1936, he proclaimed, "We want to make Spain, not destroy it; we want to build it." Rather than imperial conquests—he held— "we had another great achievement to accomplish. Which? To conquer Spain [...] Spain is entirely to be done."

Franco's dictatorship, with its sectarian and exclusivist nationalism supported by control and repression, just destroyed any basis of consensus in the construction of the nation. The emphasis on attaching the patriotic symbols to militarism and clericalism, the persecution of all dissidence and alternative allegiance, was lethal for future attempts at resuming Spanish patriotism.

Political scientist Juan Linz, as mentioned, saw "limited success in state-building and failure in nation-building" in modern Spain. Somehow following his inspiration, a broad agreement has been formed among some historians in identifying the weakness of the Spanish state as the main factor of the persistent territorial, economic and cultural fragmentation of Spain and the frustrations of the project to build a unified national state.

Santos Juliá showed how the dominion of the army and the church did not build "the Nation, because Spain was characterized [...] by the deep fragmentation of civil society, crossed by multiple lines of fracture and the lack of a central and modern civil power." Borja de Riquer viewed the "weak Spanish identity" as the result of the "ineffectiveness of the state nationalizing process." He suggested embracing Linz's hypothesis in terms that "Spanish nationalism as a whole failed because it did not attain to build a solid and fully accepted nation-state" and led to "the partially frustrated construction of the Spanish nation." Juan Pablo Fusi, already cited, also saw the weak nationalization as a consequence of the fact that "the 19th-century Spanish state was weak, poor and inefficient [...] The administrative machinery, the size and powers of government were, in general, limited, if not decidedly small." José Alvarez Junco posited, likewise, that the fact "that this juridical unifying endeavor was not wholly successful was due more to the weakness of the State itself than to the existence of forces that questioned the unity of the nation." He remarked that "Spanish nationalism confronted a problem at least as serious as the imprecision of its political objectives: namely, the weakness and lack of involvement of the State."[2]

The Imperial Burden

The Spanish cultural nationalism that has developed since the early twentieth century has been largely based on the vindication of past imperial glories rather than on a modern concept of civic nation and citizenship. The cultural and political shock of the loss of Cuba, Puerto Rico and the Philippines, which was highly disproportionate to their importance in comparison with the previous losses of most American colonies, indicated that any "national" standing was largely associated with the reverie of the empire. The defeat of the Spanish Empire came precisely at the peak of imperialist competition among the great powers, especially Great Britain and the emerging United States, for the dominion of the world.

A spirit of withdrawing from the world and reconcentrating in isolation and self-absorption was intensely elaborated by some writers who sometimes are placed together under the label "generation of the 98." Their common feeling was that the historical cycle initiated by the Catholic monarchs had ended and Spain had suddenly found itself excluded from the actual world arrangement. It was a move against the tide, precisely when broad new international economic relations were developing thanks to new advances in communication and transport.

Essayists and philosophers prone to embrace a tragic sense of existence and to engage in agonizing meditations wondered about the identity and essence of Spain. Some, like the self-inspective poet Antonio Machado, damned "the old and cheater, tinker and sad Spain." The melancholic José Martínez Ruiz, better known as Azorín, complained about "the unfortunate destiny of Spain, defeated and battered beyond the seas." From that moment forward, many Spaniards developed low levels of national self-esteem.

Professor Miguel de Unamuno also saw Spain "in collapse and doldrums." But, in reaction, he proposed to reject the "so called civilized and modern" ways of life to revive the immortal Spain of Philipp II, Saint Ignacio and the counterreform and "to Spainize Europe by imposing on them our Saint Juan de la Cruz, our Calderon, our Cervantes, and even in a certain sense and to some extent, our Torquemada [the Grand Chief of the Spanish Inquisition]."

Journalist and diplomat Ramiro de Maeztu made an ideological elaboration better fit for political and rhetorical uses and abuses. His aim was that Spain would "recover its 16th-century sense of Roman Catholic mission." The expression "Hispanity" (Hispanidad) had already been used, inspired by the notion of "Lusitanity" and Mussolini's version of "Italianity." But it was

Maeztu who developed and spread the idea, which would become a staple for Spanish imperial nostalgia throughout the twentieth and twenty-first centuries. Maeztu took the word in 1928, while being ambassador in Buenos Aires, from chaplain Zacarías de Vizcarra and an Argentinian nationalist group that followed the reactionary ideas of Louis de Bonald and of authoritarian nationalist Charles Maurras, the founder of the group *Action Française* that became the model for Maeztu's group *Acción Española*.

The idea of Hispanity refers to an imagined community of all the former Spanish colonies and whoever can speak Spanish. But the motherland (*la Madre patria*) is, of course, Spain. The central ideological element is the union of the Spanish imperial expansion with the Catholic religion that blessed it and gave it spiritual content. In a providential coincidence—observed Maeztu— the year 1492 witnessed the expulsion of the Jews, "the arrival of the Cross to the Alhambra" confronting the Muslims and the transatlantic discovery. In his words, the day of 1492 when Columbus and his crew landed near the Caribbean, "it was a 12 of October, the [same] day the Virgin appeared to Santiago at the Pillar in Zaragoza" (of the year 40 AD, according to ancient Spanish tradition). Santiago and the Virgin of the Pillar are the saint patron and patroness of Spain.

A complementary contribution came from Cardinal Isidro Gomá, who would be appointed archbishop of Toledo and primate of Spain during the Civil War in the late 1930s. In a speech given on October 12, 1934, in a theater fittingly called Colón, also in Buenos Aires, he held that "there is a relation of equality between Hispanity and Catholicism" and called for the union of "all living forces of the race" to make it prevail. Later on, he, together with other bishops, would proclaim General Franco's military uprising against the Republic "a Crusade." After the rebels' victory, the leader of the traditionalist Carlists, Victor Pradera, identified "the new State" with "the Spanish State of the Catholic Monarchs."

The founder of the fascist party Falange, José Antonio Primo de Rivera, son of the former dictator, also proclaimed its "will of Empire" because the "historical plenitude of Spain is the Empire." He postulated that Spain is a "unity of destiny within the universal," thus using the concept of "destiny" as something providential, predetermined, alien to the idea of people's sovereignty and "the universal" as a reference to the former empire. The Falangists pretended to develop the spirit of the generation of the 98 to its "ultimate consequences," whatever they were. But they conceded, according to Ramiro Ledesma, that, given the weakness of Spanish fascism in such a poor and agrarian country, they had to join the fascistized traditional right in support of the reactionary enterprise.[3]

During the Civil War, the rebel side was known as "the Nationals," in contrast to "the Republicans," which exposed a sheer division among Spaniards regarding, respectively, their national and civic allegiances. The winners used the adjective for their political organization, the National Movement. But in most Francoist authorities' speeches, proclamations and decrees, the references to the Spanish "nation" were sporadic. The more traditional notions of "patria" (homeland) and "patriotism" prevailed, together with "God," "the Crusade" and "Christianity," including "the patria's religion" and "through Empire toward God."

Revealingly, the two books written by General Franco focused on imperial obsessions. The first was a memoir of his colonialist military action in Africa. The second, *Raza* (Race), was published under pseudonym and became the script for a movie subsidized by the Council of the Hispanity that was used as a propaganda tool all across Spain. *Raza* is partly a disguised self-biography of Franco as the heroic member of a "hidalgo" family. The feats of several of his ancestors include the defeat by the British at the Battle of Trafalgar, the defeat in Cuba and, as a kind of revenge against their own countrymen, the military rise from Morocco that provoked the Civil War. Generalissimo Franco always tried to present his proclamation of "Caudillo by the grace of God" in strong connection with the imperial Catholic history of Spain.[4]

There still exist numerous symbols of the lost empire in current Spain. The most visible one is the celebration of the 12th of October as Spain's national holiday. As mentioned, the date commemorates both the imperial feat of Columbus's arrival to the New World and the religious, patriotic patronage of the Virgin of the Pillar.

Spain began to honor the symbolic founding day of the empire as a frustrated nationalist reaction after the last imperial remnants had disappeared. First, it was the Day of the Race, for 40 years from 1918, through the monarchy, the republic and the dictatorship, until 1958. Then, years after the Nazi experience had anathematized the notion of "race," Franco's government changed the label into the Holiday of the Hispanity, which became a public holiday, a nonworking day. As mentioned, race, Hispanity and Catholicism were considered equivalents by the founding ideologues of the invention. The Holiday of the Hispanity was confirmed in the first years of democracy. Only in 1987 the festivity was renamed with the more self-contained appellation of National Holiday of Spain.

Up to now, every 12th of October, whatever the political regime, there is fanfare and a military parade in Madrid with a few thousand infantry soldiers, motor vehicles and aviation. The main attraction is always the foreign legion, led by its mascot, a horned goat wearing a legion cap, followed by the legionaries signing their hymn: "I am the Bridegroom of Death." In recent years, the spectacle marched between spots with aptly chosen names, Emperor Charles V Square and Columbus Square, as well as along the Castilian Boulevard. The parade is chaired by the king, the royal family, the president of government and the heads of all other bodies of the state.

In the 1980s, some people proposed to replace the outdated imperial commemoration with the new public holiday of December 6th, the day a new democratic Constitution was approved by popular referendum, but the two holidays remained. To prevent too much interference into working schedules, the government of the moment tried to suppress instead the traditional public holiday of the Immaculate Conception, which lies just two days after the Constitution day, on December 8th. But the Spanish Episcopal Conference severely resisted the change, contending, among other lines, that the papal dogma of the Immaculate Conception of Mary had largely relied upon arguments elaborated by Spanish theologians from the sixteenth century.

Many people confuse the Immaculate Conception with the Doctrine of Incarnation that holds that Mary was virgin when she gave birth to Jesus. What the popular female names Inmaculada, Inma, Concepcion, Concha, Conchita and other variants refer to is not the conception of Jesus by Mary but the conception of Mary free from original sin by her mother, Anne. That is why Mary's Immaculate Conception is scheduled nine months before her nativity on September 8th. Most years the two holidays on December 6th and 8th plus the appropriate "bridges" with the two adjacent weekends imply that for many people there may be up to nine consecutive nonworking days. If other bridges are added between the traditional Catholic holidays of Christmas, New Year and the Wise Men on January 6th, it turns out that many Spaniards can enjoy about 30 days in a row of low-intensity work or just plain idleness.

As Spain keeps 12th of October as the main celebration, it is the only country in the world whose national holiday does not refer to feats like a rebellion against oppression, the winning of liberty or the achievement of national unity but to its imperial, colonial experience of conquest and domination of other peoples and lands. When you arrive at the Madrid airport, the highway leading to the city is called Avenue of the Hispanity. Nobody has ever suggested changing this name, in spite of lengthy and controversial discussions to change street names and monuments from the Franco era all across Spain.

The main counterpoint can be found in London and Paris. The central square and monument of each of the two cities directly memorialize two major defeats of the Spanish Empire: Trafalgar with Nelson and the Arc de Triomphe for Napoleon.

The Damned "Mili"

Although this may sound rather strange to many Spaniards, the compulsory military service—usually called "the mili"—has been successfully used in other countries as a platform for instilling and unifying patriotic sentiments among previously dispersed and uncommunicated populations. Conscription was introduced in most European countries by the mid-nineteenth century when railroads covering large territories made the rapid transportation of masses of solders feasible. Serving in the army was a modern form of a citizen's egalitarian contribution to the state, which was expected to foster sentiments of belonging to the nation.

Interstate wars fought by forced conscripts also strengthened internal national sentiments when people with different backgrounds faced a common enemy. As developed by political scientists Keith Darden and Harris Mylonas, "When states face threats to their territorial integrity through military conquest, governing elites have a strong incentive to nation-build to ensure loyal population." But, as we have seen, the weakness and impotence of the Spanish state left Spain absent from the two World Wars and other foreign territorial conflicts for about one hundred years, which produced the opposite effect. It was "a disadvantage for the nation-building process because the feeling of unity derived from being under attack diminished without being replaced by any other sense of common purpose," as phrased by historians Borja de Riquer and Enric Ucelay Da-Cal.[5]

In Spain, the new system of recruitment of soldiers was biased from the beginning and never produced massive nationalizing effects. Initially, a system of lotteries was established in the nineteenth century as well as the option to escape from the service by paying a certain amount of money—two mechanisms that sent the poor to die in the colonial wars and secured massive exemptions, deserters and runaways. Later on, at the beginning of the twentieth century, a system of quotas permitting payment for shortening the period of service was introduced. During Franco's dictatorship, college students were exempt from regular service and served, instead, as temporary officers during three summer seasons—except those who were reprisaled against for political activities. Most men not favored by those exemptions or reductions were under direct military jurisdiction from 21 to 40 years of age, counting both the years in the ranks and barracks and those subjected to immediate mobilization and reserve.

In the last few decades of the twentieth century, many boys submitted to compulsory military service were sent far away from their homes to strategic posts, especially the Sahara (the favorite destination for punished students), Majorca and the Canary Islands. In Majorca in the 1970s, for example, there were about one-third of conscripts from Majorca (who were able to keep their other occupations during the afternoon and to dine and sleep at home), about one-third from Catalonia and about one-third from Andalusia. Most of the "peninsulars," as they were called by the islanders, traveled by ship or, on some break periods, by airplane as a first-time experience. Some Andalusians saw the sea for the first time in their lives. The mixing permitted some mutual knowledge but also revealed unsuspected cultural differences. For instance, the Majorcans and the Catalans spoke in their common mother tongue within the barracks, including with some officers and subofficers from the island, a language that the Andalusians, some of them illiterate, had never heard before. In fact, the cohabitation promoted "national" solidarity mostly against the military system and some despicable officers and chiefs.

The military service was by then scheduled for 18 months, but in practice it was shorter, mainly to make savings and to allow some lieutenants and sergeants to pocket money from meals that were budgeted but not served. The soldiers were regularly submitted to physical punishment and solitary confinement in guardrooms for their clumsiness or indiscipline. Periodically, all the troops were retained in the barracks as a matter of urgency, especially when the general in charge suspected that the Friday evening meeting of the council of ministers might declare a new state of exception in reaction to protests or strikes somewhere in Spain. On some occasions, the soldiers were mobilized into trucks to patrol the city during the night. Rather than feeding patriotic sentiments, everybody was counting the days left to leave.

All young Spanish men subjected to military service had to pledge allegiance to the national flag. Entire families traveled to attend the mass and witness their sons' oath:

> "Soldiers!"—shouted the Colonel.
> "Do you swear to God and promise to Spain,
> kissing your Flag with unction,
> respect and always obey your chiefs,
> never abandon them,
> and spill, if necessary, to the last drop of your blood
> in defense of the honor and independence of the Fatherland
> and of the internal order within it?"
> "Yes, I swear!," shouted the youngsters.

As can be seen, the formula referred the issue to God, repeated the medieval and imperialistic motto for spilling the last drop of blood and made the internal target of the military mission explicit.

Typically, more than one girlfriend or sweet sister shed a little tear. Most soldiers would never forget, however, the experience of the damned "mili," which traumatized several generations of young Spaniards, together with their friends and relatives.

Once in democracy, mounting campaigns for conscientious objection and insubmission, that is, massive desertion and rebellion, eventually led to the suppression of the conscription. All in all, the Spanish military service was rather counter-effective to the effect of inducing "nationalization" of the conscripts, in contrast—apparently—to other countries with better institutional environments.

Parochial-Catholicism

The first institution that seriously attempted a cultural unification of Spain was the Inquisition. From the fifteenth to the nineteenth centuries, the Spanish Inquisition, which was a long arm of the absolutist monarchy, pursued racialism and the "purity of blood" by means of ethnic cleansing or "limpieza." Fighting the Muslims, the Jews, the heretic Protestants, as well as the converts and their descendants, could create common enemies to the Catholics of the diverse territories of the peninsula and promote some uniting links among them.

The so-called Black Legend or negative propaganda about Spain developed in rival colonial powers, especially Britain. It presented tricks and deceits as crucial mechanisms of the Inquisition's processes, arrests and sequestrations, secret prisons, forced confessions, torture, fraudulent trials and ritual Autos-da-Fe leading to public executions of infidels and heretics by burning at the stake.

In recent times, some revisionist historians have held that some of those claims were exaggerated and that, in fact, the ethnic cleansing was very limited in its effectiveness. This relative failure in imposing true religious fervor all across Spain could be interpreted as one more frustration in the aim of building a unified nation by a weak state. The Inquisition would have not established solid religious foundations for a "national" unification of Spain.

Yet, it has also been acknowledged that, beyond the numbers of direct victims, the threat of persecution by the Inquisition and the deterrence that it created among larger groups of the population diffused a superficial allegiance to Catholicism, which has survived plenty of superstitious traditions and cults. This point is persuasively argued, in particular, by the most encompassing historian of the Inquisition, Henry Charles Lea, whose monumental work was initially published in 1906 but apparently not read by any Spanish scholar during the following 80 or so years. In Lea's words, the Inquisition was a tribunal of which the real importance is to be sought, not so much in the awful solemnities of the auto-da-fe, or in the cases of a few celebrated victims, as in the silent influence exercised by its incessant and secret labors among the mass of the people and the limitations which it placed on the Spanish intellect.

In particular, as a consequence of the censorship and the arduous elimination of prohibited books in shops, monasteries, universities and private libraries by the joint action of "the State and the Inquisition, the intellectual development was stunned and starved into atrophy, the arts and sciences were neglected, commercial and industrial progress was rendered impossible." At the same time, while the Inquisition "failed to inspire genuine respect for religion," it induced conformity and external signs of devotion among the population that has endured much beyond its abolition.[6]

According to Juan Linz, "The identification of the state and even the nation with Catholicism [...] would be an obstacle to secular state and nation-building." The religious glue proved insufficient on its own to cohere national politics. But it was also sufficiently pervaded and entrenched with the state to mar a resolute progress of the alternative secularization of politics. Like in other aspects of the frustrated modernization of Spain, there was too little religion to unify the population and too much to permit the success of an alternative cultural cosmovision.

The modern panorama of religiosity in Spain can be largely understood as derived from that historical legacy. It is characterized by an implicit predominance of Catholicism as "the true religion," scarce faith and transcendental religious experience, a ubiquitous presence of folkloric practices and rites, and very varied traditions of local-Catholicisms rather than of a "national" one.

During the late twentieth and early twenty-first centuries, the proportion of self-declared Catholics in Spain has decreased more than ever. Nowadays, few Spaniards are believers and regular practitioners. More than 50 percent of those surveyed declare themselves nonpractitioners, and near 30 percent confess to be nonbelievers or atheists (or a few, believers of other religions). Yet, about 40 percent of the population still consider being Catholic something "important" or "very important" in order to be "truly Spanish."[7]

Traces of the Catholic cultural tradition are on display, including, in particular, the numerous religious holidays and local patron saints' festivals that are heartily kept. In addition to Christmas, St. Stephen, the Wise Men, Palm Sunday and the Holy Week processions, most popular events include the processions of Corpus Christi, All Saints in commemoration of the martyrs of Rome, the Feast of the Dead, the feasts of the Apostle Santiago who is the

Patron of Spain and of the Cavalry Corps and the Blessing of St. Anton when a few drops of holy water bless all kinds of animals, including the hawks of the Civil Guard, the municipal guard horses, the dogs of the National Police and the guide dogs of the National Organization of the Blind.

A series of festivities are in honor of local versions of the Virgin Mary, including the Virgen of the Pillar in Zaragoza, who is patroness of Aragon, Spain, and the Hispanity, as we have said, the Virgin of Carmen, patron of the Sea and of the Spanish armed forces, the Immaculate Conception, also mentioned, the Assumption of the Blessed Virgin Mary to the Skies where it was crowned and, in no particular order, the virgins of Covadonga, patron of Asturias and dawning of the Reconquista, Guadalupe of Extremadura and Queen of the Hispanity, Montserrat or "Moreneta" of Catalonia, Desamparados or "Geperudeta" of Valencia, Rocio of Andalusia, Aranzazu of the Basque Country, the Candelaria or another "Morenita" in the Canary Islands, as well as Almudena of Madrid, Merce of Barcelona, Begoña of Bilbao and a very long list proving that as God is one and triune, the Virgin Mary is one and multiple.

All this is, of course, mixed up and in harmonious coexistence with several other hundred patronal or semi-pagan local and parochial festivities, such as the Sanfermines in Pamplona, the Feria de Abril in Seville, the Fallas for Saint Joseph in Valencia, Saint Jean's verbenas along the Mediterranean coast, La Tomatina in Buñol, the Carnivals in Cadiz and the Canary Islands and a long etcetera.

A few imperial-Catholic traditions, initially derived from the Inquisition's mission, deserve special mention. Until the 1960s, each parish organized gatherings to "kill Jews" for the Holy Week. During three days, the children of the neighborhood, led by the parish priest, rattled carracas, matracas and other noisemakers evoking the thunder that, at the moment of Jesus' death on the cross, had killed so many Jews. The show further declined, although there are still many towns where, on Easter Saturday, an effigy representing Judas is burned in a ritual inspired by the Inquisition's autos-da-fé. In some places, people still drink a cocktail of wine and fruit called lemonade at the motto: "Lemonade that I rattle, Jew that I pulverize."

Even if very few people in Spain have ever met a person of Jewish confession, anti-Semitic prejudices are widespread. Jews are considered deceitful, stingy, mean and not to be trusted. A "judiada," or an action done by a Jew, is a dirty trick or a cruel thing such as extortion, including by the Dictionary of the Royal Spanish Academy that define it as "trick or action that harms someone."

Much livelier are the xenophobic and racist festivals of "Moors and Christians" that take place in the spring and the summer in a few hundred towns in the south and east of Spain. The tradition was invented in the nineteenth century, at the same time that the myth and the word "reconquista" were also forged, in commemoration of local battles that were supposedly fought around the thirteenth century. It intensified in the dictatorial 1940s, and it has achieved, again, a surge in the disarrayed twenty-first century. In some towns, the festival is scheduled for a patron saint, such as Saint George, who killed the infidel dragon, or Santiago "Matamoros" (Moor killer).

There are many local versions, but, basically, the participants, all of them white male Christian Spaniards, are divided into two sides called "the Moors" (pejorative for Muslims) and "the Christians" (appreciative for Christians), each wearing luxuriously expensive and colorful custom-made costumes like those of medieval times.* Watches, sunglasses and cigars may be, nevertheless, permitted. Soldier squads march to the rhythm of music bands prepared for the battle to defend against the Moors and for the Christians to reconquest the town. They combat one another for a few days with harquebuses, muskets and blunderbusses producing clouds of gunpowder smoke and enormous noise, until the Moors are defeated. Women are, of course, excluded. Thousands of spectators line the streets to cheer on the combatants. Traditionally, the final ceremony in some towns included the explosion of a puppet called "La Mahoma" (Mohamed) by firecrackers from inside his head.

Some Spanish Muslim organizations have labeled these traditions Islamophobic and called for their suppression, a proposal that has found, naturally, resolute resistance from the locals. In fact, several of those local festivities are officially recognized as "Spanish cultural patrimony."

These manifestations of popular culture can be related to widespread Spanish people's attitudes toward foreigners, immigrants, infidels and, in particular, Muslims and Arabs. There has never been a member of Parliament, a minister of government or a mayor of a large city born in any former colony of Spain, in contrast to regular occurrences of the kind in the institutions of the former colonial powers, Great Britain and France, and even of Italy.†

In a study directed by sociologists Manuel Pérez Yruela and Thierry Desrues, it was found that, in interviews and focus groups with Spaniards, "there are rare elements of empathy or a certain admiration for Islam and Muslims. The difference is perceived rather as distance, backwardness,

---

* The Dictionary of the Royal Spanish Academy defines "Moore" (Moro) as follows: "It is said of the Muslim who lived in Spain from the eighth century to the fifteenth century." As noted by linguist Anne Cenname, "It is interesting that this long-lived Muslim, who lived in Spain for so many centuries, does not seem to ever reach to become Spanish."

† In the last few years, a prime minister of France and the mayor of Paris were born in Spain, but an analogous occurrence for a head of government of Spain or a mayor of Madrid not born in Spain seems unthinkable.

transient cultural inferiority; transient since it could be resolved if they abandoned their culture, religion and customs to adopted 'our' norms." The researchers also found relevant echoes of old passions: "The sentiment of threat, invasion, reversal of legitimate hierarchies of power between 'autochthonous' and the 'Others' in the Spanish society, although it appears very little reasoned in the speeches."[8]

The social weight of both the church and the army is heavily diminished in current Spain in comparison with past periods. Neither of them was very successful in building solid bonds of national identity in modern times, beyond the above-mentioned widespread prejudices and folklore. But, in their weaknesses, their traditional ties remain close. Each corps of the armed forces maintains its military chaplain and a patron saint. In recent years, the Ministry of the Interior awarded the Gold Medal for Police Merit to the Blessed Virgin Mary of Love and to the Brotherhood of the Christ of the Good Death, patron of the Legion, the Great Cross of the Civil Guard to the Virgin of the Pillar and the Silver Cross to the Lady of Sorrows of Achicona. As a confirmation and testimony of the traditional link between clericalism and militarism, each year for Easter all military units, bases, centers and barracks, as well as the central headquarters of the Ministry of Defense in Madrid, wave the Spanish flag at half-mast, in mourning for the death of Jesus.

Multiple Languages

Together with the unity of religion, the unity of language is another essential element of a cultural nation. The Castilian and the Spanish Crowns began very early to try to impose the Castilian linguistic patterns as the only national ones all across Spain. But their achievements have always been limited, and Spain has remained a multilingual country.

Already in the late fifteenth century, Queen Isabel promoted the codification of the Castilian way of speaking Latin, which was then just one among multiple romance parlances, as a way of writing and, as such, as the only literate norm in her dominions. Castilian was elevated to the level of imperial-national written language and put at the top of hierarchical positions regarding all the other parlances of the Crown's subjects.

Antonio de Nebrija, who was given the title of Chronicler of the Catholic Kings, published both a *Dictionary from Latin to Romance* and a *Castilian Grammars* in the fatidic year of 1492. He famously asserted in the Preface of the *Grammars* that "the language was always the companion of the Empire." Asked by the queen what the benefit of such work would be, the bishop of Avila responded with more specifications on Nebrija's behalf: "After your Highness brought many barbarian peoples and nations with odd tongues under your yoke, with the victory those [peoples and nations] needed to receive the laws that the winner puts on the defeated and with them our language."

Thus, linguistic imperialism explicitly accompanied political imperialism. A few years later, the Crown ordered the burning all the books written in Arabic characters and forbade any further publication.

Emperor Charles V, who was born in the Dutch provinces, spoke Flemish, French and German, and only after becoming King of Spain did he begin to learn and speak the Castilian romance. Yet he was soon aware of the imperial vocation of the language and proclaimed, at a Pope's reception in his honor as the military victor over "infidel" Muslims, that "the Spanish language is so noble that it deserves to be known and understood by all the Christian people." The religious allegiance also accompanied the imperial one as far as language was concerned. The language was the companion of the empire and of the church.

Yet, the actual linguistic uses never fulfilled the imperial and religious ambition, which was at the same time unifying and exclusionary. The different ways of speaking Latin across the peninsula were increasingly differentiated from each other as long as the Spanish nationalism affirmed itself and faced replicas from Portuguese, Catalan and other nationalisms. But for a long while, what current linguists call "passive bilingualism" was relatively common in conversations because the speakers of the diverse parlances derived from Latin did not have much difficulty in understanding each other. For example, one of the enigmas about the origins and turnabouts of Christopher Columbus is that he wrote and supposedly spoke in a mix of Latin and of Genoese, Portuguese, Castilian and other dialects, which does not help to clarify what his mother tongue was.

The expansion of Castilian was widely accepted as a replacement for Latin as a new lingua franca, especially for written communication. But not necessarily at the expense of the other Latin-originated parlances in the diverse traditional communities. Political theorist Montesquieu reports an interesting anecdote showing how passive bilingualism was an accepted practice among people from different crowns in the peninsula during the seventeenth century:

> It is said that a king of Aragon, having assembled the estates of Aragon and Catalonia, the first sessions were spent in deciding in what language the deliberations should be held: the dispute was lively, and the estates would have broken up a thousand times, if they had not hit upon the expedient of putting the question in the Catalonian tongue, and the reply in that of Aragon.

St ill in the nineteenth century, at the moment of the independence of the Spanish colonies in the Americas, most people there did not use or even understood Spanish.

Even in Spain, the consolidation of Castilian as the national Spanish language was a goal that was more seriously pursued only later, with weak means and with incomplete results. Primary education was the key instrument.

As presented by Eric Hobsbawm in a comparative perspective, the primary schools "were institutions of crucial importance for new nation-states, for through them alone the 'national language' (generally constructed earlier by private efforts) could actually become the written and spoken language of the people [...] The primary schools' purpose was by general consent not only to teach the rudiments of literacy and arithmetic but, perhaps even more, to impose the values of society (morals, patriotism, etc.) on their inmates."

Political scientists Keith Darden and Anna Gryzmala-Busse concur. They specify that "the critical aspect of mass literacy is timing: the national ideas instilled in a population during the first round of mass schooling—when a community first shifts from an oral to a literate mass culture—are durable, as the first schooled generation will transmit those values in ways that previous or subsequent cohorts do not."

These and other scholars report the great advances of mass schooling by state school systems in Britain, France and Prussia during the second half of the nineteenth century, when around 90 percent of children were taught to read and write in the national language. Typically, the task was in the hands of state-trained schoolteachers who imposed the same type of education and values across the country, including, in some cases, harsh repressive measures against the use of family languages at the school.

However, this was not the story of Spain. As reviewed by political scientist Laia Balcells, "People were never massively educated under a strong and well-organized Spanish state." When the first Spanish law establishing compulsory and free primary school was introduced in 1857, about three-fourths of the population was illiterate. The administration of primary schools was given to the municipal councils, which would never have, by far, the necessary resources for such an endeavor. In fact, Castilian was not officially imposed as the single language in schools until 1888. A Ministry of Public Instruction and Beaux Arts in charge of funding state schools was not created until 1900. In practice, most of the primary education remained in the hands of religious and private schools of different cultural allegiances. "The Church, of course, did not create 'Spaniards' but 'Catholics,' even if that required teaching in Catalan or Basque," as put by Alvarez Junco. The Catalans, Galicians and some Basques never attended national schools and kept speaking their own languages. In the rural areas, many children were not sent to school because their poor parents needed them to work in the fields or stables for the family. The schoolteachers were legendarily low-paid and lacked the most elementary means—"you will be hungrier than a schoolteacher" was a common curse. Only in 1931 was Castilian declared "the official language" of Spain, when still about one-third of the population could not read or write. The central decades of the twentieth century, under Franco's dictatorship, were times of regression regarding primary schooling.

By the 1960s, after more than one hundred years since the first modern attempt at organizing a national system of basic education, the results were meager, to say the least. Historian Carolyn Boyd carefully reviewed the contents of textbooks that had been used with the aim of providing common national values to the children and summarized the fallout:

> Historically, the weak Spanish state could neither provide a sufficient number of state schools [...] nor effectively impose uniform standards on its own schools and teachers [...] In Spain, a chronically weak state, a divided and largely undemocratic political class, and an increasingly polarized social and political climate impeded the construction of an effective system of national education and the emergence of a consensus on the shape and meaning of the Spanish national past. This, in turn, contributed to one of the most striking features of modern Spanish political and cultural life: the absence of a strong sense of Spanish, as opposed to local or regional, identity.

Only in the 1970s did Spain achieve levels of literacy and primary schooling of the population similar to those of most European countries. It was very late, indeed, to expect that it could produce similar levels of nationalization to those of France, Italy, Germany or Britain, especially because, as remarked by Laia Balcells, at that time Catalan, Basque, Galician and other languages had already been standardized and were supported by broad cultural and political nationalist movements.[9]

Against some expectations by Spanish liberal nationalists, the linguistic and cultural homogenization of Spaniards has significantly decreased during the current democratic period. Nowadays, around one-fourth of the people of Spain use a language other than Castilian as the main language in their family and private relations, and about 40 percent live in the six territorial autonomous communities with two official languages. The multilingualism of the Spanish citizens includes not only Castilian, Catalan, Galician and Basque but also Asturian, Aragonese, Arabic, Occitan and Portuguese.

When the minister of education declared, in 2013, that his interest was "to Spainize the Catalan students," he provoked reactions of outrage but mainly of mock and dismay. One did not need much insight to realize that the Spainization of the Catalans would require a broader acknowledgment of Catalan and the other living languages as parts and components of "Spain." In truth, the mentality behind such aspirations is not an integratory Spainization of the Catalans but an exclusionary Castilianization of the Spaniards.

The tension for unconcluded linguistic nationalization, thus, has not disappeared. The Royal Spanish Academy was created by the Bourbons, under French inspiration, by the early eighteenth century and it soon produced the first *Dictionary of the Castilian Language*. Only during Primo de Rivera's dictatorship, in 1925, did the new editions begin to be titled *Dictionary of the Spanish Language*, a very tardy attempt at verbal national unification, perhaps in response to the recent modern standardization of the Catalan language.

Still today, the most recent edition of the *Dictionary*, published in 2014, includes speaking "in Christian" as synonym of speaking in Castilian or Spanish:

"In christian

1. Loc. Adv. Coloq. In flat and easily understandable terms, or in the language that everyone understands. *Speak in Christian because I do not understand you.*

2. Loc. Adv. Coloq. In Castilian."

As remarked by linguist Anne Cename:

"With the confusion between Castilian and Spanish the idea is propagated that to be Spanish you have to be Castilian, with the consequent exclusion and marginalization of all those who do not classify themselves as Castilians. The use of the three terms Spanish, Castilian and Christian as synonyms seems to imply that one has to be both Castilian and Christian to be Spanish."[10]

Some other aspects of the current language policy and certain linguistic uses by the public administration also reflect the exclusionary origins of the project of making Castilian the only Spanish language. This can be seen not only regarding the other languages within Spain but, even more, in some external uses regarding the other world languages.

The cultural consumption of the Spaniards is externally dependent to an enormous extent, but sometimes it seems that the Spanish government makes every effort to keep the Spaniards alien to any other language. The publishing industry in Spanish is one of the most foreign-dependent ones of the world. The number of books translated into Spanish every year is about four times higher than the number of books originally published in Spanish that are translated into other languages—a gigantic cultural deficit.

The deficit is even higher in audiovisual products. Nearly 90 percent of films available in Spain are foreign. Among the developed countries, the proportion is only surpassed by Australia and Canada, two English-speaking countries that routinely import English-speaking movies from the United States without the need to translate them. But in Spain almost every foreign film or TV series is dubbed into Spanish. This deprives the audience of the original voices, that is, the most exclusive and characteristic feature of actors and actresses, who are replaced with ventriloquists. At the same time, the spectators miss the opportunity to have access or practice English or other languages; they remain culturally constrained by dubbing or translation filters.[11]

Dubbing movies was imposed by Franco in 1941, officially to defend the Castilian language but also to have a way to censor some morally or politically dangerous dialogues, and it has remained the most common practice up to now in both movie theaters and TV. As dubbing is expensive and is paid by the Spanish audience, in practice it is like a commercial tariff that divests resources from potential domestic jobs and productions in the film and audiovisual industry. It favors both provincial cultural dependence and remoteness from original creations. That is, the consumers are heavily dependent on foreign cultural creations, but they do not even get directly connected with them.

At the same time, there is persistent and sometimes pathetic stubbornness at promoting Spanish as if it could work as a single common language in international and worldwide exchanges. Some data about the diffusion of Spanish in the world seem to confound the number of native Spanish speakers, mostly residents in Hispanic America, with the users of Spanish as an international language of communication between people with different mother tongues. More than 400 million people speak Spanish as a first language, but barely one hundred more million can use it as an additional language for international exchanges. In contrast, while over 400 million people speak English as a mother tongue, near the same number speak English as their first foreign language. This makes English, with about 800 million speakers, the dominant language in higher education, academic publications and conferences, science, technology and medicine, international business, finances and commerce, internet and diplomacy as well as the language of airports, sports, pop music and advertising.

This confusion, or perhaps some patriotic myopia and narrowness of mind, supports the Spanish government's resistance to using English as a lingua franca in some international cultural settings. In the popular Eurovision Song Contest, in which more than 40 countries participate each year, the contestants have been permitted since 1999 to choose what language they will sing in, and all but two of the following 20 winners came from non-English-speaking countries singing in English. Spain was the last country to begin presenting songs entirely in English, in 2016 and 2017. The illustrious members of the Royal Spanish Academy publicly avowed their protest and declared that any song from Spain "ought to be integrally interpreted in Spanish." As if the rest of Europe were waiting for it. The academics did not seem to care, in contrast, about the deplorable low quality and embarrassing self-humiliating attitude of some of the Spanish participants.

The Spanish government also maintains the *Television Española Internacional* TV channel broadcasting only in Spanish. This is in blatant contrast to the numerous international TV channels that broadcast in English, including not only the American CNN and Fox News and the British BBC but also government-sponsored channels of non-English-speaking countries such as France, Germany, Russia, India, China, Japan, Iran, Qatar, Turkey or Israel. As it has been said of some campaigns of the "Marca España," the governments of nationalistic Spain tend to do foreign promotion mostly for the domestic audience and to reinforce its isolation.

Tribes with Flags and Chants

National symbols are the main diffusers of nationalist values among the citizens of a state; they simplify ideological national identities and also contribute to shaping their contents. Together with historical myths and heroes, monuments and maps, festivities and commemorations, the main national symbols are the flag and the national anthem.

Diplomat and journalist Tim Marshall explains that "flags are a relatively recent phenomenon in human history," as they became feasible only after the Chinese invention of silk, a light fabric that, in contrast to traditional weighty standards in cloth, could be held aloft even in battlefields. With its spread in modern times, "a nation's flag fluttering in the wind is a sign of power, hope, history, and often war […] For thousands of years, flags have stood for our identities and ideals. We have them, burn them, and march under their colors. And still, in the 21st century, we die for them […] They represent the politics of high power as well as the passions of the mob." In the particular case of Spain, flags are a dramatic representation of political power in its factionalism and the wicked passions of divided mobs.[12]

The choice of a Spanish national flag was divisive from the beginning. By the late eighteenth century, the Royal Navy had replaced the traditional insignia in white with the Bourgogne cross with a flag with two horizontal stripes, one in red and one in yellow to make it more visible on the open sea. But at the Parliament of Cadiz or at the popular uprisings against Napoleon by the early nineteenth century, there was not a single flag that could identify all the Spaniards and encourage national patriotism. The navy emblem was adopted as the flag of the army and the militia in 1843. But still by the end of the nineteenth century, many inhabitants of Spain did not know of it and even some recruited soldiers were unable to identify it when they arrived at the barracks.

The further entrenchment of the bicolor or "rojigualda" flag in the minds of the Spaniards during the twentieth century involved its mixing with religious ceremonies, wars and repression. The Law of military Jurisdictions of 1906, above mentioned, established prison penalties for those who, by any means, "outrage the Nation, its flag, national anthem or other emblem of its representation." Soon thereafter, the bicolor flag began to be raised in all public buildings, especially on religious festivities such as Easter, Corpus Christi, Santiago and the Immaculate Conception. The dictatorship of Primo de Rivera in the 1920s adamantly associated the flag with the colonial adventures in Northern Africa and it added "offenses to national emblems" to the criminal code. The bicolor Spanish monarchist flag was also adopted by the rebels against the Republic and became the official flag of the Franco dictatorship. In the 1940s, it introduced the crime of propaganda by any means aiming at "destroying or relaxing the national sentiment." Up until the late 1960s, students could be condemned to several years of prison for "outrages to the national flag." The new Code of 1973 expanded the penalties to the "offenses proffered against the National Movement, its Chief, and its heroes, martyrs, flags, and emblems." In democracy, the Code of 1995 suppressed many of those crimes, but it kept "offenses or outrages of speech, in writing or in action to Spain, to its Autonomous Communities or to its symbols or emblems."

Obviously, all these provisions have been directly targeted against the hypothetical internal enemies of the symbols of Spain. There have been many, indeed, because the official national symbols have not been shared by large sectors of the population. The main alternative Spanish flag to the bicolor has been the tricolor, in which one red stripe is replaced with a purple one. It had been used by some republican city councils since 1869 and became the first constitutional flag of Spain in 1931. In retribution to previous persecutions, the Law of Defense of the Republic made a crime of "the use of the emblem, badges, or symbols allusive" to the monarchy, including, thus, the bicolor flag. The two "national" flags, the bicolor and the tricolor, have remained symbols of the traditional and civic alternative nations of Spain.

Other nationalist movements developed their own symbols. The medieval Catalan emblem with four red stripes on a yellow background became a vindicating flag since the 1880s. The Catalan flag or *senyera* would be prohibited by the Franco regime and relegalized at its end, near 40 years later. Yet, since the 1920s the activists for an independent Catalonia had added to the flag a Masonic triangle in blue with a white star—inspired by the independence of Cuba and Puerto Rico. A new pro-independence flag with the star in red would also be invented by leftist groups in the late1960s. So, three different flags would be widely weaved in Catalan nationalist rallies and demonstrations in recent times.

Likewise, the Basque flag or *ikurriña* was invented in the 1890s. It consists of a white cross over a green saltire on a red field, which represents, respectively, religion, the old laws and the Basque race. The *ikurriña* became the flag of the Basque nationalists in 1910, would be a vindicating tool against the two further dictatorships and would become official in the 1970s. Other traditional nationalist banners, such as those of the other former members of the medieval Crown of Aragon, that is, Aragon, Valencia and the Balearics as well as Galicia, Andalusia and others, would also become the official flags of the autonomous communities.

In most public buildings, the Spanish flag now waves next to those of the European Union, the autonomous community and, if it applicable, the city or town. On the one hand, symbolic Spanish nationalism has been energetically promoted by the central government. Specifically, the biggest Spanish flag ever was installed at the Columbus Square of Madrid, where a gigantic drape of 21 × 14 meters and 35 kilos waves over a 50-meter-high mast. On the other hand, compliance with the regulations is irregular and sloppy. Numerous town councils, especially in the Basque Country and Catalonia, neglect to include the Spanish flag in their menu.

As summarized by historians Javier Moreno Luzón and Xosé M. Nuñez Seixas, "The symbolic consensus, even among those who recognized the existence of the Spanish nation or at least a common State, became impossible for a long time." The symbolic divisiveness has not been only the result of political instability and frequent regime changes but also an expression of weak national cohesion. The smaller and more homogeneous Portugal and Greece, for instance, whose modern historical trajectories have also been full of political instability and breakdowns, have never changed their national flags or anthems.

For most of the population, the democratic consensus has become "a banal acceptance of the national emblems compatible with a subtle distortion: solemnity is called in frivolity or, at least, in a spontaneity of playful boundaries. In no case this transmutation is more apparent than in the recurring presence of the Osborne bull as a representative symbol of Spain, to the extent that it moves its own shield in the center of the flag in multiple festive and sporting events," in historian Rafael Nunez Florencio's words. But even this banal patriotism is not general. The shades of popular sentiments regarding the national symbols run from limited enthusiasm to passive or resigned acquiescence, emotional indifference, embarrassment and rejection and belligerence.[13]

* * *

Similar stories of divisiveness and confronted sentiments can be told regarding the national anthem. The military *Grenadiers March*, which had been sponsored by the Crown since the eighteenth century, began to be performed in religious processions by the mid-nineteenth century and went to be called *Royal March*. But it had multiple rivals as the national anthem. The *Cadiz March*, rooted in the resistance against Napoleon, fell into discredit after the political defeat of its liberal promoters. Most of the further alternatives focused either on past imperial glories or banal references. A long-living favorite for children goes, "Isabel and Fernando, the spirit prevails, we will die kissing the sacred flag." A frivolous *pasodoble*, in contrast, restrains itself to the following: "Little flag you are red, little flag you are yellow, you have blood, you have gold, in the bottom of your soul."

The *Royal March* was proclaimed Spain's official national anthem by Franco during the Civil War and has remained as such ever since. During the dictatorship, the main rival was the Hymn of Falange, *Cara al Sol*, which exalted the combatants who kept "impassible the gesture," while the Carlist *Oriamendi* called to fight "For God, for the Motherland, and for the King." Until the mid-1970s, the *Royal March* opened the only authorized radio news twice a day, at lunch and dinner times. Together with the Falangist and Carlist hymns, it was also routinely broadcasted every mid-night at the end of the black and white programs of the state monopoly Spanish Television under the background of the three flags and rather sinister portraits of monarchist Calvo Sotelo, Falangist José Antonio and Franco. Then the broadcast close was replaced with only the *Royal March*, the single Spanish flag and images of King Juan Carlos and the royal family until the 1990s.

The main problem of the *Royal March* is that it does not have lyrics and therefore cannot be sung. During the 1920s, King Alphonse XIII had commissioned playwriter Eduardo Marquina to write lyrics, but its chorus, "purple and gold: immortal flag," did not catch on. An alternative commission to poet José María Pemán produced a call to the Spaniards to "raise the forehead," which the same author changed later to "raise the arms" in a wink to the Falangists. A more popular version, however, borrowed from the catechism:

> The Virgin Mary
> Is our Redeemer
> And our Salvation.

There is nothing to fear.
The World, the Devil, and the Flesh,
Hate, always hate to Lucifer.

In the 1960s, a version in the children's *Encyclopedia Alvarez* said of Spain that it had been "the regal pedestal of Christ the Redeemer; you were of glories delightful garden." But as the meaning was rather enigmatic, in Catalonia some children sang, instead, in Catalan:

Up with Spain
Hanging from a cane.
If the cane falls,
Spain good byyye.

During the twenty-first century, the attempts to give the march some lyrics that the masses, the politicians and the sport winners could sign onto have proliferated. None has been formally accepted, and all have fallen into oblivion. President of Government José María Aznar commissioned a group led by writer Joan Juaristi, who could not avoid a reference to the imperial glories: "Wings of linen opened you the way from one to another confine of the immense sea." The Spanish Olympic Committee, concerned with the contrast between devoted singers from other countries and the silent Spaniards at medal ceremonies, also tried, but the attempt only delivered verses like "from the green valleys to the immense sea." Still, nonconformist poet Joaquim Sabina made a nice try with the lyrics "at war for peace and the goddess reason."

In truth, some of these and other lyrics were no more opprobrious than those of the national anthems of some other countries.* But, in contrast to them, in Spain it is not the warmongering or the low quality of the lyrics that makes them unattractive, but rather it is the patriotic detachment of the people that deprives them of interest and moves to mockery.

For many years, the main rival of the *Royal March* had been *The Marseillaise*, which calls "to arms, citizens, form your battalions." The *Hymn of Riego*, in honor of the colonel who rebelled against the absolutist king Ferdinand VII and became a martyr of freedom in the 1820s, originally referred to "the children of the Cid" ready "to win or die" for the homeland. But it eventually became the chant of the republicans and adopted more crass tones. In the

---

* Compare, for example, the anthem of Italy, which repeats the call to "be willing to die" (*Siam pronti alla morte*), or that of Mexico, which begins with "Mexicans, to the cry of War" (*Mexicanos, al grito de guerra*) and repeats the chorus "War!, War!". Etcetera.

late 1920s, when Prime Minister General Primo de Rivera was replaced with Admiral Berenguer, some people sang,

> The King was taking a shit
> And he had no paper.
> Berenguer passed by there
> And he cleaned himself with him.

Soon thereafter, when the Republic was proclaimed, some of its supporters warned,

> If the priests and nuns knew
> The beating that we are going to give them
> They would go out on the street yelling
> Freedom, freedom, freedom!

As the latter occurrence did not happen, the first threat was widely enforced. The *Hymn of Riego* became the Spanish national anthem in 1931. But it usually rivaled with *The International*, the hymn of the socialists and communists, which calls to "Make a clean slate of the past [...] The world's foundation will change," and *The Varsovian*, which was adopted by the anarchists to calling to struggle "to the barricades."[14]

Els Segadors ("The Reapers"), currently the official national anthem of Catalonia, is a war song against "the enemy [...] those people who are so conceited and so arrogant"—supposedly the Castilians. Equally war-like and religious are several Basque chants, such as the *Eusko Gudariak*, which asserts, "We are the Basque warriors to liberate Euskadi," the *Gernikako arbola*, which was originally an homage to the tree "planted by God about one thousand years ago," and the *Eusko Abendaren Ereserkia*, which became the current national anthem but without the traditional lyrics referring to "the Holy Cross" and "Glory to good God." The official anthem of Galicia, *Os Pinos*, argues that "the ignorant people, and weak and hard, the idiots and dark do not understand us, no." Other regional anthems are more pro-Spanish: the anthem of Valencia says to fight "to offer new glories to Spain," while the Andalusian one proclaims, "Andalusians, get up! Request land and freedom! Be for free Andalusia, Spain and Humanity!"

The last autonomous community to adopt its official anthem was Madrid, although it has been less than discreetly used. Composed by Professor Agustín García Calvo, it acknowledges that, as the other communities, "each one wants to be itself; I will not be less," and, thus, Madrid declares itself "the last autonomous entity, the pure and sincere one [...] that only for being something I am from Madrid."

Everybody, except the whole of Spain, was entitled and no one could fail to intone its own local anthem.

National-Footballism

In certain circles of the anti-Franco resistance, it was a relatively common comment that football was the opium of the people. It should be expected— some of those resistants reasoned—that, with the disappearance of the dictatorship, the popular masses would be enlightened and much less hooked on such a "drug." The implicit intellectual reference was, of course, Karl Marx, who had said that religion was the opium of the people, that is, "the heart of a heartless world, and the soul of soulless conditions."

The prediction of those anti-Francoists could not be more wrong. They were even more wrong than Marx, because, after all, in democracy religion has declined to some extent. Football, in contrast, has thrived. Every Spaniard can watch one or more football matches every day on TV, the programs with biggest audiences are always football matches, updated information is available through the internet and networks 24/7 and football is the favorite topic of conversation in offices and bars.

In fact, the Marxian reference had a point, because in Spain football has become the most popular cultural substitution for religion. The fall could not be harder: from the highest spiritual pursuit of the realization of the human essence to kicking with the feet. At a much lesser level, football provides, like religion, phony happiness. A Marxian would say that it gives people pleasant illusions, but it also reduces their energy and their willingness to confront the adversities of reality—which is why hopeful anti-Francoists wished that its decline would enhance social combativeness. Nowadays, "myriad alternative religions flourish" everywhere, as observed by the *Economist*. In particular—the influential magazine pointed out—"football fans flock to stadiums in rain or snow and spend thousands on season tickets" like many people do with other religious-type entertainments.[15]

The maximum level of Spanish football nationalism was attained in 1964. On the 25th anniversary of Franco's victory in the Civil War, which was ominously celebrated as "25 years of peace," the national team of Spain won the European Championship by beating the Soviet Union—the main enemy of the Francoists—in Madrid, with the Caudillo in the main box. The Spanish team was formed only by native-born players, excluding nationalized ones such as Di Stefano or Kubala; it displayed the classical imperial style of

"Spanish fury," which basically meant that the only tactic was for all to run after the ball with low technique and much stamina; and the players wore not traditional red, because it was also the color of the communists, but blue like the Falangists.

There have been a few further episodic explosions of Spanish football patriotism. Among Spaniards, however, such a widespread common devotion is not a spring of national cohesion. Rather on the contrary, as happens with other national symbols, Spanish football has become a primary playground for the development of internal localism. In Spain, it is usually said that a person can change one's husband or wife, political party or even religion but never football team. This fidelity is not as strong in other countries where football attracts broad followings, like England, Italy, Germany or Brazil, where some people may choose to follow one or another club at different times of their life depending on the team's performance, new players, coaches or owners or other changing circumstances. Perhaps only in Argentina are the local football allegiances as intense as in Spain, although the Argentinian list of major clubs is simpler than the one in the motherland.

Competition among rival localisms is polarized, of course, around Real Madrid, which is prone to be supported by the factual powers of the central state, and Football Club Barcelona, or "Barça," which claims to be "more than a club" and to represent alternative Catalan nationalist sentiments. The local rival of Real Madrid is Atlético de Madrid, which is supposed to have more social-popular followers. The local rival of Barça is Real Club Deportivo Español, whose competing national allegiance is explicit in its name. The first clubs of the third and fourth cities, Valencia Club de Futbol and Sevilla Futbol Club, wear white, like Castilian Real Madrid. But their local rivals bend toward the other side: Llevant Unio Esportiva wears blue and red like the Catalan Barça, and Real Betis Balompié wear green and white like the Andalusian flag. Athletic Club of Bilbao also claims to be "more than a club," and all its players are native or adopted in the Basque Country or Navarre, like the national teams. Its local rival, Real Sociedad de San Sebastian, abandoned that policy a few years ago only to replace it for a while with the hiring of foreigners but not of non-Basque Spaniards. The governing body of football in Spain is the Royal Spanish Football Federation. But rather than a federal mosaic, competitive football in Spain looks like a postmodern patchwork of rival localisms, regionalisms and nationalisms of different colors and sizes.

Historian Alejandro Quiroga has observed that "no other sport has contributed to the consolidation of national identities and the spread of national narratives as much as football." But in Spain, those identities and narratives have been, above all, those of the several "football nations within a state" that have been documented by Vic Duke and Liz Crolley. In the stadiums of Barcelona and Athletic of Bilbao, the flags with the colors of the local club wave together with hundreds of Catalan and Basque flags, respectively. But when Barcelona or Athletic play in Madrid, it is the Spanish flag that is waved by the local fans, as if it meant that the Catalans and the Basques are not Spaniards.[16]

Likewise, every time that either Barcelona or Athletic or the Basque Alavés play in the final match of the King's Cup—which has happened on 9 of the last 10 years—tens of thousands of fans vociferously boo and whistle the Royal March or Spanish national anthem. Of course, nobody could counterattack with singing it, because, as we have seen, there is no karaoke for that. This is in striking contrast with the fervor of the masses, and most players of both teams chanting on analogous occasions *God Save Our Queen* at Wembley, *Fratelli d'Italia* in the Olympic Stadium of Rome, *La Marseillaise* at Le Parc des Princes of Paris or *Deutschlandlied* in the Olympic Stadium of Berlin (perhaps in this order of enthusiasm). Traditionally, the final of the Spanish Cup was played in Madrid, but after those repeated occurrences, the Real Madrid refused to cede its stadium for the occasion.

The internal local and regional rivalries are endogamous and not smoothed by international sympathies. Barça and Real Madrid and their main stars have millions of fans and followers in dozens of countries in the world, as Manchester United, Manchester City, Milan, Juventus or Bayern Munich also have to some extent. But it is extremely rare to find a single Spaniard who declares himself supporter or follower of a club outside of Spain. Local fidelities are never distracted.

In this context of internal introspection and external aloofness, one should expect that the Spanish national identity should be warmed up by the matches of the Spanish national team. Yet the results on this front have been pretty limited. To begin, the national team was created 30 years after the first domestic clubs had been founded—and several decades after the national teams of England, Scotland, Italy, France, Germany and others had begun to play.

International football matches can be a substitution for war and, as such, they can incense patriotic passions against a common enemy. However, the Spanish national team tends to avoid the use of the words "national team" or even "Spain," which have been replaced with "the Selection" and, more recently, "the Red" for the color of the uniform. During the last three decades, the mood of fans and journalists regarding the Red has oscillated between a narrative of failure, disappointment and pessimism and—when it won two European Championships and one World Cup—outbursts of pride and self-aggrandizement. These victories were achieved, under the managers Luis Aragonés and Vicente Del Bosque, by usually putting on the field a majority of the players from Barcelona, which helped many Catalans to make the two symbolic national allegiances compatible. Yet the national team of Spain has not played in Bilbao or Barcelona for more than 50 years, and there are no plans for it. When the Red wins, the main celebrations are at the Fountain of Cibeles in Madrid, the same place where the fans usually celebrate the victories of Real Madrid.

Not Very Spanish, After All

The president of government Mariano Rajoy famously ended a speech in front a few dozen party followers by exclaiming, "Spain is a great nation. And the Spaniards, very Spanish, and much … Spanish." But the available evidence gives only limited support to these brave claims.

As mentioned, the reestablishment of democracy after a long, destructive dictatorship did not reinforce the sentiments of belonging to the Spanish nation, but rather it weakened them. In addition to the imperial legacy and Franco's nationalism, major factors for this unanticipated development include the following: the discontinuity of internal migrations across Spain since the mid-1970s, the creation and growth of autonomous communities since the 1980s and the integration in the European Union and the subsequent decrease of nation-state rivalries for about the same period.

According to a recent survey, "In comparative terms with other European countries, Spain's national identity is relatively weak […] Spain is below the EU average in the percentage of those who feel 'attached' to their country." Regarding the internal prestige of each country, "Spain stands out in the last few years for its very low self-esteem."

Specifically, "all the elements that are offered to the interviewees as possible reasons for identification with the rest of Spaniards have suffered a decline" since the beginning of the century, including the Spanish culture, the Castilian language, the history and symbols of Spain and "especially the central aspects that define a State: its independence and borders, and its political and economic life," as specified by political scientist Carmen González-Enríquez for the Royal Institute Elcano.

When, in other surveys, the question of the allegiance to Spain is addressed in relation to the allegiance to the autonomous community, only 22 percent of the citizens surveyed say that they "feel only Spanish or more Spanish than of the Autonomous Community." In Catalonia, only 12 percent do. In the Basque Country, only 8 percent. If the answer of double allegiance to Spain "as much as" to the autonomous community is added, about three-fourths of Spaniards say they feel somewhat Spanish, while only one-half do in Catalonia and only a little more than one-third in the Basque Country; the rest feel more of or only of the autonomous community.[17]

At the beginning of the current century, there was some discussion about the possibility of basing allegiance to the Spanish nation not on traditional cultural traits such as those above reviewed but on the values of the democratic Constitution. According to some interpretations that at some moments were favored by both the PSOE and the PP, this would permit to develop a "constitutional patriotism" among a population with varied religiosities, languages and cultural traditions. The only basis of the new Spanish nation would be the people's fidelity to the Constitution, the democratic institutions and the law.

Yet the application of this notion to current Spain was ambiguous from the beginning. In its General Congress in 2002, the People's Party approved a position paper titled, "The Constitutional Patriotism of the 21st Century." On the one hand, it asserted that "constitutional patriotism is not based on the domain or right of history, ethnicity, race, community of beliefs and language, or any other inheritance, whether it is more or less real or imaginary [...] The Constitution has [*sic*] a historical foundation moment." But, on the other hand, it also remarked that Spain is "a nation constituted over the centuries [...] with a heritage forged along an extensive historical trajectory."

Actually, the current Spanish Constitution neither says it has (?) a foundational historical moment nor does it proclaim itself the foundation of the Spanish nation. Rather, it assumes that the nation existed before any political or legal community was formed. It is the preexisting nation that is enshrined as the foundation of the Constitution. Article 2 literally says, "The Constitution is *based on* the indissoluble unity of the Spanish Nation, the common and indivisible homeland of all Spaniards".

The Nation, with capital letter, appears, thus, as a pre-democratic traditional entity. As such, it is the continuation of the tortuous history of the previous decades and centuries, including all the imperial, militaristic, clericalist and dictatorial periods, and particularly the Franco dictatorship. Most of the heritage forged along such an extensive historical trajectory is incompatible with liberal and democratic principles or the rule of law. Article 2 of the Constitution that defines the Spanish nation does not make any reference to values of liberty or democracy.

It may be worthy to remember that the final text of this fundamental article was not the work of the parliamentary Drafting Committee of the Congress of Deputies that was elaborating the Constitution in 1978. It found its way in the form of a handwritten sheet of paper delivered from the Moncloa palace, the president of government's residence. The messenger bearing it, Gabriel Cisneros, made the other committee members see that the text contained the "necessary licenses," and that not a comma could be altered because it responded to a literal commitment between the president of government and the de facto interlocutors, who were extremely interested in the issue. This prompted another of the committee members, the centrist José-Pedro Pérez-Llorca, to stand at attention, raising his open hand to his temple in a military salute. The socialist member of the committee and future chairman of the Congress of Deputies, Gregorio Peces-Barba, frankly acknowledged that they accepted the letter of the article "to reassure the Francoist bunker and the military."

The approach was swallowed by most constituents. In fact, "the new democratic agreement was not considered the founding moment of a new political community. On the contrary, it supposedly gave a new political content to a previously existing nation, whose existence as a demos was taken for granted and not questioned by most of the political actors that shaped the Constitution," in historian Xosé M. Nuñez's words.

In particular, Peces-Barba said candidly, "We take for granted that Spain, as a Nation, does exist before the Constitution [...] To us, the Nation as a relevant fact is a matter of right which precedes the Constitution." On the right-wing side of the political spectrum, José María Aznar and Mariano Rajoy, like many other members of the People's Party, have tirelessly repeated that "Spain is one of the most ancient nations of Europe" and that the mere duration of more or less stable borders for 500 years is a source of legitimacy of the current state. This daring statement was echoed by Felipe González to try to deauthorize some Catalan demands: Spain—he said—"is a historical reality with more than 500 years within its current perimeter, one of the oldest nations in the world." In this approach, the Spanish nationalism could not be more "essentialist" or "primordialist," that is, independent of what real human beings may choose in liberty. And, of course, the argument about the perimeter strikingly overlooks Portugal and all the imperial colonies that for most of five centuries included "the Spaniards of both hemispheres," the largest component within the borders of Spain.

In practice, high patriotic praises to the Constitution and sparks of civic nationalism are frequently mixed with traditional cults to imperial glories, the Hispanity, the Castilian language, Catholic traditions, the rojigualda, the Royal March, the Roja and so on, as we have seen in the previous pages. When a few politicians and intellectuals still repeat that the democratic allegiance should be detached from history, geography or language, they usually mean any history, geography or language other than Castilian-Spanish.

The problem for the popularity of the symbols and components of the Spanish national identity comes from the previous historical trajectory: "In general terms, when a regime that has monopolized patriotism falls, its interpretation of national identity is probably delegitimized and will be incapable of acting as a cohesive element of the political unity of the state," as observed by political scientist Jordi Muñoz. And, in particular, when the monopoly of patriotism has been deeply divisive and confrontational, as it was during the long trajectory that culminated with Franco's regime, the delegitimation may be complete. To make it a cohesive element of political unity, a new nation would need to be reinvented.

In current Spain, the official national identity continues to be largely associated with inherited symbols and historical myths. Significant groups of citizens, especially, but not only, in Catalonia and the Basque Country, do not identify themselves with the Spanish patriotism. Many others feel weak nationalist sentiments or refer to dissimilar cultural patriotic references. In contrast to the above-quoted claim by the president of government, many Spaniards are not, in fact, very or much Spanish. And, as we will see, the incompleteness of the Spanish nation, in a context of weak institutionalization of the state, fatally mars the working of the current democratic regime.[18]

Chapter 4

A MINORITY DEMOCRACY

There are different levels of quality of democracy. The current democracies in Canada or Sweden, for example, are of higher quality in terms of civil rights, rule of law, citizens' participation and government effectiveness than those in, say, Paraguay or Romania. Likewise, there are also different levels of atrocity of dictatorships, as we can see if we compare, for example, totalitarian North Korea or Saudi Arabia with the softer regimes of Malaysia or Morocco. There are democracies and democracies, as there are dictatorships and dictatorships. From this perspective, the current political regime in Spain is a democracy but not of very high quality—rather low in some important respects.

Spain is not exceptional regarding the disappointment of democratic promises. All democracies based on elections by political parties in large states have limitations and produce frustrations. In general, the establishment of the modern model of representative democracy implied some loss in comparison with the classical model of direct democracy in small city-republics. But precisely, how different democratic regimes deal with the shortcomings of the modern representative formula is what gives them different levels of quality.

Let us briefly recall some basic concepts to clarify this. In direct democracies—such as ancient Athens, Renaissance Florence or the current Swiss communes, for example—the people, first, vote on policy in open assemblies and second, they select delegates to implement their decisions. The delegates are not representatives of the people but only mandataries to execute the assembly's imperative instructions. They render account of their job and could be sanctioned for their performance.

In contrast, in modern democratic states the people do not make binding decisions. The voters, first, elect representatives without any imperative mandate on public policy and, second, the elected representatives choose policy with vast discretional latitude and without legally binding pledges or electoral promises. The representatives make decisions *on behalf* of the people. They are not revocable and cannot be recalled on the basis of their policy performance. The only mechanism for accountability of the elected representatives is the following election, which has to deal with both past performances and new future promises at the same time.

The constitution maker and romantic novelist Benjamin Constant insightfully analyzed those differences. He noted that with what he called "the liberty of the ancients," people were sovereign in public affairs but slaves in all private relations. In contrast, the "liberty of the moderns" means that people lose direct decision power in public affairs, which moves them to focus on the enjoyment of private life. Constant vehemently warned against a Faustian bargain by which the entire public affairs soul would be lost. He called the people enjoying their modern private liberty to also "exercise an active and constant surveillance over their representatives, and reserve for themselves the right to discard them if they betray their trust, and to revoke any powers they have abused."[1]

The problem with representative democracy is, thus, not only the election of the right representatives with the necessary information about whether they can do the job appropriately. The problem is especially acute regarding the postelectoral period: when the representatives have large discretion in their decisions, monitoring their actions is costly and there are few institutional checks to limit their ability to act unilaterally.

Spain's current democratic regime is less than mediocre in both dimensions: electoral representation and rulers' postelectoral accountability, as we will discuss in the following pages. The current Spanish democratic regime has low quality because the governments are always based on minority electoral support; the political party oligarchies tend to control all political, legal, media and other institutions; there is a permanent confrontation between opposed minorities and exasperation politics; and the territorial autonomies tend to engage in centrifugal competition.

These meager results derive, first, from the previously reviewed weakness of the state, which produces feeble institutionalization of political relations and relatively low enforcement of the rule of law. Also, the incompleteness of the Spanish nation, which we reviewed in the previous chapter, hinders the inclusiveness of the democratic institutions and fosters interterritorial conflicts. In addition, some choices of institutions of the current regime that were intended to favor political stability have become awfully rigid and unable to adapt to social and political changes and new political demands.

Oligarchy and Clientelism

In comparison with the major countries in Europe, Spain lies at the end of the queue regarding its experience with modern democracy. Let us count only attempts at establishing a "minimal" democratic regime based on elementary requirements such as universal male suffrage, open electoral competition and a government depending on electoral results. Let us leave aside not only female voting rights, which were a late novelty in almost every country, but also other higher-quality features, such as broad and varied associations, consensual policymaking or an effective rule of law. The score for "minimal" democracy in Spain is limited to very brief periods of a few months or years after 1812, 1820, 1868 and 1931 plus the several decades' experience initiated in 1977.

In total, from 1800 to 2018, there has been minimal democracy in Spain during only one-third or 33 percent of the time. This is in contrast to much longer periods of democracy in Britain (63 percent), France (59 percent), Germany (56 percent since 1868) or Italy (45 percent since 1861). The relative scores are even worse for Spain if we accept a rather common classification of political regimes in three categories—democratic, partly free and dictatorial—and focus on dictatorships. Spain has been ruled by absolutist monarchs or military dictators during 38 percent of the time of the same modern period, in contrast to much shorter periods of dictatorships in France (16 percent), Italy (12 percent), Germany (8 percent) and Britain (0 percent).[2]

In the midst of sustained instability, the most durable political formula in modern Spain was a "partly free" or "mixed" regime with the legislative power shared by the king and the Parliament, beginning with the restoration of the Bourbon monarchy in 1874 and lasting for almost 50 years. The mixed regime's main characteristics revealed the country's institutional weakness and territorial fragmentation. Its legacy had a visible influence on further developments, including some features of the current democratic regime.

Let us review it. Initially, the Restoration regime gave voting rights to only about 5 percent of the total population. In 1890, the introduction of universal male suffrage multiplied the electorate by more than five, with most potential voters being rural, poor and illiterate. The electoral system was highly restrictive, as three-fourths of the seats were elected in districts with a single seat, which fostered the representation of narrow local interests and did not permit more than two candidates to compete effectively to obtain representation. Even more important, the government did not depend on electoral results, which were cooked up before every election by the king and some ministers.

The public notary Joaquín Costa famously characterized the real working of the Restoration regime as a combination of "oligarchy and *caciquism* (or rule by local political bosses)." Politicians and voters were exchanging personal favors for loyalty and votes, like patrons and clients by means of brokers. We will see that some of these exchanges evoke political party practices in current Spain.

The clientelist exchange implied that, on the one side, politicians' favors were granted in priority to friends, relatives and professional and economic partners. The favors included private goods, such as recommendations, appointments, transfers and promotions for plum public jobs, dispensation from the military service, exemptions from taxes or influence over judicial sentences as well as small-scale public goods, such as a local branch of a road, a bridge, a railway station, a marketplace or even a provincial university. Likewise, for nonfriends and enemies, the exchanges could imply the loss of documents in a bureaucratic trap, threats of reprisals or arbitrary lawsuits, fines and imprisonments. On the other side, the beneficiaries gave the providers deference, submission and votes.

Of course, this was not a mechanism for democratic representation of different social groups and interests. The members of Parliament and other elected officers were not responsive to citizens' demands. It was patronage and clientelism. But, as Costa said, besides the official legal structure, it was the skeleton of the actual "government of the country by a minority of the worst that tends exclusively to their personal interest, sacrificing the good of the community."

The system worked with three layers. First, the national oligarchs were the deputies and senators and the editors of large circulation newspapers—a political oligarchy rather than an economic one, although with direct links with the latter. Second, the local caciques, who were not big landowners, but mostly lawyers, local bureaucrats, journalists, physicians or pharmacists, were typically recognized as the notables, bosses or "lively forces" of every town, province or electoral district able to recruit and secure some fidelity of votes. They controlled mayors, local judges and public functionaries, and sometimes some of them could also become members of the political oligarchy. Third, the provincial prefects appointed by the central government were the crucial brokers between the oligarchs and the caciques, the main ways of communication and the instruments for reaching deals and monitoring their enforcement.

The Conservatives and the Liberals colluded on a "peaceful turn" in government. To enforce the periodical transfer of power between the two parties, electoral fraud was indispensable. In many districts, "the electoral contest—if that is the term—took place in the negotiation before the election [...] Usually the opposition candidates, after a show of fight that preserved their bona fide for the next time round, withdrew and secure there was no contest," as explained by Raymond Carr.

At the end of the elongated experience, the Catalan leader Francesc Cambó looked in retrospect:

> Who does not remember elections in which the provincial prefects used the police to steal the voting urns or in which the counts of votes were falsified in the very rooms in which justice is administered? Who does not remember that vote of the elected deputies to the Cortes declaring valid a gross and obvious falsification, as a result of which we saw a number of respectable people accepting as their colleague in Parliament an individual whom they would never permit to enter their private houses?

A similar structure in the late-nineteenth-century Italy motivated political theorist Gaetano Mosca to coin his concept of "political class"—a concept still useful nowadays. In the critical analysis of Joaquín Costa, there was an "adverse selection" of the members of the political class, that is, "the conscious, reflexive and systematic exclusion of the fit by the inept."

In this view, the word "oligarchy" fits standard Aristotelian concepts. In contrast to classical democracy, which should be the rule by the many, the "aristocracy" should be the rule by the best few. But when the modern form of representative government is perverted by the adverse selection of the ruling few, it becomes a mere oligarchy, that is, the power of a minority for its own benefit.

The prevalence of clientelist political exchanges between the rulers and the voters through local caciques tends to emerge and survive in countries where the state is weak and centralized while the building of a modern nation has been frustrated by the endurance of fragmented localisms. In the absence of a robust, professional public administration and of ideological parties with a mass membership, the national rulers can try to keep some control over the society by way of clientelist exchanges through local caciques.

The Spanish caciques system did not contain actual political parties in competition or rivalry. The Conservatives and the Liberals, "nor can it even be said that they were parties of notables but chattering caciques, formed by the accumulation of personal clienteles," in the estimation of historian Javier Tusell. In fact, "the cacique of caciques was the boss of the party," as put by historian José Varela Ortega.

In Juan Liz's view, the Spanish clientelist system was the result of a failed attempt by urban elites to introduce an "early political modernity in an economically and culturally backward society." In historian Gabriele Ranzato's version, it is "the story of the forcible transformation of an ancient regime's country instilled by modernization, [where] no social component of national significance permeated by the values of liberal democracy had become the bearer of change."

The backwardness of the society is also an explanation of why in Spain, unlike almost any other West European country, politicians enjoy a social prestige and reverence disproportionate with the actual power of the public offices. Still nowadays, according to Linz, "this explains the important role of politics in our society."

The Restoration system somehow evolved, as in other European countries with comparable structures, especially with the broadening of suffrage rights, a slow growth of electoral participation and the competition of other parties in the few electoral districts with multiple seats. But even if control of elections by the central government weakened and fraud was reduced, in most of the country the role of local networks increased, including new practices of direct purchase of votes. The mechanism was described by Mosca:

> The enlargement of the suffrage certainly increases the number of voters. But the caciques, the prefects, the political organizations, and all those who are used to manipulate the so-called urn results, see how the volume of dough that they have at hand increases, while it becomes softer and more malleable.[3]

Almost 60 years later after the end of the Restoration experience, a new democratic regime in Spain brought about big increases in both voters and dough at hand. In the new context, several of the features of the old political system reappeared and expanded, including oligarchical parties, adverse selection of politicians, local caciques and clientelism and disproportionate social reverence to the members of the political class.

Party-Cracy

Through a highly accidental trajectory of about one hundred years, the political parties in Spain have gone from being "caciques chattering" to becoming electoral apparatuses. There have never been mass parties like those that built modern democracy in the most advanced European countries, especially after World War II.

The most recent reconstruction of a party oligarchy has its origins in the path of the transition to democracy in the 1970s. After a long dictatorship, all political parties, both those formed from the ranks of the authoritarian regime and those emerging from opposition movements, had to be created or recreated almost from scratch. The secret negotiations that led to compromises and pacts for political change were highly personalized by a handful of party leaders; in order to make credible commitments, they had to prove their capability to implement the agreed decisions through the measly ranks of their new pygmy parties. The other way around, the party leaders obtained the support and control of the party affiliates thanks to the achievements negotiated with other parties. External pacts among party leaders and internal authoritarianism within their parties were, thus, two facets of the same game.

The consequences were that many choices of new institutions were custom-made for their authors: they intended to confirm the paramount role of political parties and their leaders in the new political regime and eventually consolidated the parties' oligarchical structure.

Partisan leadership is constitutionally and legally overprotected: The parties are generously funded with public resources based on taxes whose spending is barely controlled by any impartial body. They enjoy regulated broadcasting time on public radio and television, reduced postal rates and public places for their propaganda and public meetings. The electoral system gives them absolute control to select candidates for public office, as neither in the local or regional, Congress or European elections can the voters express any preference for individual candidates on the electoral ballot. And about two thousand office holders, including all senators, national and regional deputies and many appointed high officers, are legally exempted from ordinary judicial prosecution.

This partisan and institutional power is highly concentrated: Spain is possibly the only democratic country in the world in which the same person is the party leader, the head of the party parliamentary group and the president of the government. Electoral campaigns strongly focus on the party candidates for president of the government, up to the point that most voters do not even know the top name on the list of candidates to Parliament in their electoral district.

Let us examine some successive steps of the political process. The formation of the electoral candidacies, the parliamentary groups and the Government as well as the relations between the legislative, the executive and the judicial powers are strongly subjected to the dominance of the parties and their leaders.

To begin, the choice of electoral candidates is the privilege of the party leadership. Already for the first election in 1977, the secretary general of the official candidacy Union of Democratic Center (UCD) and later president of government, Leopoldo Calvo Sotelo, implemented president Adolfo Suárez's choice of candidates by "imposing on the leaders [of the parties in the coalition] an agreement by which they gave power only to me to present the lists in all the electoral districts."

Some years later, the vice secretary general of the Spanish Workers' Socialist Party (PSOE) and vice president of government, Alfonso Guerra, was in charge of implementing president Felipe González's choice of candidates. He cautioned potential candidates that "those who move don't appear in the photo," a motto he adopted from Fidel Velázquez, boss of the Workers' Confederacy of the Mexican authoritarian single party, PRI. González himself early cautioned the public that the PSOE was suffering a process of "oligarchization."

Later on, the president of government for the People's Party (PP), José María Aznar, bragged about secretly writing the names of future candidates for public offices in a blue notebook that he frequently waved closed. Aznar privately designated his successor with his big finger. The favored aspirant, Mariano Rajoy, acknowledged in the further period that crafting the electoral lists is "an undesirable and rather uncomfortable job," but he also warned his party fellows that "the one in charge of approving the lists is me."

Once the candidates have been selected, appointed or elected through closed electoral lists, top-down decisions within the party and the parliamentary groups also prevail regarding the launch of electoral promises, policy proposals or legislative initiatives. The activity of most members of Parliament is extremely limited. The parliamentary rules strongly restrict the role of parliamentary committees and make legislative decisions largely determined by the agenda of the government and, in practice, of the leadership of the governing party. Only the partisan parliamentary groups are authorized to introduce bills. Any amendment proposed by an individual deputy has to be endorsed by the party spokesperson. Even questions to government members, though they are formulated by individual deputies, are always previously decided upon within the parliamentary group.

At the heart of each party group, there is strong voting discipline, upheld through explicit instructions, signals by the whip's hands within the parliamentary chamber, controls and fines of several hundred euros to the occasional disobedient member. In practice, individual members of Parliament work as a mechanical mouthpiece for top-down partisan directives.

A former member of Parliament for the PP, Jesús López-Medel, explained that "one day, before leaving the Chamber, the deputy spokesman of the Popular Group took me by the arm and said to me: 'Jesús, you applaud little.'" This was in contrast to most of his party fellows who could interrupt with frenetic applause up to 20 times in a few minutes speech of their president, chairman and boss. This reproach or threat reminded López-Medel of "an unexplained but real prohibition of thinking for oneself." His reflection: "The Parliament is valid only to applaud, cheer or insult. But making laws, even voting, is a thing of the past. The interference of the Government in the legislative function of the Cortes has broken all records."

After being president of the constitutional court, political scientist and jurist Manuel García Pelayo had made it a general point:

For the elected representative, exercising his freedom of judgment and voting, formally guaranteed by the Constitution, becomes a personal decision for which he must weigh the loyalties, values and roles in conflict, as well as the political costs of the decision, including, in most cases, the exclusion from the political class.

The next level is the formation of government. The selection of ministers is a reserved field of the president. The council of ministers does not operate on a collegial basis. Coordination is essentially hierarchical through the government's delegated commissions, interministerial commissions and undersecretaries' commissions work, which adopt many decisions that are put to the council only for ratification.

Over the years, one can observe a "de-parliamentarization" of the members of government, an increasing dominance of professional politicians and low specialization and subordination of the ministers to the president. "From appointment to departure, the ministerial condition reveals a subordination to the head of government which is incompatible with a sufficient level of political autonomy to turn the minister into the true leader of the political machine of his respective ministry," as observed by political scientist Juan Rodríguez-Teruel.

High concentration of power causes high personalization of politics, rather than allegiance to policy or ideology. The mere appellation of "president" of government is a rarity in parliamentary countries, where the chief executive is most often called prime minister or similar names implying collegial work. Through the years, this has generated political emotions of servitude and reverence called Suarism, Felipism, Aznarism, Zapaterism, Maríanism and so on, for the names of the successive heads of the executive.

The party-cracy erodes the separation of powers by also giving the ruling party far-reaching control of the appointments for the top of the judiciary and other autonomous bodies. All members of the General Council of Judicial Power (CGPJ) are appointed by the Parliament with the aim of achieving "political coherence" with the governing party majority, as was made clear when the rule was established. The CGPJ nominates the presidents of the Supreme Court, its lower courts and the high courts of the autonomous communities.

"The horse trading between political parties for the appointment of magistrates and members of the higher organs of justice," according to the jurist Francisco Rubio Llorente, former vice president of the constitutional court, "has produced the progressive degradation of our political uses, so ingrained that, apparently, its actors have even lost consciousness of it [...] Considerations based on the preparation, intelligence or integrity of the candidates disappear or go to a very second term, and everything is reduced to bargaining between parties, to a simple struggle between political rivals, for which the only factor that counts, the only relevant feature, are the political "sympathies" of those candidates."

This has generated, in administrative law professor Alejandro Nieto's view,

the implacable dismantling of the so-called Judicial Power: its alleged constitutional independence has almost completely disappeared, and judges, abandoned without protection, are dangerously vulnerable to the pressures and temptations of governments and political parties [...] Appointments [of magistrates] are made in an outdoor fair where the booty is distributed in scrupulous installments.

Likewise, the members of the constitutional court are appointed by the Parliament, the government and the CGPJ, typically producing partisan majorities in favor of the government party and allotment of appointments with the other party, by turns. As political scientists Pablo Oñate and Juan Rodríguez-Teruel observed in their comprehensive survey of magistrates' recruitment,

Given the control political parties exert over the bodies that nominate the magistrates, the nomination is made under partisan-line bases, negotiated by party leaders every time new appointments are to be made. Even if magistrates are independent, their political "orientation" is usually well known before they are appointed.

The Group of States against Corruption (GRECO), which is formed by the 48 members of the Council of Europe and the United States, has evaluated corruption prevention rules with respect to members of Parliament, judges and prosecutors in Spain every four years since 2001. The group has repeatedly recommended to introduce objective criteria and evaluation requirements for the appointments of the higher ranks of the judiciary, that is, the General Council of the Judiciary, presidents of provincial courts, high courts of Justice and Supreme Court judges, "to ensure that these appointments do not cast any doubt on the independence, impartiality and transparency of this process." Its most recent compliance report issued in 2018 concludes that "none of the recommendations has been implemented satisfactorily or dealt with in a satisfactory manner by Spain," which appears as the country that has complied the least with the recommendations regarding prevention and fight of judicial politicization and of corruption out of the 21 countries evaluated.[4]

Likewise, the government or the political party majority in the Spanish Parliament also appoints most members of the boards of many regulatory bodies, including the Bank of Spain and the public Spanish Radio and Television, as well as the National Commission of Markets and Competition, the Council of State and the Accounting Court, with comparable consequences.

* * *

All these vast controls of institutions are managed by party organizations with copious financial and administrative resources but very few affiliates, who are mostly current, former and aspiring officeholders. Party membership in Spain is paltry, although there are not well-verified data about such membership. Out of the about 25 million voters in recent general elections, the parties' public declarations would amount to about one and a half million party members in total or about 6 percent. But the more formal party censuses for voting in so-called party primaries or the election of delegates to internal party congresses in 2016–17 amounted, in total, to less than one-third of that number, about 400,000 or less than 2 percent of the voters. The compulsory fees that every member must pay to the party are to be discounted from the income tax statement; but according to the Finance Ministry, less than 100,000 people do so, or 0.4 percent of the voters.

This series of numbers suggests different layers in the party organization from bottom to top. As presented by political sociologist Robert Michels,

The participation in party life has an echeloned aspect. The extensive base consists of the great mass of electors; upon this is superimposed the enormously smaller mass of enrolled members of the local branch of the party, numbering perhaps as few as one-thirtieth [3.3 percent] of the electors; above this, again, comes the much smaller numbers of the members who regularly attend meetings; next comes the group of officials of the party; and highest of all [...] the half-dozen or so members of the executive committee.

This is how the increasing concentration of power upward to the party summit creates an oligarchy. In Michels' famous words,

> The fundamental sociological law of political parties may be formulated
> in the following terms: It is organization which gives birth to the dominion
> of the elected over the electors, of the mandataries over the mandators, of
> the delegates over the delegators. Who says organization, says oligarchy.[5]

For most party members, being enrolled in the party and passively abiding
by the party discipline is only a way to wait to be enlisted for public posts.
It does not come as a surprise that the recruiting of professional politicians
has become—again, like in past historical periods—an adverse selection.
At the beginning of the current democratic experience, a number of high
officers, whether elected representatives or appointed executives, were
professors, lawyers or economists who had exerted their professions before
entering politics. Gradually, they were replaced with younger people whose
entire work experience was in a political party or a low-level public office.
More recently, some social activists and a number of media pundits with
neither professional skills nor public job experience have also become full-
time politicians. The wages of the Spanish parliamentarians are among the
lowest in Europe, but, for many of those people, the opportunity cost of not
having taken an alternative job is zero. Many years after they were written,
the words by Joaquín Costa have renewed validity: the recruitment for the
political class is based on "the conscious, reflexive and systematic exclusion
of the fit by the inept."

In the light of all this, it may not come as a surprise either that political
parties currently enjoy the lowest popular reputation in Spain. According to
recurrent surveys by the Center for Sociological Researches (CIS), the most
important problems of Spain are, next to the economy and unemployment,
the politicians in general, political parties and politics. Political parties score
next to last in sympathy on a list of 12 social movements or organizations, only
above squatters.

* * *

The overcontrolling, overprotected, internally authoritarian, lowly affiliated
and self-centered Spanish political parties do not spend many resources to
develop broad and solid social networks. In contrast to classical mass parties—
like the social democrats or the Christian democrats in Northern and Central
Europe, for example—most of the Spanish parties' campaigns are not based
on personal interactions between affiliates and potential voters, the local
party branches' direct influence or the leadership of social organizations and
movements. Their messages are, in contrast, concentrated on the main leader
and mostly diffused using commercial propaganda, communication media
and electronic networks.

Yet, the electoral effects of these means may be relatively volatile. For more durable electoral support, some traditional forms of clientelism have also reemerged, this time less based on individual caciques like one hundred years before than on party and local governments' patronage and a neo-cacique system. Like in the past, private favors certainly remain operational, including recommendations and appointments to plum public jobs; but local public goods are now also widespread, including high-speed train stations, local airports and provincial universities.

It is not that traditional individual caciques have completely disappeared. Famous cases from the PP include, for example, Carlos Fabra, fifth-generation president of the provincial Council of Castellon (since his great-great-grandfather occupied the office for the first time in the family in 1874). Carlos held the office from 1995 to 2011 and explained his subsequent fortune by claiming to have won the lottery nine times in 12 years—before finally going to jail. Another example is José-Luis Baltar, president of the province of Orense from 1987 to 2012, who called himself "a good cacique," is remembered with a trombone animating the tune "if you're not from the PP, fuck you, fuck you" and appointed his son as successor.

Former vice president of Galicia, Xosé-Luis Barreiro, who had personal, very direct knowledge of the matter, stated, "If one were to make the list of councilmen, deputies, senators, senior officials of the Administration [...] who follow the party's obedience in exchange for perks, positions, posts of influence [...] we would fill a thick tome!" Only counting the employees of provincial councils who are not recruited by formal procedures but hired at the boss discretion, the number goes up to about 35,000 jobs.

Political scientist Antonio Robles Egea holds,

The patrons and the clients have always been, with more or less intensity and under different modalities, protagonists of our political scene and of our contemporary history. Surviving in the turmoil of changes brought about by the transformation of the agrarian society into an industrial and service one, by the processes of urbanization and growth of the middle classes and by the democratization of the country, the clientelistic structures have shown an enormous capacity of adaptation which resembles that of the chameleon, which varies the pigmentation of his skin depending on the color that predominates in his environment.

Several scandals, judicial prosecutions and convictions in Andalusia, in particular, have revealed the extent of modern forms of party caciques. The rocky electoral support of the PSOE in the region has been partly explained by the spread of the party control of municipalities, provincial councils, agencies, public companies, foundations, local newspapers and a variety of associations that are vastly dedicated to provide thousands of plum jobs, retirement pensions, food stamps and other perks and pork barrel benefits to their clients.

Political scientist José Cazorla explained the basic party clientelist mechanism through the example of the Rural Employment Plan (PER), one of the many public subsidy programs implemented through municipal governments, which benefitted several hundred thousand people for many years:

> The Plan "grants wages to agricultural workers provided they have worked a minimum number of days in the year. Given that the local mayor is responsible for certifying the number of days worked, the potential for local politicians to ensure electoral support in exchange for approving the payment of these subsidies is obvious, and it appears that the PSOE, the majority party in the areas covered by the PER, has made use of this power to secure a faithful electoral clientele."

The historically derived civic and organizational weakness of large parts of Spanish society is reflected in these examples of low collective participation, stunted democratic procedures and servitude and dependence on political parties' power.

This explains again, like it did one hundred years ago, the disproportionate deference and public attention devoted in Spain to politicians. The following words by José Ortega y Gasset's may be perfectly accurate for current Spain, just replacing his reference to out-of-date social gatherings with the current presence in the media and social networks:

> In Spain, the political man who has been a ruler or is so appropinquated to being, enjoys a great social power. Any jackanapes who for twenty-four hours has settled his buttocks in a ministerial armchair remains socially consecrated for the rest of his life. All specifically social springs work to his advantage. Not only he has political influence, but when entering a private ball or sitting at a convivial table he seems to be "someone" [...] I do not think there is another country in Europe where the politician enjoys equal power. It is not that the former Spanish minister possesses more social force than [for example] the French, but because of the absence of other forces, he is monstrously prominent.[6]

* * *

All in all, the particization of all forms of politics in current Spain drastically alters the tenets of modern representative democracy. As we said, in contrast to classical direct democracy, the current elected representatives are not subject to imperative mandates from the electors on public policies or other collective decisions. But rather, the elected representatives appear subject to other imperative mandates or, in other words, to unilateral orders from the party oligarchies in charge of forming electoral lists of candidates and the subsequent local, provincial, regional and national parliamentary groups and ruling teams.

The rise of political party oligarchies as the main agents of representative democracy has been analyzed by political scientist Bernard Manin. In his assessment, "there is not any sign that the new elites are in a position to inspire feelings of identification on the part of voters. More than the substitution of one elite for another, it is the persistence, possibly even the aggravation, of the gap between the governed and the governing elite that has provoked a sense of crisis" of political representation. The power that the citizens had in ancient democracy to mandate their representatives has been taken, in the current representative democracy, by a narrow political class.[7]

Minority Governments

Spain is the only country in Europe where, in more than 40 years of democracy, there have always been, at the state level, governments controlled by a single party, no coalition government has ever formed and all governments have been based on a minority of popular votes.

The average electoral support of the Spanish governments formed after the first 13 elections was 40 percent. This feature makes the democratic regime appallingly exclusionary, as it implies that there is always a minority of voters who are absolute winners because the party they voted for controls all government, while a clear majority of voters are total losers because the parties they voted for do not share power at all. Such a high concentration of power on the basis of a minority support in popular votes favors polarization, hinders the institutionalization of the division of powers and political pluralism and hampers the regime's social legitimacy.[8]

Minority governments result from restrictive institutional rules, basically the electoral system and the requirements for the appointment and dismissal of the president of the government. Let us briefly analyze these procedures.

The current electoral system replicates the basic elements that were established by decree by a nonelected government before the first election in 1977. The main author of the first draft of the decree was constitutional lawyer Oscar Alzaga, who, many years later, explained the electoral design in a colloquium at an Italian university, which he probably did not expect it was going to be recorded and published. Responding to a question from the audience, he confessed,

The actual political order [from the government led by Adolfo Suárez] was to write a law by which the government could get an absolute majority [of seats]. Since pre-electoral survey polls gave the future Union of Democratic Center [the government party UCD] about 36–37% of votes, we intended to make a law in which the absolute majority [of seats] could be located at about 36–37% [of votes]. And with a mechanism that partly favored the rural areas, where in the pre-electoral projections the UCD prevailed, in respect to the industrial areas, where there was greater favorable vote for the Socialist Party, we intended that the attainment of the absolute majority [of seats] for the Socialist Party were not at 36–37%, but at 39–40% [of votes].

As suggested by Alzaga's confession, not only would an electorally minority party be expected to be allocated a majority of seats but also a party well established in rural districts could easily gain a greater number of deputies than another, more urban-based party that might have received more popular votes.[9]

Although the electoral system is based on the principle of proportional representation, in fact a dual electoral system operates. On the one hand, about 50 percent of all deputies are elected in small districts with very few seats, in which only one or two parties can receive representation. On the other hand, the remaining 50 percent of deputies are elected in a few districts with higher numbers of seats, which permit a degree of multi-partyism.

So far, the system has favored the two most voted electoral lists. No party has ever won an absolute majority of votes in any Spanish election. But in the first 13 democratic elections since 1977, the electoral system produced four absolute majorities of seats in Parliament for a single party: two for the PSOE and two for the PP.

In eight of the other nine elections, the larger party was able to impose its candidate as president of government, in spite of controlling only a minority of members of Parliament, thanks to the rules for parliamentary "investiture." In the first round of voting, the favorable vote of an absolute majority of the deputies for a presidential candidate is required. But if such a majority is not attained, then only a plurality or relative majority can do the job. This means that the president of the government does not need the support of more than 50 percent of the deputies, but he only needs more votes in favor than against so that a sufficient number of abstentions can make a winner. A minority government, both in popular votes and in support from the Parliament members, is the determined outcome.

Minority governments can survive because, in contrast to those low requirements to appoint a president, the rules to overthrow him are much more demanding. Opposition parties can present a motion of censure against the president of government, but the censure must be "constructive," that is, it can succeed only if there is an absolute majority of deputies in support of an alternative candidate. It is, thus, possible for a single-party government with minority support in the Parliament to survive if its opponents are sufficiently competitive with each other and do not agree on a common candidate. In practice, the censure motions that have been presented (by PSOE in 1980, PP in 1987 and Podemos in 2017) have been mere denunciations of government and party propaganda exercises in front of a TV audience.

For many years, the political system of Spain was one of "adversary politics," as it was branded by political scientist Samuel Finer. Although the model was intended to explain the British system, which is based on a different electoral system, Finer's characterization also fit Spanish democracy very well: "Our system—he said—is one of alternating single-party government."[10]

Two major consequences of an adversary political system have been identified. First, it tends to produce socially minority and biased governments that satisfy only the preferences of small groups of citizens and are prone to be captured by minority interests. This can be well observed in Spain, especially regarding some of the biggest banks that were the result of mergers strongly facilitated by government intervention and former state-owned monopolies that were privatized under political control.

The second consequence must be qualified. In the British experience of many decades, the complete alternation of parties in government without intermediate bridges—such as coalitions with centrist parties—caused a series of policy reversals and instability, including nationalizations and privatizations of industries and services and frequent changes of tax, commerce, labor and other policies. However, even in Britain the distance between major economic policies implemented by the two alternating parties in government was greatly reduced since the late 1990s when the Labour Party renounced proceeding with further renationalizations of privatized companies and adapted to basic requisites of a market economy.

The convergence of the two major parties of Spain on macroeconomic policy was earlier and precocious, as it was mostly derived from the PSOE's policy choices after its first electoral victory in 1982. Felipe Gonzalez's first minister of economy, Miguel Boyer, immediately announced "ten years of stabilization," a strategy that was followed by subsequent economy ministers, Carlos Solchaga and Pedro Solbes. In periods of expansion, the basic policy orientation meant privatization of state bureaucratic monopolies producing private goods (such as automobiles, transport, energy or telecommunications), liberalization of capital and labor markets, opening to foreign investment and expansion of social transfers and spending, while in periods of recession within the European Union, it involved balancing public budgets by means of raising taxes, reducing wages, cutting spending and other "austerity" stances.

Of course, the PP was broadly identified with these policy orientations. "The strikingly small partisan and ideological conflict over the size of the welfare state in Spain" has been documented by political scientists José Fernández-Albertos and Dulce Manzano. In contrast to the challenges faced by the British Labour Party and other European social democrats, which were stuck to their previous experiences of high governmental intervention, the PSOE had the advantage that its pro-market choices did not openly contradict any past performance. The PSOE also benefitted from the political autonomy of the party oligarchy from relatively weak social movements, as we remarked before. The party leaders had, thus, wide latitude to give priority to electoral motivations, that is, to compete for support from the middle-class voters, in the confidence that its core voters would not shift to support the Conservatives when they were still stained by the authoritarian past.

In the most recent periods, the lack of strong controversy around major macroeconomic and social policies and the renovation of the PP's leadership has moved the parties to choose other issues that are able to provoke confrontational and adversarial campaigns. The PSOE largely moved the public agenda toward moral issues, such as abortion or gay marriage, religious teaching at schools or the revision of the "historical memory" of the Civil War. Meanwhile, the PP developed symmetrically aggressive campaigns following the conservative commands of the Catholic bishops and tried to obtain political benefit even from terrorism, sometimes with counter-effective results. As mentioned, the two major political parties have also rivaled in denouncing the other's corruption, with the unintended effect that the arousal of scandals eventually eroded the voters' confidence in both parties and decreased their electoral support.

In a kind of paradox, the PSOE and the PP have viciously attacked each other on these issues, precisely because they are too "close" in their policy positions on other issues—especially the economic and social policies that had marked traditional ideological differences between left and right.[11]

* * *

After the traditional party system was abraded by the Great Recession, a series of scandals and continuous confrontational campaigns, the general election in 2015 produced an unprecedented result: the two larger parties, PP and PSOE, which on some previous elections had obtained together up to 80 percent of the votes, barely collected 50 percent. Two new parties emerged, Podemos on the left and Citizens (Cs) on the center-right, while regional parties kept or increased representation.

As, for the first time in almost 40 years, no single party could reasonably expect to obtain sufficient support in the Parliament, there was an uproar in public opinion in favor of the formation of a grand coalition. Multiparty coalition governments formed by parties from the center-right and the center-left existed at the time in 14 European countries, beginning with Germany and including other countries with both older and more recent democracies and higher and lower living standards than Spain. Also, broad coalitions constitute the typical consensus politics of the European Union, where the European Popular, Liberal and Socialist parties account for about two-thirds of the votes and seats in the European Parliament and form the European Commission. The 2015 election was an opportunity for Spanish democracy to begin matching European mores.

In reaction to these demands, there was a lot of posturing and conversations among party leaders. The PSOE and the Cs signed an initial government agreement, of which the speaker for the largest party, the PP, said it could accept about 70 percent. However, politicians' arrogance, animosity and narrow party internal interests prevailed; no further negotiations were undertaken; and, as no majority was formed in the Parliament, a new election had to be called six months later, by mid-2016. This time, a single-party government was—again—appointed. The PP obtained parliamentary support from Cs through an agreement that included about two-thirds of the previous agreement between the PSOE and Cs and the last-minute abstention of the PSOE and other parties to prevent the third election within a year. The new government was supported by the smallest electoral minority ever: only 33 percent of the votes. A further censure motion replaced the government by one formed by the PSOE with support from less than 25 percent of the votes.[12]

Further developments dramatically showed the weakness of the Spanish state, which we analyzed in the previous chapter, making it close to impotence. The Parliament lost, in practice, most of its legislative budgetary and control powers. The government routinely makes resource to decree-laws. Even the most competent and honest politicians might feel frustrated and impotent.

Yet, the political show goes on as usual. In Spain today, numerous political actors continue to act the gesticulation and crispation part of adversary politics, even if most of its substance has dramatically vanished. Party officers replicate old grinds and clichés with no context or relevance. Political parties consume themselves in inward-looking curling.

At the same time, many media and social networks project the cockney culture that blows off steam without pursuing any constructive result: the eternal bravado, the insults, the inability to listen, the automatic reflex to interrupt the speaker to bar any new point of view, the impulse to repeating the same words and the same phrases over and over again. Sometimes the spectacle of politicians, pundits and talk-show guests keeping their speeches, rhetoric, gestures and other routines while they ignore or pretend to ignore the background of the political institutions' colossal impotence can be astonishing.

One could apply to current Spanish politics what Henry Kissinger said when he was a professor at Harvard and was asked why the disputes on college campuses are so bitter: because the stakes are so low. Spanish politicians can afford the luxury of bitter feuds because, after all, not much happens. Even if the government does not do anything, or no government is formed for many months, the consequences are not very serious: the European Union, the central administration, the Social Security, the autonomous regions and municipalities continue operating as usual. Nowadays, the difference between a government elected by the Parliament and a caretaker government is not big. As in campus politics, the stakes are rather low. Many important decisions are increasingly made in Brussels, Washington or New York, including on monetary, fiscal, financial, migration, anti-terrorism, security or climate change policies, while local and regional governments administer almost all public services, including education and health. The Spanish democracy looks adversarial, but the regular management of many issues is rather banal. The current democracy is, by far, not what, in another historical context with a stronger state and a more robust nation, it could have been and was not.

Centrifugal Autonomies

By far the most adversarial issue in Spanish politics is the territorial distribution of power. When, in the early 1990s, the PSOE did not have a majority in the Parliament and sought support from the Catalan and Basque nationalists, the opposition PP chose a confrontation strategy and harshly criticized the PSOE for yielding to the nationalists at the expense of other regions. When, a few years later, it was the PP, also lacking a parliamentary majority, that sought the support of the Catalan, Basque and Canary nationalists and accepted some of their demands in contradiction with its previous denouncements, it was the PSOE that promoted Spanish nationalism and reversed its past compromises. When, in contrast, the PP achieved an absolute majority of seats in 2000 and launched a program of recentralization of the state, the PSOE formed a common front with the nationalists and promised to support a new Statute of Autonomy for Catalonia. Then, when the PSOE got back into power in 2004 and relied upon support from the left republicans of Catalonia and the Galician nationalists, among other groups, the PP responded with a campaign to collect signatures for a Spain-wide referendum against the Catalan statute and in defense of a "single Spanish nation." This generated even more open confrontations after the PP won the Spanish election in 2011 and when the PSOE got back in government in 2018. All in all, the result of letting the territorial issue be used by parties without strong institutional constraints has been sustained bipolar controversy between the two larger Spain-wide parties and increasing centrifugal moves by the regional governments.

The autonomous communities are also engaged in permanent competition among themselves. The Basque Country, Catalonia and Galicia were initially given special rights, but there are also differences among these and other communities based on languages, civil law, fluvial waters, insularity or the relative importance of different economic activities. Most autonomous governments have always wanted to approach or reduce the level of autonomy of the Basques and the Catalans in search of uniformity, while the latter try to maintain a difference. This game of rivalry, which has been called "comparative grievance," is like a greyhound race in which the dogs chase after the hare, who escapes and provokes acceleration of all the players. The chasers, however, are not keeping up: certain surveys show that the population of the communities that want and have higher self-government perceive that they have too little (especially the Basque Country, Navarre, Catalonia and Balearics), while those who would like little perceive that they have too much (especially Madrid, Castile-Leon, Castile-La Mancha and Extremadura). The race for power creates deviating paths and centrifugal trends.

All this is feasible, first of all, because the definition of the form of the state in the 1978 Constitution is extremely ambiguous. It maintains the provinces that were shaped as the basic instrument of centralized control in the nineteenth century, acknowledges special rights to the three historical nationalities above mentioned, adds special fiscal privileges to the Basque Country and Navarre and includes an optional decentralizing formula for communities of the rest of Spain—all at the same time. The state is not clearly defined as federal, regional or unitary—as neither was the Second Republic with its equivocal "Integral State." Neither the number and list of autonomous communities nor even the usual expression "State of autonomies" are included in the constitutional text. In practice, the decentralization of the state has been the result of party strategies, competition and bargaining, rather than a process regulated by previous planning and predictable procedures.

Usually, in federal countries built from bottom-up—like the United States, for example—the constitution leaves all competences in the hands of the territorial governments except those explicitly allocated to the central government, while in top-down decentralized states, like Spain, it is the other way around: everything remains in control of the central government except the list of powers to be transferred to the territories. However, the Spanish

Constitution provided two lists of areas delimiting the minimum activities of the central and the autonomous institutions, respectively, which opened the gate for broad competition on nonregulated issues.

At the same time, the governments of the autonomous communities enjoy a fiscal illusion. Except in the Basque Country and Navarre, the autonomies collect very few taxes directly and most funds are transferred from the central Ministry of Finances. This, of course, encourages irresponsible waste and profligacy, as the regional rulers pretend to appear to the voters as providers of public services at no cost, while it hinders the possibility to make them accountable for their management.

As a consequence of lowly institutionalized competition, Catalonia was able to build its own police like the Basque Country, an achievement that was soon imitated by other autonomies; all of them were transferred powers in education and health; some of them accused the central government of reserving framework legislation to itself and leaving the autonomies with only its development and execution; and the constitutional court accumulated hundreds of conflicts and case laws. Eventually, the race provoked a venturous sprint of the Basques toward a confederal relation with the Spanish state and of the Catalans toward independence, both ending in direct conflict.[13]

In the process, competition also developed about national symbols— with the background of the weak Spanish nationhood that we analyzed in the previous chapter. After the Basque Country, Catalonia, Galicia and the Canary Islands asserted themselves as historical "nationalities," several other autonomies followed up. So did, through reforms of their statutes in the years 2006 and 2007, the former members of the Crown of Aragon, that is, Aragon, Valencia and Balearic Islands as well as Andalusia referencing the medieval Muslim kingdoms of Al-Andalus before the Christian Reconquista.

A triggering occurrence was the introduction of the words "nation" and "national reality" in the preamble of the new Statute of Catalonia in 2006 (a reference that the constitutional court took care to specify did not have "juridical interpretative efficacy"). For the educated reader, no neat conceptual difference may exist between "nation," "national reality" and "nationality," since the first two expressions refer to a collective group and the other to the condition of the individuals who are part of it. Most people would accept, for instance, that the citizens of the national reality of the French nation are of French nationality. Is that not clear? But Spanish politicians entertain themselves with quarreling for the honor of such words.

During the Great Recession, most autonomous governments went broke and, for many years, they sustained their finances on periodical transfers of liquidity from the central Ministry of Finances. Yet, the threat to follow an endless race for more powers and resources continued. It had been made official by the new Valencian Statute of 2006; in a unique clause in the worldwide experience of federal or decentralized countries, it proclaims,

> The Valencian Community will ensure that the level of self-government established in this Statute is updated in terms of equality with the other Autonomous Communities. For this purpose, any extension of the powers of the Autonomous Communities that are not assumed in the present Statute or have not been previously attributed, transferred, or delegated to the Valencian Community will oblige, where appropriate, the legitimated institutions of self-government to promote the corresponding initiatives for such updating.

Likewise, the vice president of Catalonia, Oriol Junqueras, assured, "There is no reason, no single one, for us to be satisfied with less than any other nation in the world."

Permanent competition among autonomous communities for increasing powers is also feasible because there are very few institutional bodies to negotiate and arbitrate with the central government. In contrast to the typical feature of federal countries, the Spanish Senate is not organized on the basis of the political majorities in the autonomous communities; on the contrary, it is even more prone than the Congress of Deputies to produce a single-party absolute majority in seats and has no significant legislative powers. Legally, the autonomous communities have the power to initiate legislation before the Spanish Parliament, but in practice they never exercise it. The joint Conference of Presidents of the central government and the autonomous communities, and the Fiscal and Financial Policy Council and other gatherings of central and regional ministers should promote multilateral agreements on policymaking, including on Spain's government positions in the European Councils. But as they can only achieve "recommendations" or "commitments" by unanimity, they have become occasional stages for a confrontation between the institutions controlled by the central government's party and those in the hands of the opposition. Rather than general cooperation, many issues have been addressed by bilateral negotiations between every autonomy and the central government in Madrid.

As summarized by political scientist Michael Keating,

> Competition among regional elites to gain more symbolic status and substantive powers creates centrifugal dynamics. The dominance of parties is also a reflection of the weak institutionalization of territorial relations and intergovernmental conflict.[14]

Like in most spheres of Spanish politics, a poorly institutionalized framework does not provide regular mechanisms for appropriate management of the territorial distribution of power. The issue is particularly open to confrontation due to the weak nationalization of the country that we analyzed before. The consensus among actors committed to interplay under formal rules has been substituted with party competition, opposing nationalist claims and strategic action. This has hindered interinstitutional cooperation and fed sustained political conflict.

The Catalan Roller Coaster

Many of the territorial conflicts in Spain have involved the relations between Catalonia and the Spanish state. This is because an independent political action from Catalonia is doomed in Spain, basically due to its relative mid-size. On the one hand, Catalonia has never been sufficiently large to lead Spain. Many Catalans have seen themselves more prosperous, clever and entrepreneurial than most Spaniards and thus capable of leading them. But the relative size of Catalonia in population and the economy (now at about one-sixth and one-fifth, respectively) has never been sufficiently large, and the other qualities not great enough, to succeed in leadership attempts.

On the other hand, Catalonia has never been sufficiently small for Castile and the rest of Spain to let it be on its own or to negotiate a path toward self-determination. The loss for Spain would have been too big, and the Spanish central rulers have never been willing to permit to Catalonia the very high levels of self-government that they have accepted, in contrast, to a smaller community like the Basque Country.

At the same time, Catalonia is doomed by its internal divisions. On the one hand, the Catalan society has been sufficiently middle class and mediocracy to permit the Spanish state to try accommodations with moderate Catalan sectors around a limited autonomy. After all, the two languages are close derivations from Latin and bilingualism and the mixing or switching of cultural references imply low costs.

But, on the other hand, there are sufficient domestic social divisions and political rivalries to generate frequent changes of political strategies. The disaggregation of social structures produced by the Great Recession and the challenges of globalization have increased both political fragmentation and polarization. Through a series of cycles of ups and downs, which repeat themselves like a roller coaster, they tend to produce endless instability.

The three just mentioned alternative strategies have been tried once and again in modern Catalan history: to lead and modernize Spain, to settle on some accommodation with limited self-government or to seek Catalan independence from Spain—always leading to failure and frustration.[15]

To face this continuing tension, many of the rulers of the Spanish state have tended to rely upon the doctrine of "conllevancia." According to the Spanish Dictionary, the word means to get along well, to muddle through, but also to endure something adverse or painful. As it was elaborated for the Catalan question by Ortega y Gasset in his discourse against the project of Statute of Autonomy in 1932, the attitude is based on the belief that "the Catalan problem cannot be solved, it can only be carried out; it is a perpetual problem, which has always been, before the peninsular unity existed and will remain as long as Spain will subsist." This view implies that Castile-dominated Spain is too weak both to assimilate the Catalans and to be confident about its appeal and recognize Catalonia's self-determination; it can only try to attain arrangements to kick the can down the road.

That is why the historical cycles in the relations between Catalonia and the Spanish state have repeated again and again in modern history. Like in the *Begin the Beguine* song, "To live it again is past all endeavor." Or, as the protest singer Raimon put it, "When you think it's over, it starts again!"

In every historical cycle, the three mentioned Catalan strategies have been tried at the same time by different groups or parties, but each of them has prevailed at different stages: either leading Spain, or focus on self-government, or the search for independence. Each stage has implied a reaction to the disappointment or failure of the previous one, the replacement of the leading group and the choice of an alternative course of action and a new institutional formula. If the Spaniards were not sufficiently supportive of the Catalan lead, let us—thought some Catalans—tend our own garden; if this also became insufficient and frustrating, let us fly away on our own.

In between the cycles, Catalonia has been a less distinguished province of Spain, sometimes a subjugated one. Relative fast processes of switching strategies have also generated more limited and slower processes of change of national identification among sectors of the population, usually requiring a generational renewal to be clearly visible. But sooner or later, the cycle starts again.

In fact, every cycle has been shorter than the previous one, and each time the full sequence has restarted sooner than the previous time. This acceleration may be mostly due to the increasing speed of information and action induced by socioeconomic and technological changes, which also change some action forms. As in Marx's famous correction of Hegel's dictum, history repeats itself but "first as tragedy, then as farce." Nevertheless, "the traditions of all the dead generations burden, like a nightmare, the minds of the living," as certainly it is the case in Catalonia.

After the failure of the most recent campaign for independence, these rhythms might, thus, augur a new cycle to start again relatively soon, as soon—or as late—as a new generation of politicians may be able to engage on refreshed developments. Recent processes of domestic disaggregation of traditional economic, social and cultural structures have reduced constraints for the launch of new strategic campaigns; now they may be more "transversal" in society than in past periods and thus more hazardous and unpredictable. Yet, the current European and international context would make the old formulas less fitted, and new political initiatives may require innovative strategies and institutional designs to be successful. Meanwhile, there may be a new parenthesis of subjection, confusion or bewilderment.[16]

* * *

Three historical cycles of relations between Catalonia and Spain, in which many events and pitfalls have reproduced again and again, can be observed: from the early sixteenth to the eighteenth centuries, from the mid-nineteenth to the early twentieth centuries and from the late twentieth century on.

The first cycle began, after the widowing of King Ferdinand of Aragon from Isabel, with his access to the Regency of Castile in 1506 (and the further annexation of Navarre). The mythical motto "tanto monta, monta tanto, Isabel como Fernando" referred to an alleged prenuptial agreement to co-rule over a unified monarchy. It could have been expected, thus, that, once widowed, Ferdinand would rule the entirety of Spain. But in truth, although the couple was cooperative, both realms had remained separate during their lives. After the death of Isabel, Ferdinand left, in practice, the Kingdom of Castile in the hands of chancellor Cardinal Cisneros. His successor, Charles I, easily established the dominance of Castile, which at the time encompassed three-fourths of the population of Spain.

In the following, second stage, however, the Kingdom of Aragon kept its traditional laws and institutions of self-government. Catalonia, in particular, kept the Parliament (*Corts*) and the Generality or permanent committee acting as the executive of the Parliament accords. The Aragonese Parliament was a counterweight to the Spanish Crown's powers. But after a hundred years or so, they began to be curbed by the king and, especially, by his prime minister Gaspar de Guzmán y Pimentel Ribera y Velasco de Tovar, better known as Count-Duke of Olivares, who was trying to impose the laws, taxes and military recruitments of Castile onto all the provinces. With the empire in ruin and decline, the Crown was in fiscal and military necessity and it aimed at extracting resources from the Eastern lands of the Peninsula. In historian John Elliott's words, the inhabitants of the Kingdom of Aragon, "increasingly parochial in their outlook, even began to derive a perverse satisfaction from ruminating upon the neglect and the injuries they suffered."

But the loss of the Spanish Empire in Europe and the subsequent centralizing pressures of the Spanish Crown eventually triggered the first Catalan insurrection for independence, the third stage of the first cycle. The "Reapers' War" was initially, in 1640, a revolt against the Castilian recruits of soldiers and its troops before becoming a general political and social rebellion. After a year of fights, the president of the Generality, the canon of the cathedral of La Seu d'Urgell, Pau Claris, proclaimed an independent Catalan Republic under French protection. It lasted for a week. Then the Catalans transferred allegiance from the Spanish Kingdom to the French Kingdom, in the expectation of keeping its institutions, but the French troops occupied Catalonia after six months. The conflict became a war between France and Spain until 1652. During the later peace treaty, France annexed the Northern Catalan territories of Roussillon, where the traditional Catalan laws and language were forbidden.

This first Catalan attempt of independence was defeated, as would occur during further attempts, in both external isolation and internal quarrels. The Reapers' revolt encouraged the revolt of the Portuguese, who had much more advantageous external cards, especially their own African, American and Far Eastern Empire, in contrast to the locking of Catalonia in the Mediterranean. Portugal also greatly benefitted from the foreign support of England, an enemy of Spain, which did not imply the annexation of the distant territory in contrast to the expansionism of contiguous France regarding Catalonia.

Internally, "the Catalans themselves did much to ensure the failure of their experiment. The Principality's potentialities for lapsing into social confusion and anarchy were fully realized," according to John Elliott. "Catalonia lacked the social cohesion and political unanimity in which a stable governmental system could alone be established [...] By its internal divisions, Catalonia destroyed itself." It would not be the last time.

Yet, the conflict was also a big defeat for Spain, as would happen again in further editions of similar cycles. As the revolts of 1640 were closely followed by the Westphalia treaty in 1648, which established a new order in Europe, they "marked the disintegration of an entire economic and political system," the European Imperial Monarchy of Spain.

An aggravated replication of the defeat of Catalonia and a new start for Spain took place a few years later, at the end of the War of Succession to the Crown of Spain. The political aspirations of many Catalans were again defeated at the hands of France, now in the paramount form of the victory of its dynasty in all of Spain. The new king of Spain, the French Philip V of Bourbon, who had been appointed by his grandfather, Louis XIV, the archabsolutist "Sun King," dictated decrees of New Plant for the "rebel kingdoms" of Aragon, Valencia, Majorca and Catalonia along the period 1707–16. They had their institutions abolished and were submitted to uniform control, analogous to the overseas colonies: a captain-general and a royal audience.

The mythicized chronicle of the two days after the final entry of the French troops in Barcelona, on September 11, 1714, as written by the captain of the Resistance, Francesc de Castellví, holds that "the inhabitants generally opened all the shops and returned to run the commerce and the artisans to their work with calm, as if inside the city nothing had happened." Yet, Castellví wrote this story from exile, like many thousands of other defeated Catalans, while a few hundred were executed in place.

Doubly defeated by both Spain and France, first by the mid-seventeenth and then by the early eighteenth centuries, Catalonia was, definitely, a frustrated Portugal.[17]

* * *

The second cycle began by the mid-nineteenth century, when Spain lost the American Empire, an incipient industry fed Catalan interests in the Spanish markets and new support for liberal ideas emerged. Many Catalans participated in the earliest liberal movements for change and modernization of Spain. But the first stage of this cycle, when Catalan groups more clearly tried to lead the reform and renewal of Spain, can be located at the so-called Revolutionary Six-Year term, in 1868–74.

The Catalan general Joan Prim i Prats, who was directly subsidized by the owners of Barcelona's España Industrial, the first cotton company in Spain, led a *pronunciamiento* to overthrow the monarchy. Prim became prime minister and hired prince Amadeo of Savoy to be elected king of Spain by the Parliament. Somehow, this Catalan initiative toward Spain paralleled the leading role of the Piedmont, a Savoyan land, in the unification of Italy: both Catalonia and the Piedmont were peripheral northern, industrial regions within their peninsulas, trying to modernize a backward, mostly agrarian country through a liberal monarchy. Yet, the day after the Parliament voted for Amadeo, Prim was shot to death. The new king reigned for a little more than two years but, puzzled by factionalism and conspiracies, abdicated and went back to Italy in 1873. Catalonia was a frustrated Piedmont.

Then the First Spanish Republic was established, also under strong Catalan influence, now to adopt a federal structure. The first president of the Republic, the Catalan Estanislau Figueras, was in office for only four months. Facing perennial fights and altercations among the republicans themselves, during a meeting of the council of ministers Figueras banged his fist on the table and, as he was angry, said in Catalan, "Gentlemen, I can no longer stand it. I'll be frank: I am fucking fed up with all of us"; then he said to go to walk into the

Retiro Park, went to the Atocha station, caught the first train and did not get off until Paris.

His successor, the also Catalan Francesc Pi i Margall, was more adamant about introducing a federal, top-down constitution, but it was sunk by cantonal insurrections from the bottom-up, including an ephemeral proclamation of a Catalan Republic promoted by the "intransigents" of his own party. He was in office for only five weeks. The Republic lasted for only five more months under two more presidents and was overthrown by a new *pronunciamiento*. A few months afterward, Pi i Margall was shot at home; by chance, he was only slightly injured, which moved the attacker to kill himself in place.

The fate of federalism in Spain also depended on the relative weakness of the state. For some, the state was strong enough to be taken as the platform for top-down territorial decentralization; for others, it was weak enough to be overlooked and to start building a new bottom-up structure from cantonal, local and regional republics. None of the two projects found sufficient institutional and social support.

The second stage of this cycle was the result of the retreat of the failed Catalan industrialists and federalists who had tried to lead outward in Spain and their replacement by a subsequent regionalist inward-looking movement. The final loss of the Spanish Empire in America in 1898 moved Catalan manufacturers and lawyers, historians and poets, to act together in search of a new path. From 1901 on, the regionalists began to achieve some power by winning mayoralties against the two established cacique parties.

Their main success was the establishment of an administrative Commonwealth of the four provincial councils of Catalonia, initially chaired by the president of the province of Barcelona, Enric Prat de la Riba, in 1914. Very soon, however, the regionalists and some republicans began campaigning for an autonomy with legislative powers, a demand that was harshly rejected by the Spanish Parliament. The leader of the regionalists, Francesc Cambó, kept intervening in Spanish politics, for which he would be accused of trying to be, at the same time, the Bolívar or liberator of Catalonia and the Bismarck or ruler of Spain, an endeavor in which he failed—especially the second part.

In the middle of workers' general strikes, terrorism and political violence, the captain general of Catalonia, Primo de Rivera, made his *pronunciamiento*, which was supported by the king, as we saw, and also by the then chairman of the Commonwealth, Josep Puig i Cadafalch. It was a terrible mistake: a few months later, Puig i Cadafalch exiled himself to Paris and the Commonwealth was dissolved.

This failure of consolidating Catalan self-government within Spain generated radical movements for independence, which formed the third stage of the cycle. The best political opportunity had been missed when, at the end of World War I, the United States president, Woodrow Wilson, had favored something that could be interpreted as the nations' right to self-determination as a way to pacify Europe. With the defeat of expanded Germany and the collapse and dissolution of the Austro-Hungarian, Ottoman and Russian empires, up to nine new states were formed and internationally recognized. Some Catalan nationalists renamed the conflict "War of the Nations." According to historian Enric Ucelay Da-Cal, "The petty-bourgeoisie, the Catalan left—the left-wing Catalanists and the Catalan republicans—dreamed of the Wilsonian 'new world' of nations, progress and peace."

But as Spain had not been belligerent in the war, the Catalan demands were not included in the agenda. Some Catalan activists pretended to have sent thousands of volunteers to fight for the Allies as a platform for their claims. Francesc Cambó planned an interview with Wilson in Paris, where he was visiting for the creation of the League of Nations. But the Allies' diplomacy recommended the Catalans not to try; it was, instead, the Spanish prime minister, Romanones, who met the United States president and the French prime minister, Clemenceau, to prevent any interference.

The real action for self-determination of Catalonia began after the establishment of Primo's dictatorship and the dissolution of the Commonwealth. It involved, again, the emergence of a different set of politicians and activists. Somehow, the new movement was still trying to catch the last wagon of the international train. Ireland was still running its own armed insurrection against the British Crown away from the continental empires and achieved the Irish Free State in 1922. Inspired by that, a former Catalan lieutenant-colonel of the Spanish Army, landowner and obstinate conspirer, Francesc Macià organized, as late as in 1926, a small armed band to cross the border in the Pyrenees from France with the expectation of provoking a mutiny of soldiers, a general strike and the subsequent proclamation by radio of the Catalan Republic. All participants were arrested by the French police before arriving at the border.

A new political opportunity emerged with the municipal elections that provoked the proclamation of the Second Spanish Republic in 1931. Two days after the election, Macià went out to the balcony of the historical Palace of the Generality, where the provincial Council of Barcelona then had its seat and, without any loudspeaker, addressed the improvised audience in the plaza to proclaim "the Catalan State and the Catalan Republic" to go "with all our affection towards a Confederation with the other Republics of Spain." A few hours later he signed a statement declaring "the Catalan Republic as a member State of the Iberian Federation" (thus including Portugal). Celebrating the strategic turn, some people shouted in the streets, "Up with Macià! down with Cambó!" Yet the mess ended three days later in an agreement with the provisional government of the Republic, which led, first, to rebranding Macià's provisional government with the historical name of Generality of Catalonia and, one year later, to the approval of a regional Statute of Autonomy of Catalonia within the "integral" Republic of Spain.

Soon thereafter, Lluís Companys, the new president of the Generality, made a new proclamation during the strikes of October 1934, this time of "the Catalan State of the Spanish Federal Republic." There were 80 deaths and the president and all members of the Catalan government were imprisoned.

Like the old cantonalists, both Macià and Companys made references to a federation or confederation, whether Spanish or Iberian, as if it had to be built from the bottom-up by the creation of other states across the peninsula. But, as neither another region in Spain imitated such a unilateral declaration nor did the Constitution of the Republic become federal, in practice, the Catalan proclamations were declarations of secession.

In the mid-1930s, the international context had dramatically changed, and there could not be a worse aspiration than to break apart a democratic state. Portugal with nationalists, Italy with the fascists—from whom both Primo de Rivera had taken inspiration—Germany with the Nazis, even several of the newly created states at the end of World War I, had become dictatorships, while the League of Nations was in fatal decline. As we reviewed, the coups, countercoups, revolutions, insurrections and spurious elections in Spain since 1923, in which the Catalans were outstanding participants, generated increasing conflict until the military uprising of 1936.

Some people have maintained that, during the first months of the Civil War, as the government of the Republic was unable to exert effective control of the territory, a workers' revolution exploded and the Catalan government established a war economy, Catalonia achieved considerable political independence. However, the situation reversed when the government of the Republic, besieged by the rebel military, left Madrid and Valencia and moved to Barcelona, with its 250 thousand employees and their families, in 1937.

The third stage of this cycle ended, of course, in total defeat before the troops that occupied Catalonia at the shouts of "¡Arriba España!" and "¡Viva Cataluña Española!" The reprisals included thousands of exiles, imprisonments and executions by firearm, including of president Companys.[18]

* * *

We could locate the beginning of the third cycle around the 1960s, when some new Catalan groups launched innovative, leading initiatives toward Spain. By that time, Catalonia was again one of the leaders in economic innovation when the contagion from development in more advanced countries crossed the Pyrenees. The cultural creativity of Barcelona was admired by broad intellectual sectors. In the political field, the most visible Catalan influence over the rest of Spain came from anti-Franco movements, including those formed by students, workers, professionals and cultural activists. They largely gathered together in the Assembly of Catalonia, founded in 1971, with a basic program that was synthesized in many demonstrations with demands of "Liberty, Amnesty, and Statute of Autonomy." Yet the more forgotten fourth of the four points of its foundational statement was "the coordination of the action of all peninsular peoples in the democratic struggle." Barcelona was considered the Spanish capital of the resistance, and Spain-wide unitary platforms, especially the Democratic Coordination or Plata-Junta, were largely inspired by that seminal experience.

The Catalan momentum reached all the way to the parliamentary Draft Committee of the Constitution of 1978, which, out of seven members, included two Catalans: communist Jordi Solé-Tura and nationalist Miquel Roca-Junyent. It was also present in the deputy prime ministership of the government of Spain by a former mayor of Barcelona, Narcís Serra, in 1991, and reached its peak during the Olympic Games in Barcelona in 1992, an event that the new mayor, socialist Pasqual Maragall, greeted with the thesis that "what is good for Barcelona, it is good for Catalonia, and it is good for Spain." Yet, the results, all in all, were rather modest. No Catalan has been president of government of Spain since 1873. Leading Spain was not exactly what the Catalans have done best.

The Catalan nationalists' message, "Then, let us tend our own garden," was heard. The reestablishment of the Generality with the return of president in exile, Josep Tarradellas, in 1977, before the Spanish Constitution was approved, the new Statute of Autonomy in 1979 and, especially, the first election to the Parliament of Catalonia in 1980 had drawn a parallel line and opened the second stage of this cycle. Under the presidency of Jordi Pujol, the main focus of Catalan politics was—like the Commonwealth of 60 years before—the building of a more homogeneous Catalan language and cultural nation within the Spanish state. Pujol's nationalist party supported the Spanish Parliament minority governments of both the PSOE and the PP, in exchange for more transfers of powers and resources to the Generality of Catalonia in the race with other autonomies. During this stage, like at the beginning of the century, the Catalan intervention in Spanish politics was less conceived as an attempt at leading Spain than as a form of pressure and negotiation for the protection and reinforcement of Catalan autonomy.

The second president of the Generality in this period, Pasqual Maragall, also tried to intervene in Spanish politics, but he supported only the PSOE and was in open confrontation with the PP. The bid, under pressure from his government partners, the left republicans, was a new Statute of Autonomy that would give Catalonia more significant legislative and judicial powers. According to the constitutional procedures, the statute was initially approved by the Parliament of Catalonia, negotiated and revised by the two chambers of the Spanish Parliament and submitted to a ratification referendum by the people of Catalonia in 2006. However, the PP launched a campaign all across Spain to collect signatures "against the Catalans" for the nullification of the statute and, at its demand, some of its articles were partly invalidated by the Spanish constitutional court in 2010.

The subsequent reaction in Catalonia was less for gain than for justice. Regarding the "gain," the PP leader, Mariano Rajoy, had declared that the Catalan statute "unilaterally liquidated the model of the State, changing it from the present State of Autonomies into an asymmetric confederation that only privileges Catalonia." However, the constitutional court rejected most of the PP's resources and made relatively limited invalidations on the initially approved statute. It accepted that Catalan would be a language of "normal use" in the Catalan public administration, but not "preferential" to Spanish, a ruling that did not have any practical consequence on actual language uses. It favored a structure of government with multiple levels by preserving the powers of the Spanish ombudsman, the General Council of Judicial Power and the constitutional court itself, while accepting "non-exclusive" Catalan counterparts of the three institutions. It also preserved autonomous fiscal powers of local governments and limited the Catalan participation in Spain-wide tax and other policies.

Had these cuts been introduced during the parliamentary process, the statute most probably would have been approved anyway (after all, neither the Spanish right wing of the PP nor the Catalan pro-independence left republicans supported it in the referendum). Still, it could have been a temporary arrangement, a new kick to the can down the road, which may have lasted for perhaps one more generation.

But the problem was "justice," that is, the breach of the political agreement and an ostensible violation of regular procedures. In the words of constitutional law professor Javier Pérez Royo, "The sentence does not lack legal argumentation and one can even agree with some of the things that are said in it. But that is not the problem. The problem is that the Constitutional Court overruled the pact between the Catalan Parliament, the Spanish Parliament and the people of Catalonia."

The constitutional court, which in practice acted as a third chamber, was widely seen as illegitimate. Out of 12 magistrates who should form the tribunal, only seven were in the post on regular basis, while another had passed away and had not been replaced, another was recused by the PP, two remained in the office after the deadline of their mandates because the PP delayed the appointments of their substitutes, which, as we reviewed above, are made on partisan bases, and the president had also extended her term. The full sentence was backed by only five magistrates, four of them directly or indirectly appointed by the PSOE, including the prorogued president, and one by the PP that remained beyond his term. Four of the five dissidents had been directly or indirectly appointed by the PP and wrote particular votes, which were not enforced, in favor of more invalidations or more restrictive interpretations of articles in the statute.

This created the occasion to launch the third stage of this cycle, which was openly oriented toward independence. More than 500 municipalities (not including Barcelona and the largest cities) had already organized informal referendums for independence during the years 2009 and 2010, before the constitutional court's sentence, with total participation around 30 percent of the electoral census. Several campaigns about deficient transport infrastructures such as the Barcelona airport or commuter trains, a series of different reports on the fiscal balances between Catalonia and Spain or some criticisms of the language policy at schools had also been presented as if they did not leave any other way out but secession and the creation of a Catalan state. Since 2012, a series of rallies mobilized several hundred thousand people on Catalonia's Day every year.

Under the presidency of nationalist Artur Mas, the government of Catalonia called, first, a "participative process" in 2014, which mobilized about 37 percent of the electorate. Then, a "plebiscitary election" in 2015, with the aim, as pronounced by the leader of the left republicans, Oriol Junqueras, of not being satisfied with a bird in hand but only with "flying, free, with all the birds in the world." The votes for the candidacies for independence amounted to 37 percent of the electorate again (48 percent of the votes with 76 percent turnout). Under the new president, Carles Puigdemont, it was called an illegal referendum for independence in 2017 that, according to the organizers' data, attracted about 38 percent of the electorate once again (90 percent votes for "yes" with 42 percent turnout).

A few days later, Puigdemont interpreted that he had "the people's mandate to convert Catalonia into an independent State with the form of a republic," but he proposed "to suspend the effects of the declaration of independence." He made front-page headlines all across the world, although nobody understood what exactly he meant. Two weeks later, the Parliament of Catalonia voted a resolution to constitute "the Catalan republic, as an independent and sovereign state." Then, the Catalan ministers and deputies took the weekend off. The government of Spain dissolved the Catalan government and Parliament and called a regional election. The Catalan president fled the country while several members of his government were imprisoned. In the elections, the parties for independence received, for the fourth time, the support of 38 percent of the electorate (48 percent of the votes with 80 percent participation). Against a background of high division and polarization of the citizens, with a permanent draw between the supporters and the adversaries of independence, Catalonia—like, increasingly, Spain itself—appeared to be ungovernable and developed lasting political instability.

As in the Catalan campaigns for independence in past historical cycles, the international context was rather adverse. When the Soviet Union had dissolved and 15 new republics had been created around 1991, the political opportunity to follow the trend and call for the independence of Catalonia had been explicitly discarded. President Jordi Pujol held then that "we have the same rights as Lithuania, only that they exercise them through the path of independence, and we, of autonomy." He noted the differences: Spain was "a more solid, democratic reality" than the USSR, and the Baltic republics "want to flee to Europe, [while] Catalonia already belongs to it."

Later on, references to other countries were casual and diffuse. Quebec and Scotland were hopeful examples because their governments had signed agreements with the Canadian and the British governments, respectively, for legal, enforceable referendums on independence, but the "no" vote won in both cases. Artur Mas said that Catalonia "was the Holland of the South" and it should be "the Denmark of the Mediterranean" but also that he wanted it to be "like Massachusetts," which is not an independent state as far as it is known. The diplomacy of the Spanish state was much more effective than the foreign service of the Generality, and no state supported the independence of Catalonia. The European Commission and the European Council were particularly receptive to following instructions from the Spanish government to declare that Catexit from Spain would mean Catexit from the EU and that an independent Catalan state should apply for membership anew. Several calls for international mediation were not successful.

In fact, many participants in the Catalan movement did not care much about international links or the foreign environment; they had culturally disconnected from Spain and also from the rest of the world and lived in a kind of self-centered and endogamic bubble that they purported to be self-sufficient. Often, the public debate in Catalonia tends to emit an old, well-known courtyard smell.[19]

* * *

The story of the political relations of Catalonia with the Spanish state, which have been cycling like a roller coaster, has been one of failure and frustration.

The Catalans have not been able to lead the Peninsula, like the Piedmont; they have not achieved the development of a durable self-governing state within a federation, such as, say, Massachusetts (or even a privileged enclave like the Basque Country); nor have they managed to be a separate country from Spain, like Portugal.

The historic "experience of external dissociations and internal contradictions has ended up constituting a psychological spring of collective behavior," observed Catalan historian Jaume Vicens-Vives. The strategy of leading Spain failed due to "the coercive impotence of Catalonia." The accommodations that were initially accepted as common sense were eventually rejected for insufficient, which may reveal the importance of fear and myopia, also called prudence, in the initial choice. Then, when the reality looks displeasing, "the anger, the rudeness and the bursting arise, the attitude of saying enough! [...] the whole or nothing, the negation of the ideal of compromise and pact dictated by collective common sense."

Vicens-Vives wondered,

> It is not easy to understand how we can pass, in hours (historical time), from the darkest alignment with the world of minimized realities to the iconoclastic exuberant bootfighter [...] We break into a few hours the work of years of reconstruction. And then, to start again, plotting ourselves in the stumbling block, but without thinking about it, avoiding the political, social and spiritual analysis of the facts.

The succession of historical cycles fed the feeling among many Catalans that the trials and failures would be permanent, that—as Ortega y Gasset held from the other side—the Catalan problem could not be solved, that it was and would be perpetual.

A number of comments and reactions in crucial conjunctures can illustrate the point. Regarding the insurrection and proclamation of the Catalan state in 1934, jurist and Parliament member Amadeu Hurtado reflected, "For the parties in the government of Catalonia, the important thing was to follow the tradition of our struggles, preferring the adversity to the success as a sure food for one more protest." Then, the leader of the Catalanist conservatives, Francesc Cambó, addressed the members of the Spanish Parliament this way: "Do not delude yourselves. This Parliament will pass, all the parties that are represented here will disappear, regimes will fall, and the living fact of Catalonia will subsist." When a year and a half later, in 1936, President Lluís Companys, upon exiting prison, returned to the balcony of his office, he asserted, "We will suffer again, we will fight again, and we will win again".

Nearly 50 years later, in 1984, when the president of Catalonia, Jordi Pujol, was involved in a lawsuit for a previous misappropriation of funds in his bank, the Catalan government secretly subsidized newspaper ads calling a demonstration in solidarity; one of the most repeated ones said, "We will have no right to complain if we do not know how to respond now." When President Carles Puigdemont announced the call of a referendum for independence in 2017, he augured, "Although they want to see us beaten or defeated," in the end "we will be defeated soldiers of an invincible cause." The Catalan minister of economy, Andreu Mas-Colell, summarized his vision of the problem with this pronouncement: "We the Catalans have spent 300 years sinking stone [it is understood that this means against the Spanish State] and most likely we have to continue doing it for 300 more years." He justified his support of the 2017 referendum with this objective: "On October 1 it is necessary that a great and peaceful demonstration of democratic dignity be deployed, and that we can be in a position to wake up, on October 2, with the head and morale very high." After the suspension of the declaration of independence, the speaker of the anti-capitalists proclaimed, "Neither we nor many people think about giving up, there is no defeat whatsoever, we begin a new stage of struggle!"[20]

Note that any expectation to achieve any concrete success tended to be absent from those commitments and convocations; the most common forecast was defeat and the resuming of complains. Years, governments, parliaments and parties will pass, and the problem of Catalonia will remain unsolved; we will follow the tradition of our struggles; we will suffer once and again, but we will retain the right to complain and to wake up with the head held very high; we will keep stinging stone for 300 more years, beginning, once and again, new stages of struggle, and we will be, once and again, beaten and defeated in an invincible cause. That these statements were pronounced during two separate historical cycles over a period of more than 80 years confirms that this was what actually happened almost all the time.

* * *

Building a large state and dealing with territorial differences in the construction of a common political community, like Spain, are the inside face of the outside relations among states. The modern concept of "sovereignty" has precisely these two faces: internal monopoly of power and external noninterference and mutual recognition with other sovereigns. For the territorial conflicts within the Iberian Peninsula, especially between the central Castile and the peripheral Portugal and Catalonia, the fate of the transcontinental empires has been determinant, as we have seen in previous chapters.

Particularly adverse consequential factors for the relations of Catalonia with the Spanish state have included the vicinity with centralizing and statist France, the treaty of Westphalia that consolidated the sovereignty of existing states, the redrawing of the map of Europe after the collapse of the continental empires in World War I from which the Catalans were ignored, the rise of dictatorships in the ride toward World War II which ran against the attempts to revamp the Spanish democratic Republic and the dissolution of the Soviet Union and its Eastern European Empire whose opportunity was discarded.

Nowadays, the actual sovereignty of states is fatally challenged by transnational technological and economic developments, global institutions and, in particular, the increasing integration of the European Union. As a consequence, new foreign opportunities for further territorial changes in Spain may emerge.

It may seem paradoxical that the EU permitted Brexit, that is, the secession of Britain from Europe, but, following Spain, it did not permit Catexit, that is, the secession of Catalonia from Spain. A simple explanation may be that the EU is less integrated than Spain is. Yet, it may not be so neat. In fact, the EU was strongly against Brexit, and the European Commission adopted a very harsh position in the further negotiation, especially with the intention to prevent the temptation of exit by other countries (Hungary or Poland, for example), up to the point to make many Britons think about the possibility to reverse their decision.

Also, the EU did accept the referendum for independence of Scotland, which had been agreed with the British government. The Scottish government planned a transitory period remaining within the UK before enacting independence in order to reenter the EU without a break. The EU had already monitored the referendum for independence of Montenegro, which had also been agreed with the government of Serbia, by setting the requirements of 50 percent turnout and 55 percent of votes "yes" (which were fulfilled). So, one can wonder whether the current constraints on redrawing borders in Europe could be formally lessened for everybody.

It can be helpful to compare the evolution of the EU on the issue with the historical experience of the United States. About seven decades after the approval of the Constitution, the United States government did not accept state secession from the Union. The attempt to leave the Union by 11 states in the south was answered with military action and triggered an extremely lethal Civil War. Something like a Brexit could not happen in the United States.

At the same time, many internal borders were redrawn. The US Constitution had established that a new state could be "erected within the jurisdiction of any other State" with "consent of the Legislatures of the States concerned as well as of the Congress." Then, during the Civil War, West Virginia split from Virginia, Nevada split from Utah, and Montana was created by putting together several lands from Oregon, Washington, Idaho and Dakota; all the new entities were admitted as member states of the Union.

In this light, the United States seems to have been more integrated by the mid-nineteenth century than the European Union is now. This is not true on other issues, as the EU is now more integrated on monetary, financial and some political issues than the United States was by then. But through the Civil War, the American Union became sufficiently strong not to allow exits from the Union while at the same time permitting the redrawing of internal borders between its member states. The crucial point is that the member states were not recognized as sovereign anymore—neither for exit nor for fixing their borders.

What could change, thus, in Europe, that would make a qualitative difference regarding interterritorial relations in Spain? If we try to take inspiration from the United States experience, a higher integration of the European Union should prevent more Brexits and, at the same time, be more open to internal redrawing of borders. More specifically,

- The level of EU's integration should be one at which the Union would not recognize the sovereignty of the member states.
- Referendums of self-determination should be consented to not only by the parliaments involved but also by the European Parliament.
- For new opportunities to emerge there should be a major internal transformation of the European Union. Alternatively, the international context could change as the result of some major political crisis, as occurred in the above-mentioned cases the Civil War in the United States, the dissolution of Yugoslavia or the collapse of the Soviet Union.

All this may happen one day. Or it may not.

The Basque Pendulum

In contrast to Catalonia, the Basque Country has been blessed in Spain due to its relative small size (less than one-twentieth of the population, tightly packed within a tiny territory bordering France, and one-sixteenth of the economy). Because of the small dimensions of the peripheral country, no Basque political party or politician has ever dared to try to lead Spain.* Almost every Basque

---

* Only conservative Eduardo Dato, who was born in Galicia and grew up in Madrid, was a member of the Spanish Parliament for the Basque province of Alava and prime minister of Spain for a few years by the early twentieth century before being shot by an anarchist patrol.

intervention in Spanish politics has been, conversely, in resistance to Spanish nationalization, whether by the *foralists* or defenders of the *fueros* or medieval laws and the Carlists in the nineteenth century or by moderate nationalists pleading for autonomy and radicals for independence since the early twentieth century. All the Spanish central governments, whatever the political regime or party ideology, have conceded to some extent on unique forms of Basque self-government, in contrast to the more usual centralizing or reluctant attitudes toward Catalonia and other territories in Spain. The cost for the Spanish state of the Basque special formulas has always been affordable.

The Basque Country and Navarre, which had belonged to the historical Kingdom of Navarre and have acted as a united movement on several contemporary occasions, are highly internally divided: between territories, such as Alava, Biscay, Gipuzkoa and Navarre (plus Lower Navarre and two more former provinces in Iparralde, within the current French state), between bilingual Basque speakers and unilingual Spanish speakers who cannot understand a conversation or a speech in Basque and by several social and political cleavages that, at some moments, have produced high levels of fragmentation, polarization and violence.

Thus, the Basque political strategies are bounded within the common aim of achieving, maintaining and enhancing self-rule, but they have oscillated between two orientations: either toward special rights and autonomy negotiated with the Spanish state or toward radical self-determination and independence. In practice, the latter breaches and movements, including those using violent means, have been used by the former, moderate mainstream as a threat and negotiation tool with Spanish governments to obtain high rates of legal self-government, but the evolution of the question has been lurching.

The history of Basque nationalism is "ultimately the history of the confrontations, separations, and reunifications of these two blocs," as put by legal historian Javier Corcuera. As a result, the relations between the Basque Country (often including Navarre) and the Spanish state have been shifting like a "patriotic pendulum." Always "maintaining its anchorage in the defense of the Basque national identity, have alternately oscillated between the different possibilities that were presented, depending on the external circumstances and the internal balance of options and interests," according to the metaphor by historians Santiago de Pablo and Ludger Mees.[21]

* * *

The surviving *fueros* or medieval laws and institutions of the diverse territories of the Peninsula had been abolished in the former kingdoms of the Crown of Aragon by the early eighteenth century, as we reviewed. But they had subsisted in the lands of the former Kingdom of Navarre thanks to their support for the Bourbon candidate in the War of Succession to the Crown of Spain. They included a particular civil law, complete fiscal autonomy and the exemption from serving in the Spanish Army. During the nineteenth century, through three bloody Civil Wars, the Carlists, that is, the supporters of the candidate Carlos María Isidro to the Crown of Spain (against his niece Isabel II), defended the validity of such traditional entities against the liberal attempts at unifying laws in all Spain.

At the end of the first Carlist War, in 1839, a convention was achieved with the Spanish liberal government for Navarre to keep its traditional *fueros*. At the end of the third Carlist War, in 1876, the *fueros* of the provinces of Alava, Biscay and Gipuzkoa were abolished by the Spanish government. But the traditional institutions, formed by a General Junta and a Foral Council in each territory, remained and led immediately to a fiscal pact, called the Concert, by which they would be able to raise and collect all taxes and pay a "quota" to the central government. These outcomes were certainly a defeat of Spanish liberal nationalism. The old *foralists* and the Carlists resisted the weak central authority of the Spanish state and confirmed the steady entrenchment of traditional institutions.

By the end of the nineteenth century, a new Basque Nationalist Party (PNV) was formed under the slogan "God and Old Laws." Its leader, Sabino Arana, coined the name of the imaginarily unified country, "Euskadi," and designed its flag. The party's first manifesto pointed to "full reintegration of the *fueros*." But it gradually adapted from resistance to participation in regular politics with more limited goals. The so-called Euskalerriacos fraction, close to the emerging industrial bourgeoisie in Biscay, used the label Nationalist Communion and joined Navarre's clerical Carlists in a campaign for "a broad autonomy" for the Basque-Navarre provinces and municipalities "within the unity of the Spanish nation" in 1917. The campaign, in parallel to a Catalan campaign for autonomy previously mentioned, failed, which provoked the split of the more radical, secularist "Aberri" or Arana's extreme separatist followers.

As the PNV did not join the Spain-wide for the establishment of the Republic in 1931, a new pro-republican split formed a liberal, lay party called Basque Nationalist Action. Although the PNV did not support the Constitution of the Republic either, it presented a project for an "autonomous State within the totality of the Spanish State." It was sold to its followers as a bonus sprint in the race toward the full *fueros*, but it caused, again, the separation of a small radical group, this time around the Bilbao-based weekly magazine *Jagi-Jagi*.

The Basque Statute was finally approved, as late as October 1936, when the Basque nationalists decided to bend on the side of the Republic against the military and fascist insurrection that had already generated the Civil War. The statute established that "the Basque Country may adopt the tax system that it will judge fair and convenient," remaining exempt even from the Spain-wide income tax. As has been acknowledged by legal historians Gregorio Monreal and Roldán Jimeno, this was an exceptional, unique formula, affordable to the Spanish state due only to the small magnitude of the Basque Country's fiscal contribution: "The extension to other autonomous territories of the Concerts and Convention systems was simply unimaginable, since with the broad financial ruling that the central power would be deprived of, it would be unrecognizable not only the 'integral State,' but even a genuine federal State."

For a few months during the Civil War, to the Basque government headed by nationalist José Antonio Aguirre "the isolation of the Northern front from the rest of the republican Spain allowed him to widen enormously the autonomy until forming a semi-independent State in Biscay," according to historian José Luis De La Granja. "Lehendakari [president] Aguirre did not even control the three provinces that officially constituted the autonomous Euskadi, since Alava and nearly all of Gipuzkoa were in the hands of the Francoists. Nevertheless, during the eight months preceding the [Francoist] conquest of Bilbao, Aguirre organized the free Basque region as a semi-independent state, even counting on its own army," in the concurrent analysis of Ludger Mees.[22]

It is interesting to observe, thus, that the same *foral* medieval root eventually developed into Basque nationalists fighting on the republican side of the Civil War and, in parallel, Carlist militias or Requetés joining the Spanish nationalists on the fascist side. Both branches had in common a premodern tradition, anti-liberal stance that succeeded to resist, survive, recover and thrive over a weak Spanish state. The divergence also showed the traditional and persistent territorial fragmentation of the former Kingdom of Navarre. The "very loyal" province of Navarre as well as Alava on the basis of "its very valuable contributions to the National Cause" were rewarded by Franco with the maintenance of their fueros institutions and fiscal privileges, while the "traitorous provinces" of Biscay and Gipuzkoa, where "the most cumbersome anti-Spanish politics" had prevailed, were punished with submission to the general rule of Spain.

* * *

The political void left by the Basque Nationalist Party during Franco's dictatorship was filled by a radical split from its youth organization in the late 1950s, which would become the radical pro-independence group "Basque Homeland and Freedom" or ETA. Initially, the group considered adopting the name "Aberri," like the radical branch of the PNV in the 1920s, but it was discarded for euphonic reasons. In its first assembly in 1962, ETA issued its principles. It defined itself as a Basque Revolutionary Movement of National Liberation. It was in pursuit of self-government of the six historical regions with "a democratic and unequivocally representative regime," together with "the maximum decentralization in the structure of Basque political society." It aimed at "the development and invigoration of the Basque Nation in all its fields" by "the most appropriate means that each historical circumstance will dictate."

ETA also declared itself favorable to European federalist integration, promising that "if Euskadi, with full freedom, considers most convenient to its ends and existence the assignment of various rights to supranational organizations, so will it," while it embraced the final goal of "the progressive suppression of state borders all around the world." The old prestate *fueros* were trying to be made compatible with a poststate world. Very soon, however, ETA broke with the PNV, adopted an anti-colonialist revolutionary inspiration, promoted armed struggle and experienced several splits for diverse versions of combatant Marxism.

From 1968 on and continuing for 40 years, ETA assassinated policemen, civil guards, militaries, employers, politicians, judges, professors and journalists and launched terrorist attacks by installing bombs in military and police headquarters, airports, department stores and other public spaces. The total killing was estimated as 857, two-thirds of them within the Basque Country and most of the others in Madrid and Catalonia. There were also 86 people kidnapped, 3,421 victims of attacks that were officially indemnified and a few thousand who left the Basque Country after being threatened or targeted. On the other side, it was alleged that police persecution and "dirty warfare" by paramilitary squads, somehow supported by members of the Spanish security forces and secret services, had caused about 200 mortal casualties, while 3,300 ETA militants were imprisoned.

With a total of about 1,000 mortal victims, the conflict barely qualifies as a minor civil war, as we discussed before. The death toll was immensely lower than the previous four Carlist Wars (including the Civil War of 1936 on the list, as has been suggested). A comparable conflict during about the same period for about the same population size, "The Troubles" in Northern Ireland, that is the contest between the Irish Republican Army or IRA, the British security forces and diverse paramilitary groups, produced near four times more deaths, about 3,700.

The aim of the Basque insurgents was not the violent conquest of power, as is the case of major revolutions and civil wars, but the development of an attrition strategy aimed at outlasting the armed forces of the Spanish state. As put in an ETA's internal document, "The function of the armed struggle is not to destroy the enemy, for that is utopian, but it is indeed to force him, through a prolonged war of psychological and physical attrition, to abandon our territory due to exhaustion and isolation."

Most ETA killings were produced after Franco's death. The peak took place just after the amnesty that freed all ETA and all other Spanish political prisoners and exiles in 1977, especially during the three years in which the new Spanish Constitution and the new Statute of Autonomy of the Basque Country were approved and the first election to the Basque Parliament was held. The violent secessionists sensed that the settlement of the new institutions could hold off a political opportunity for independence for a long while.[23]

* * *

Indeed, the political opportunity existed, and it was eagerly taken by the revitalized Basque Nationalist Party. Before the first open Spanish election in 1977, the PNV presented its program for an "autonomous Basque State." It did not participle in the further elaboration of the Constitution and called not to vote in the referendum for its ratification, which, together with the boycott by ETA's followers, made the Basque Country the only region of Spain where the Constitution was not backed by a majority of the electoral census. However, the Basque nationalists—in a revival of the tactics of the 1930s—managed to develop a bilateral negotiation with the Spanish central government to have a few special clauses included in the Constitution: it repealed the law that had abolished the *fueros* in 1839, it established protection and respect of the historical rights of the *foral* territories and it introduced a procedure for the incorporation of Navarre to the Basque Country at the former's initiative.

The subsequent Statute of Autonomy of the Basque Country restored the *foral* institutions, that is, the three General Juntas and *Foral* provinces, while the Navarre *Fuero* was "ameliorated." The *foral* provinces have full fiscal normative and management powers, as they "collect, manage, liquidate and inspect all taxes" (with the only exceptions of customs duties and monopolies). The Basque Country, as well as Navarre, contribute to the state with a "quota," which now is not proportional to fiscal revenue—as it was in the traditional *fueros*—but estimated to complete the financing of the state's general expenses (basically diplomacy, defense and payment of debt interests).

The new Concert including Biscay and Gipuzkoa was explicitly inspired by the one previously surviving for the province of Alava, which made Gregorio Monreal and Roldán Jimeno say that "it is necessary to consider as something *providential* the maintenance of the Alava Concert and the Navarre Convention during the dictatorship, since it made possible the rebirth of the institution in Bizkaia and Gipuzkoa during the Transition." They might not have been wrong because, although the dictatorship was not directly ruled by Providence, it may have been it indirectly through the Caudillo of Spain by the Grace of God.

The same authors acknowledge that "the system presents remarkable singularities, not only with respect to the rest of autonomous communities of the State, but comparing it with those of other politically decentralized States." In fact, it is a unique arrangement, which also creates an interesting challenge to the Basque Country rulers.

The citizens of all the other autonomous communities, like those of some other territorial units in decentralized countries that mostly rely upon financial transfers and grants from the central government, suffer, as we mentioned, what public economics call a "fiscal illusion." They may perceive that most of their taxes are paid to the central government, while the regional government appears as if it provided a broad set of public services almost for free. A consequence is that the citizens may demand more of those "free" services and support increases in the size of the regional government. Naturally, the regional leaders can take political advantage of this type of situation by blaming the central government for the costs, bragging about themselves for the benefits and trying to expand the resources under their control.

But in the Basque Country it is the opposite. The Spanish central government is almost invisible and the Basque government has to take full political responsibility for its performance. This has helped to improve its efficiency and has also tamed public corruption. The government's political accountability increases the popular legitimation of the Basque autonomous community, while the Spanish government fades away. The system of Concert and quota must be a very good deal, because it has unanimous political support in the Basque Country from both the Basque moderate nationalists and radical independentists and the Spain-wide Socialist and People's parties. It would be very difficult for the Spanish leaders of the PSOE or the PP to promote an alternative formula because the Basque sections of their parties would openly oppose it.

One of the very first initiatives of the Basque government, under the presidency of Carlos Garaikoetxea (a Basque nationalist from Navarre), was the restoration of the Carlist militias in Biscay and Gipuzkoa, the "Forales" and the "Miqueletes," respectively, which, together with the existing "Miñones" in Alava, were the basis for the creation of the Basque police force, known as the *Ertzaintza*. The *foral* police of Navarre remained independent. Contrary to the law, the *Ertzaintza* first officers were not previous members of the Spanish security forces, whom they replaced for all tasks except border control.

The PNV craftily argued that as, in contrast with the national policemen and civil guards, the *ertzainas* and their officers would be Basque natives and

Basque speakers, they would form the best corps to prosecute ETA and control violent nationalist activists. From the side of the Spanish government, "if there have been no objections to force the constitutional framework, it is because it was believed that this way would help to solve the so-called 'Basque problem', which is a difficulty motivated by the existence of ETA [...] Since its [PNV's] concurring has always been considered essential to end terrorism, it [the autonomous police] has been believed to be a suitable instrument for the resolution of that problem," as explained by Javier Corcuera. Seen in perspective, the ETA armed squads did not become, as they had dreamed, the armed forces of the Basque Country themselves, but they were indirectly determinant for the creation of such a corps.

Once the autonomous Basque government was well-established, the nationalist pendulum kept swinging. Lehendakari Garaikoetxea led a radical split from the PNV, initially motivated by his will to reinforce the Basque government rather than the *foral* provinces, and created a new party, Basque Solidarity (EA), in 1986.

A swing in the other direction was pushed in the following years, when the PNV, back in power under the presidency of José Antonio Ardanza, coalesced with the Basque Socialist Party, sponsored a pact with the Spain-wide parties against ETA and attained several deals in the Spanish Parliament with both the PSOE and the PP, always in exchange for further transfers of powers to the Basque government and better deals for the fiscal "quota."

The following turn toward the radical side led to the Pact of Lizarra, which brought the PNV and the EA with the addition of minor leftist groups and workers' unions, closer to ETA's political branch, Popular Unity (HB), in 1998. After the PNV signed a secret political agreement with ETA for a ceasefire, there was the expectation to replicate the type of pacifying negotiations that were held at the time in Northern Ireland with the IRA. But the attempt failed due to the exclusion of the Spanish government from the deal and ETA's impatient resumption of its bombings.

The PNV's new lehendakari, Juan José Ibarretxe, launched, nevertheless, a major initiative of institutional reform with the parliamentary support of HB, in 2002. The project of Political Statute of the Basque Country Community claimed the right of self-determination of the Basque Country and proposed a "free association" with the Spanish state. It would have given Basque citizenship and nationality to all inhabitants of the Basque community, while, at the same time, keeping the Spanish nationality only as an optional choice. The fundamental elements of continuity included the fiscal Concert and keeping the king of Spain as head of state.

"The Ibarretxe Plan was intended to find a new way between the alternatives of restricted autonomous self-government within a larger nation-state and full-blown independence," in political scientists Michael Keating and Zoe Bray's view. It took some inspiration from the Northern Ireland Good-Friday Agreement that had been signed in 1998 by the British and the Irish governments and the Northern Irish political parties. However, the differences were crucial. The Northern Irish Agreement, first, was centered on the dissolution of the armed IRA, in contrast to the sustained bustle of ETA. Second, it made power sharing between pro-British and pro-Irish parties compulsory by establishing a proportional allocation of government ministries to all parties in Parliament, in contrast to the exclusive nationalist control of the Basque government.

For Spanish speakers, "free association" also evokes the relation between Puerto Rico and the United States. However, the official name in English for such a formula is "Commonwealth" (and nobody knows exactly what the translator in the 1950s meant). In fact, the situation of Puerto Rico in the United States is almost the opposite of the Basque Country in Spain: instead of accepting financial responsibility in exchange for political responsibility, Puerto Rico is financially dependent on the federal government in Washington and is politically less than a state in the Union, as it does not have representation in the federal Congress or in the Presidential Electoral College. In a series of recent referendums, the most voted alternative has been to become a state of the Union, while independence has marginal support.

The Ibarretxe Plan aimed at the Basques having "direct" representation in the institutions of the European Union. As the debates for the plan coincided with the referendums on a project of European Constitution, "the European context might have saved the Ibarretxe Plan had it been linked to a coherent program at the European level," in Keating and Bray's view. However, "just as the political parties fought over identification with Basqueness, so they also wrangled with each other over identification with Europeanness, each with their own understandings of what these two concepts signify." Strangely, no international context was taken into consideration for such an ambitious territorial redistribution of power not even regarding Europe.

The statute was harshly rejected by the Spanish Parliament in 2005. (Even the Spanish Episcopal Conference declared it "morally unacceptable.") Ibarretxe threatened with calling a unilateral referendum, but he was eventually defeated in a further Basque Parliament election that produced the first nonnationalist lehendakari of the Basque Country, Patxi López, from the PSOE, for the period 2009–12.[24]

* * *

Two main questions are open on the future of the relations between the Basque Country and the Spanish state. The first is about the potential consequences of the disappearance of ETA and its violence. For several decades, there had been multiple bilateral negotiations between the Spanish government, whether from the PSOE or the PP, and ETA for the latter's disarmament and a political settlement. All of the negotiations broke down, time and again, after new terrorist attacks. In the end, neither ETA nor its political branch negotiated a farewell to arms, like in Northern Ireland. ETA stopped killing, hijacking and rioting in 2009, unilaterally announced the "definitive cessation of armed activity" two years later and handed over the weapons after five more years. It left the further pursuit of its political goals in the hands of the political parties.

This may create new opportunities for new editions of the traditional patriotic pendulum, which were more difficult to manage when the radical wing was associated with terrorism. PNV's lehendakari Iñigo Urkullu has followed a moderate pro-autonomy line since 2012. But new broad coalitions between the PNV, the remnants of EA, the successors of the former political branches of ETA, most recently under the name of "Basque Country Unite" or Bildu, and other groups, like the ones that have already been formed with particular success in Navarre and many local councils, might reintroduce proposals for self-determination and independence in a pacified future. The current "period of electoral ascendancy provides little incentive to shift away from a territorial goal that (as in earlier years) is deliberately ambiguous, with the possible options including further autonomy, a federal or confederal state or a bilateral relation with the state through an updating of the 'historical rights' granted by the Spanish Constitution," as insightfully perceived by political scientist Anwen Elias and historian Ludger Mees.

The second question refers to the future of the traditional form of fiscal Concert. On the occasion of recent conflicts between the government of Catalonia and the central government of Spain, several voices were raised to propose the spread of such a formula. However, as we discussed, applying the Concert to larger communities than the Basque Country would involve a higher cost that no Spanish government may be willing to accept. The Spanish Ministry of Finances publishes official "fiscal balances" between the central government and the autonomous communities (or the difference between the tax revenue and the central expense in each community). According to the most recent data for 2014, the balance was positive for the Basque Country (3.4 billion euros) and negative for Madrid (-19.2 billion euros) and for Catalonia (-9.9 billion euros). More recently, in 2017, the ministry experts evaluated that applying the "quota" to Catalonia with the same criteria that are used for the Basque Country would involve an additional expense by the central government in Catalonia of 16.6 billion euros. This big difference between the Basque Country and the other communities is partly derived from the biased, undervalued calculations of the cost of the central expenses for the Basques, the exemption of the Basque Country from contributing to interregional redistributive funds and political negotiations, such as the one for the quota of the period 2018–22, which was pressured by the potential pivotal role of the PNV in the Spanish Parliament.

The political debate about the territorial distribution of powers in the Spanish state of autonomies often turns on the fairness or unfairness of each community's contributions. But the most important political variable for the central government decisions is not the amount of the communities' contributions relative to their economies but the absolute amount of money they bring to the central government. In this light, the central government's deficit with the small Basque Country may be an affordable inefficiency, while replacing big surpluses with big deficits with Madrid, Catalonia or other communities would not. As the above-quoted core defenders of the Basque Concert and quota said, its extension to other communities is simply unimaginable.[25]

The Basque Concert and the Navarre Convention might also be challenged by further developments in the European Union. A sentence of the European Court of Justice in 2008 dismissed the European Commission's suspicion that the low corporate tax of the Basque Country had violated Europe-wide market competition rules. Yet, a further fiscal union of the EU, as it is promoted by the commission, might reintroduce the revision of unique cases such as the Basque and the Navarre ones in the context of the Union. Even if the Basque Country is much smaller in relation to Europe than it is in relation to Spain, the much higher efficiency of the EU might achieve some forms of fiscal unification that the weak Spanish state has never been able to complete.

A Blocked Constitution

As we have seen, the democratic regime established since 1978 contains several rules that have proved to be exclusionary. Their implementation has turned some preventive mechanisms that tried to favor political stability into factors of erosion of the electoral and social support to the results of the political process. The incompleteness of the Spanish nation has also facilitated political competition around the territorial issue and inter-autonomous governments' rivalries.

In the light of the previous analysis, it should be possible to conceive some legal and constitutional reforms that could address such problems, including the electoral system and the regulation of political parties, the investiture with minority support and the constructive motion of censure, the particization of the top judicial bodies and the constitutional court, the divisions of powers between the central government and the autonomous communities and the uselessness of the Senate to facilitate interterritorial cooperation. Also, the greatest constraint on the actual functioning of Spanish political institutions, which is the growing reliance on the European Union, could be formally acknowledged by introducing the topic in the Constitution, where it is not even mentioned. Some of these, as well as other reform proposals, have been raised in moments of crisis as if they could fix or at least soften some of the vices of the regime.

Yet, for 40 years no major constitutional change oriented to enhance the quality of democracy has been implemented. Spain is one of the countries of Europe with highest barriers to constitutional reforms, since they require qualified majorities in the two chambers (and its replication after an election for issues related to civil rights and the Crown) as well as a referendum. It is also, in practice, the country of Europe in which there have been fewer constitutional reforms: since 1978, only two, both derived from the European Union (voting rights for Europeans in municipalities and priority to reduce the public deficit and pay the debt).

In contrast, all democratic countries tend to revise their constitutions periodically. The oldest and shortest of the current democratic constitutions, that of the United States, has added 27 amendments, at an average of one every 8.5 years. The amendments have dealt with many important issues, such as civil rights, slavery, voting rights, taxes, electoral rules or the president's mandate limit.

The country of Europe with the most constitutional changes is Portugal, whose difference with its neighbor is that the reform does not require elections or referendum but only a decision of a large majority in its unicameral Parliament. The Portuguese reforms have included major issues, such as the removal of restrictions on economic policy and the transformation of the presidential regime into a parliamentary one.

In Britain, given that the constitution is not codified in a single text, the changes are also relatively easy: there have been 51 since the end of the World War, including major issues such as the Convention on Human Rights, parliamentary procedures, hereditary Lords, freedom of information, justice or the election of mayors. In France, there have been 17 reforms in less than 60 years, which have affected issues such as EU treaties, the duration of the president's term of office, parliamentary relations and, according to the currently ongoing process, new changes on the size of Parliament, the electoral system and the legislative procedure. In Germany, there have been 14 reforms since reunification in 1990, including on the EU, environmental protection, affirmative action for women or the right of asylum. In Italy, the barriers are higher because a referendum can be called for, but there have been 15 reforms, including those that have given legislative autonomy and exclusive powers to the regions.

There is a fairly clear relationship between the length and rigidity of a Constitution and its noncompliance. Those that are shorter and more open to reforms, such as those of the United States or Great Britain, have a very high level of compliance. Spain is near the other extreme: the Spanish Constitution is rather long, that is, it regulates many issues so that over time the obsolete provisions accumulate and make it decreasingly in line with the political and social reality, which generates numerous demands for changes. At the same time, the Constitution is very rigid or difficult to reform. The frustration of demands for change due to the absence of reforms leads to high levels of noncompliance and rejection.[26]

Only a very broad reform of the Constitution, which has remained almost intact for 40 years, could prevent it from ending up exploding in its entirety. But the fear of the perils of "opening the box" of constitutional reforms—as Spanish rulers usually say—reflects the weakness and vulnerability of the state and the fragility of the nation, which have permitted to build only minority support for the results of the current democratic regime.

CONCLUSION: TRANSITIONING OUTWARD

This book has highlighted a number of continuities in the modern history of Spain. As we have observed that the current democratic regime is threatened by interterritorial tensions and attempts at secession, we have looked at the historical background of an incomplete nationalization of the country. We have also seen that the political game has become the field of oligarchical political parties whose representatives in government have never relied upon the support of a majority of voters. Together with the paralysis of the legislative and the particization of the judiciary ruling bodies, we have seen these features as expressions of the general low level of institutionalization and of compliance with the rule of law, both with very long traditions in the country. In the most recent period, both the people's allegiance to the Spanish nation and the electoral and social support for the governments have decreased. This seems to be the result of some unfortunate institutional choices in the 1970s, which have produced unintended effects and especially of the cumulative constraints on the state powers introduced by the European Union. But looking back, all of these fragilities can also be explained by the structural weakness of the Spanish state, whose main causal factor has been identified in this book as the Spanish imperial adventures that kept people busy—or rather distracted—for several centuries since the 1500s.

As has been reviewed in the previous pages, Spain was born with the empire led by Castile, and it broke with it. The multicontinental empire of the Spanish monarchy was not in itself a good business for the Spaniards or the Crown. But the main consequence was the missed opportunity to begin to build, instead, a modern state, like Britain and France at the time and, somewhat later, Germany and Italy did. Spain did not have the human, technical, financial or military resources to build a successful and profitable empire when it tried to do it. When, later on, new technological and economic developments permitted, or rather pushed the other mentioned countries to expand their markets, conquests and areas of influence overseas, Spain had already been defeated, left isolated and found itself entangled in a series of political messes. While Britain and France built early states, which gave them solid bases to build further empires, in Spain it was the opposite: an early empire frustrated the building of a modern state. The old imperial venture can help explain, directly or indirectly, many further developments.

The interpretive key of the contemporary frustration is to see postimperial modernizing attempts as unsuccessful or incomplete and sometimes counterproductive. Many innovative standards have been strong enough to challenge old standards but, due to inherited structural weaknesses, not to prevail in social uses. Thus, the broken survival of old traditions has produced results with an ambiguous continuity. Specifically, the Catholic Counter-Reformation was partly tamed by secularism, but it left quite a superstitious, rather than deeply religious, society. The traditional picaresque ways of life survived the spread of public spirit and civility and became widespread corruption. Old localisms prevented the full construction of a unified nation and generated opposing rival nationalisms. Militarism and dictatorships cut the road to democracy and ended up giving way to an oligarchical party-cracy in a low-quality liberal regime.

Nowadays, Spain is not what it once was, the core of a multicontinental empire, but neither is it something it could have been: a modern, sovereign nation-state. In the early twenty-first century Spain has struggled to decouple itself from the problems of other EU countries on the verge of bankruptcy, such as Greece, Ireland and Portugal. But for some Spaniards it has taken a while to realize that Spain, which is larger in size than the other states just mentioned, is now also a peripheral and relatively deprived partner of the European endeavor, not one of the core decision makers. Its ancillary role has a long history of frustrations behind it.

* * *

The theory of "path dependence" shows how the options taken at certain historical moments constrain or determine the future trajectory. Certain options have a high opportunity cost, as happened with the Spanish imperial adventure, which fatally postponed the construction of a modern state and a unified nation. At the same time, social practice reinforces the choices made through patterns of behavior that are transmitted through generations and make it increasingly difficult to rectify them.

Cultural continuities can also be explained with the help of game theory. We do not need to be technical. Just to identify a few crucial variables called the initial situation, the population mixture and the frequency and length of interactions among the individuals in the group, and then see whether a stable outcome can be expected and explained from those variables.

Roughly speaking, "the initial situation" in Spain, both in the sixteenth century and at the time of more crucial modernizing opportunities by the nineteenth and the early twentieth centuries, was highly disadvantageous; it was characterized by much poverty, a missed industrialization, low levels of schooling, a parasitic bureaucracy, long traditions of last-minute improvisations, a ubiquitous picaresque and permanent conflicts and revolts.

The second variable, the so-called population mixture, refers to the proportion of individuals identified with those traits or with alternative well-trained, more efficient, better-educated and more enlightened orientations; the weight in Spain rather lies on the former group's side against the repeatedly failed attempts to introduce and consolidate more modern and civilized mores.

Then, an isolated country with a population devoted to local traditions, who sanctions work as a divine condemnation, is used to scrutinize any stranger in the street, inclined to cantankerous, endless shoptalking, and to killing time in cantinas and bars, tends to produce frequent, intense and long-term durable "interactions"; adaption, imitation and contagion of the dominant mores spread.

On these bases—adverse initial situation, dominance of people attached to old mores and intense interactions—a so-called evolutionary stable strategy can be predicted to be one that aims at sustaining and reproducing those backward traits and making deviating behaviors difficult. The outcome, or "evolutionary equilibrium," which results from those strategies, involves many frustrations: the eternal Spain remains alive, sometimes temporarily subsided, but once and again revived and prevailing.

* * *

In Europe, in the well-advanced twenty-first century, the agenda is not the same as it was in the nineteenth century or a hundred years ago. In the current context of open transnational economic and cultural exchanges and increasing interdependence, trying to keep constructing, reinforcing or sustaining a sovereign national state is a futile endeavor.

In fact, "national sovereignty"—as those words are enshrined in the Spanish Constitution and frequently thrown at one other by Spanish politicians—has become one of the most obsolete political concepts in today's world. In the multilevel structure of governance that currently characterizes, in particular, the European Union, nobody is sovereign: neither the traditional states, which are "member" states of the Union, deprived of competence on important policy issues and submitted to strong constraints and controls by the EU institutions, nor any local or regional government that might claim such an ambition. The member states of the European Union have pooled or shared powers derived from their previous sovereignties, but they have not created a new European sovereignty either. Each level of government has exclusive powers on some issues, they share powers on other issues, each should be specifically financed to cover the costs of its services and none can impose its will on the others on everything—which is what sovereignty would imply. The population of Europe lives under several jurisdictions of different scopes and breadths that frequently overlap.

Nowadays, "sovereignty" is not a central concept even in the constitutional orders of the states, as can be seen with the following brief review. In the written constitutions of 10 EU member states, the word "sovereignty" is not even mentioned (Austria, Belgium, Czech Republic, Cyprus, Denmark, Germany, Italy, Luxembourg, the Netherlands, Sweden). The laws, statutes, court judgments, treaties and other sources that make up the United Kingdom's political regime embody only the principle of "parliamentary sovereignty," which has been made compatible with the adoption of the EU structure and compliance with international standards. In the current French Constitution, rhetorical references are made to the principles of the Revolution that place sovereignty in "the people." Similar expressions are used, only as a simple synonym of democracy, in the constitutions of six other countries (Estonia, Finland, Greece, Hungary, Latvia, Portugal). The sovereignty of the "state" is affirmed in only four countries (the recently decolonized islands of Ireland and Malta and the historically threatened Poland and Slovakia). The sovereignty of the "nation" appears only in the constitutions of four newly liberated republics from Soviet imperial control (Bulgaria, Croatia, Lithuania and Romania). In contrast to a common doctrine among Spanish professors of constitutional law, no constitution of any member state of the European Union mentions the sovereignty of the constitution itself.

In this context, Spain is an extreme case, since the Constitution proclaims "national sovereignty" and assigns its defense to the armed forces. The European Union is not even mentioned. Thus, a sweeping turn of orientation may become necessary. The best inspiration for a constitutional reform could be, for example, Slovenia, a recent democracy that aimed from the beginning to be a member of the EU and took the issue as a leitmotif. No less than eight times, its Constitution proclaims that the republic will "transfer the exercise of sovereign rights to international organizations."

If, on the contrary, Spanish politics kept focusing on trying to reinforce the sovereign authority of the state and the institutional capacity of political decision making at the state level, it could lead to a huge step back that would leave Spain behind again and produce more and more frustration. Regarding its political agenda, public discussion and main topics of conversation, Spain is self-absorbed in its own internal fragmentation and divisions. Although only occasional attention is given to it, the new horizon is toward Europe and toward the world; this is the key dimension to develop.

By looking outward, internal political struggles and partisan confrontations turn into poisonous tempests in a glass of water that only make it non-potable. The real new Spanish transition that remains is for greater integration into Europe and the world and toward greater participation in the European and the global institutions. It actually was already the case for many years, although it did not always look like that: for a peripheral, latecomer, weak, constrained state like Spain, the most important public policy is foreign policy. Now it is not such; that is, it is not "foreign," but it has become the essence and the key of everything else.

NOTES

Introduction: When Did Spain Screw Up?

1 Ian Gibson, Giardinetto Sessions interview, May 18, 2017: http://ilgiardinetto.blog.
2 Felipe González, January 16, 2018.

Chapter 1 A Ruinous Empire

1 For a survey of the political literature on empires:
   Josep Colomer, "Empires versus States," *Oxford Research Encyclopedia of Politics*, 2017. DOI:10.1093/acrefore/9780190228637.013.608.
   The first quote is from:
   Geoffrey Parker, *The World Is Not Enough: The Imperial Vision of Philip II of Spain*. Wako, TX: Markham Fund of Baylor University Press, 2001.
2 The quotes are from:
   Ramon Carande, *Carlos V y sus banqueros*. [1943]. Barcelona: Crítica, 1987.
   Fernand Braudel, *La Méditerranée et le Monde Méditerranée à l'Epoque de Philippe II*. [1949]. Paris: Armand Colin, 1966 (English version, *The Mediterranean and the Mediterranean World in the Age of Philip II*, University of California Press, 1995).
   John H. Elliott, *Imperial Spain 1469–1716*. [1963]. London: Penguin, 2002.
   Manuel Fernández Álvarez, "El fracaso de la hegemonía española en Europa." In *La España de Felipe IV, Historia de España*, vol. 24. Madrid: Espasa-Calpe, 1982, p. 789.
   Paul Kennedy, *The Rise and Fall of the Great Powers. Economic Change and Military Conflict from 1500 to 2000*. New York: Random House, 1987, p. 48.
   Anthony W. Marx, *Faith in Nation*. New York: Oxford University Press, 1992, p. 148.
   Henry Kamen, *Empire: How Spain Became a World Power, 1492–1763*. New York: HarperCollins, 2003, p. 508.
   Antonio Miguel Bernal, *España, proyecto inacabado. Los costes/beneficios del Imperio*. Madrid: Marcial Pons, 2005, p. 434.
   See also:
   John H. Elliott, "The Decline of Spain," *Past and Present*, 20, 1961: 52–75.
   Henry Kamen, "The Decline of Spain: A Historical Myth?," *Past and Present*, 81, 1978: 24–50.
   Jordi Nadal, *España en su cenit (1516–1598). Un ensayo de interpretación*. Barcelona: Crítica, 2011.

As Poor as Gambia

3   The data for average income per person and population for different countries and years are taken from the Maddison Project and converted to international dollars of 2016:

   http://www.ggdc.net/maddison/maddison-project/home.htm, 2013 version.

   See also his elegant survey:

   Angus Maddison, *Contours of the World Economy, 1-2020 AD. Essays in Macro-Economic History*. New York: Oxford University Press, 2007.

4   Jaime Vicens Vives, *Manual de historia económica de España*. Barcelona: Teide, 1959.

   Henry Kamen, *Empire*, 2003

   Carlo M. Cipolla, *Before the Industrial Revolution: European Society and Economy, 1000–1700*, 2nd edn. New York: W. W. Norton, 1980.

   Jan Luiten Van Zanden, "Cobb-Douglas in Pre-Modern Europe: Simulating Early Modern Growth." Amsterdam: International Institute for Social History (IISH), Working paper, 2005.

   Carlos Alvarez-Nogal and Leandro Prados de la Escosura, "The Decline of Spain (1500–1800): Conjectural Estimates," *European Review of Economic History*, 11, 2007: 319–66.

   Alvarez-Nogal and Prados de la Escosura, "The Rise and Fall of Spain (1270–1850)," *Economic History Review*, 66, 1, 2013: 1–37.

   See also:

   Regina Grafe, *Distant Tyranny. Markets, Power, and Backwardness in Spain, 1650–1800*. Princeton, NJ: Princeton University Press, 2012.

5   For factors of economic growth, see discussion and references in my blog:

   http://jcolomer.blogspot.com/2016/05/the-return-of-big-questions-in-economics.html.

   In particular:

   Douglass North, *Institutions, Institutional Change and Economic Performance*. New York: Cambridge University Press, 1990.

6   Rodrigo Manrique's letter of 1533 is translated from Latin and quoted in

   Marcel Bataillon, *Erasmo y España. Estudios sobre la historia espiritual del siglo XVI*. México: Fondo de Cultura Económica, pp. 489–90.

   Mariano-José de Larra, *Vuelva usted mañana* [Madrid, 1833]. Barcelona: Salvat, 1982.

   Santiago Ramon y Cajal, *Reglas y consejos sobre investigación biológica*. Madrid: Fortanet, 1898.

   Miguel de Unamuno, Letter to Jose Ortega y Gasset, May 30, 1906, in Epistolario complete Ortega-Unamuno. Madrid: Fundación Ortega y Gasset, 1987, and *passim* until 1912.

7   For discussion of the theory of "path dependence," see Paul Pierson, "Increasing Returns, Path Dependence, and the Study of Politics," *American Political Science Review*, 94, 2, 2000: 251–67; and Josep M. Colomer (ed.), "The Strategy of Institutional Change," *Journal of Theoretical Politics*, 13, 3, 2001, special issue with contributions by Gerard Alexander, Alberto Diaz-Cayeros and Beatriz Magaloni; Patrick Dunleavy and Helen Margetts; and Kenneth A. Shepsle.

The American Silver in Genoa Is Buried

8   Earl J. Hamilton, *American Treasure and the Price Revolution in Spain, 1501–1650*. Cambridge, MA: Harvard University Press, 1934.

   Pierre Chaunu, *Séville et l'Atlantique (1504–1650)*, 12 vols. Paris: SEVPEN, 1955–60.

Francisco de Quevedo, "Poderoso caballero es Don Dinero," 1603.

Paco Ibáñez, *La poesía española de ahora y de siempre*. Paris: Moshe Naim, 1967

Carlos Alvarez-Nogal and Christophe Chamley, "Debt Policy under Constraints: Philip II, the Cortes, and Genoese bankers," *Economic History Review*, 67, 1, 2014: 192–213.

Carmen M. Reinhart, Kenneth S. Rogoff and Miguel A. Savastano, "Debt Intolerance," *National Bureau of Economic Research*, Working Paper 9908, 2003.

Carmen Reinhart and Kenneth Rogoff, *This Time Is Different: Eight Centuries of Financial Folly*. Princeton, NJ: Princeton University Press, 2009.

For other data on finances and the military:

John Lynch, *Spain 1516–1598. From Nation State to World Empire*. Oxford: Blackwell, 1991.

Mauricio Drelichman, "All That Glitters: Precious Metals, Rent Seeking and the Decline of Spain," *European Review of Economic History*, 9, 2005: 313–66.

A Catholic Monarchy

9   Thomas Aquinas' doctrine about the sun and the moon in *De Regimine Principum*, book III, c. 1265.

Elected Kings with the Name of Presidents

10   On the feudal legacy of Spain in Hispanic America:

Marcello Carmagnani, *L'America Latina dal '500 a oggi. Nascita, espansione e crisi di un sistema feudale*, 1975 (In Spanish: *Formación y crisis de un sistema feudal: América Latina del siglo XV a nuestros días*. México: Siglo XXI, 1976).

Luis Weckmann, *La herencia medieval de México*. México: Fondo de Cultura Económica, 1984.

Luis Weckmann, *La herencia medieval de Brasil*. México: Fondo de Cultura Económica, 1993.

On the independence of Hispanic American colonies and further political instability:

Simón Bolívar, "Mensaje al Congreso Constituyente de la Republica de Colombia," 1830. In Bolívar, *Discursos, proclamas y epistolario político* (ed. Mario Hernández Sánchez-Barba). Madrid: Editora Nacional, 1975: 353–60.

Tulio Halperin Donghi, *The Aftermath of Revolution in Latin America*. New York: Harper & Row, 1973.

Antonio Annino, Luis Castro Leiva and Francois-Xavier Guerra, *De los imperios a las naciones*. Zaragoza: Ibercaja, 1994.

Eduardo Posada-Carbó, ed., *Elections before Democracy: The History of Elections in Europe and Latin America*. New York: St. Martin's Press, 1996. Josep M. Colomer, "Taming the Tiger: Voting Rights and Political Instability in Latin America," *Latin America Politics and Society*, 46, 2, 2004: 29–58.

The British Alternative

11   Areas of Spanish, British and other empires from:

Rein Taagepera, "Expansion and Contraction Patterns of Large Polities: Context for Russia," *International Studies Quarterly*, 41, 1997: 475–504.

12   Quotes from the Parliament of Castile to Philip II and by Ambassador Sessa, from Parker, *The World Is Not Enough*, 2001.

Fray Bartolomé de las Casas, Brevísima relación de la destrucción de las Indias, 1552.

Mauricio Drelichman and Hans-Joachim Voth, *Lending to the Borrower from Hell. Debt, Taxes, and Default in the Age of Philip II*. Princeton, NJ: Princeton University Press, 2014.

Miguel Bernal, *España, proyecto inacabado*, p. 434.

See also:

Nial Ferguson, *Empire. The Rise and Demise of the British World Order and the Lessons for Global Power*. New York: Basic Books, 2002.

John Darwin, *Unfinished Empire. The Global Expansion of Britain*. London: Bloomsbury, 2013.

Getting Rid of Ultramaria

13   Jeremy Bentham, "Get Rid of Ultramaria!," 1820. In *Colonies, Commerce, and Constitutional Law: Rid Yourselves of Ultramaria and Other Writings on Spain and Spanish America*, ed. Philip Schofield. Oxford: Clarendon Press, 1995. (Spanish translation: "¡Liberaos de Ultramar!," in Jeremy Bentham, *Antología*, ed. Josep M. Colomer. Barcelona: Peninsula, 1991).

Pedro Fraile and Alvaro Escribano, "The Spanish 1898 Disaster: The Drift towards National-Protectionism," *Revista de Historia Económica*, 16, 1, 1998.

Leandro Prados de la Escosura and Santiago Amaral, eds., *La independencia americana: consecuencias económicas*. Madrid: Alianza, 1993.

Quotes about Cuba, which are mixed up in several sources, are from:

Cánovas, July 3, 1891, April 2, 1895; Sagasta, March 8, 1895.

María Dolores Elizalde, "Las relaciones de España y Estados Unidos en el umbral de un nuevo siglo." In *España y Estados Unidos en el siglo XX*, eds. Lorenzo Delgado and María Dolores Elizalde. Madrid: CSIC, 2005, pp. 19–56.

14   The qualification of the political regime of Equatorial Guinea is from "Freedom in the World," an annual report of political rights and civil liberties by Freedom House, available at https://freedomhouse.org/

Rebuilding Imperial Links

15   On Spanish foreign policy toward Hispanic America:

Celestino del Arenal, *Política exterior de España y relaciones con América Latina. Iberoamericanidad, Europeización y Atlantismo en la política exterior española*. Madrid: Fundación Carolina-Siglo XXI, 2011.

Chapter 2 A Weak State

1   For survey, definition and typologies of "states" as a form of political organization, see:

Charles Tilly, ed., *The Formation of National States in Western Europe*. Princeton, NJ: Princeton University Press, 1975.

Hendrik Spruyt, *The Sovereign State and Its Competitors*. Princeton, NJ: Princeton University Press, 1994.

Martin L. Van Creveld, *The Rise and Decline of the State*. Cambridge: New York: University Press, 1999.

Miguel A. Centeno and Agustín E. Ferraro, eds., *State and Nation Making in Latin America and Spain: Republics of the Possible*. New York: Cambridge University Press, 2013.

For data and calculations on economic variables, the number of years under suppression of guarantees and states of war, the list of military *pronunciamientos* and coups, numbers of social attempts 1910–23 and political violence during the Second Republic 1931–36, see Albert Carreras and Xavier Tafunell, eds., *Estadísticas Históricas de España*. Madrid: Fundación BBVA, 2005.

The Breakdown of Public Finances

2 About the economic and financial failures of nineteenth- and twentieth-century Spain, see:

Josep Fontana, *La quiebra del Imperio español, 1700–1824*. In *La quiebra de la monarquía absoluta* [1974], ed. Fontana. Barcelona: Crítica, 2002, p. 20.

Nicolás Sánchez Albornoz, *España hace un siglo: Una economía dual*. Barcelona, Península, 1968, p. 18.

Jordi Nadal, *El fracaso de la Revolución Industrial en España, 1814–1913*. Barcelona: Ariel, 1975, pp. 9, 226.

Albert Carreras, *Industrialización española: Estudios de historia cuantitativa*. Madrid: Espasa-Calpe, 1990.

César Molinas and Leandro Prados de la Escosura, "Was Spain Different? Spanish Historical Backwardness Revisited," *Explorations in Economic History*, 126, 1989: 385–402.

Francisco A. Comín, *Historia de la Hacienda pública*, 2 vols. Barcelona: Crítica, 1996.

Francisco A. Comín, "Default, Rescheduling and Inflation: Public Debt Crises in Spain during the 19th and 20th Centuries," *Revista de Historia Económica. Journal of Iberian and Latin American Economic History*, 30, 3, 2012: 353–90.

Gabriel Tortella, *The Development of Modern Spain. An Economic History of the Nineteenth and Twentieth Centuries*. Cambridge, MA: Harvard University Press, 2000, p. 2. (*El desarrollo de la España contemporánea. Historia económica de los siglos XIX y XX*. Madrid: Alianza, 1994, p. 4.)

Albert Carreras and Xavier Tafunell, *Historia económica de la España contemporánea*. Barcelona: Crítica, 2004, p. 85.

The five stages model of economic development was initially devised by

Walt W. Rostow, *The Stages of Economic Growth*. New York: Cambridge University Press, 1960.

3 Comparative data for economic recovery after the Great Depression, the Spanish Civil War and World War II are taken from the Maddison Project, as cited above. The pick and the recovery years of per capita income were for France, 1939–49; Italy, 1939–49; Britain, 1943–54; Germany, 1944–55; for the average of Western Europe, 1943–1950; and, in contrast, for Spain, 1929–55.

José Luis González Vallvé and Miguel Ángel Benedicto Solsona, *La mayor operación de solidaridad de la historia. Crónica de la política regional de la UE en España*. Luxembourg: Publications Office of the European Union, 2006.

Enric Juliana, "Tres Planes Marshall," *La Vanguardia*, March 13, 2011.

4   International reports by the World Economic Forum:
The Global Human Capital Report, 2017
The Global Information Technology Report, 2017
The Global Competitiveness Report (2017–18), accessible at https://www.weforum.org/reports.

A Pretorian Army

5   Samuel H. Finer, *The Man on Horseback* [1962]. New Brunswick and London: Transaction, 2002.
Samuel P. Huntington, *The Soldier and the State: The Theory and Politics of Civil-Military Relations* [1957]. Cambridge, MA: Belknap Press, 1981.
Samuel P. Huntington, *Political Order in Changing Societies* [1968]. New Haven, CT: Yale University Press, 1973.
Charles Tilly, "War Making and State Making as Organized Crime." In *Bringing the State Back In*, eds. Peter Evans, Dietrich Rueschemeyer and Theda Skocpol. New York: Cambridge University Press, 1985, p. 184.
6   Stanley G. Payne, *Politics and the Military in Modern Spain*. Stanford, CA: Stanford University Press, 1967, p. 4.
Raymond Carr, *Spain 1875–1980*. Oxford: Oxford University Press, 1980, pp. 83, 84.
Manuel Ballbé, *Orden público y militarismo en la España constitucional*. Madrid: Alianza, 1983.
Josep M. Colomer, "Conversa amb Manuel Ballbé. El militarisme com a desordre públic," *L'Avenç*, 75, 1984: 78–83.
Carlos Seco Serrano, *Militarismo y civilismo en la España contemporánea*. Madrid: Instituto de Estudios Económicos, 1984.
Julio Busquets, *El militar de carrera en España* [1967]. Barcelona: Ariel, 1984.
Julio Busquets, *Pronunciamientos y golpes de Estado en España*. Madrid: Planeta, 1982.
Gabriel Cardona, *El poder militar en la España contemporánea hasta la guerra civil*. Madrid: Siglo XXI, 1983, p. 52.
Ramon Serrano Suñer, *Entre Hendaya y Gibraltar* [1957]. Barcelona: Planeta, 2011.
The quote from the Royal Commission of military chiefs is taken from Josep Fontana, *La época del liberalismo*, in *Historia de España*, vol. 6. Barcelona and Madrid: Crítica and Marcial Pons, 2007.
7   The labeling as civil wars of conflicts producing 1,000 deaths corresponds to the categorization of armed political conflicts and other types of organized violence, which is used by the United Nations. It is based on data and analyses provided by a number of annual reports, namely States in Armed Conflict (Department of Peace and Conflict Research, Uppsala University), SIPRI Yearbook (Stockholm International Peace Research Institute), Human Security Report (Simon Fraser University, School for International Studies) and the Journal of Peace Research. See, in particular, the dataset of the Uppsala project at http://ucdp.uu.se/.
The numbers of deaths in late nineteenth and early twentieth century wars are taken from:
John Lawrence Tine, *War and Genocide in Cuba 1895–1898*. Chapel Hill: University of North Carolina Press, 2006.
David S. Woolman, *Rebels in the Rif*. Stanford, CA: Stanford University Press, 1968.

David Long and Bernard Reich, *The Government and Politics of the Middle East and Northern Africa*. Boulder, CO: Westview Press, 2002.

Michael Clodfelter, *Warfare and Armed Conflicts. A Statistical Reference to Casualty and Other Figures 1500–2000*. Jefferson, NC: McFarland, 2002.

The number of Franco's military ministers is given by Robert Graham, *Spain: Change of a Nation*. London: Michael Joseph, 1984 (which increases by six the number of such ministers listed and classified by Ramón Tamames, *La República. La era de Franco*. Madrid: Alianza, 1988, Appendix 1). The number of 955 procurators in *Cortes* that were also military is from Julio Busquets, "Las Fuerzas Armadas en la Transición Española," In *Fuerzas Armadas y poder político en el siglo XX en Portugal y España*, ed. Hipólito de la Torre Gómez. Merida: UNED, 1996, both cited by Narcís Serra, *The Military Transition. Democratic Reform of the Armed Forces*. New York: Cambridge University Press, 2010, p. 91.

8   The reforms of the military since the 1970s are mostly explained in

Felipe Aguero, *Soldiers, Civilians, and Democracy. Post-Franco Spain in Comparative Perspective*. Baltimore, MD, and London: Johns Hopkins University Press, 1995.

Raquel Barrios Ramos, *El proceso de transición democrática de las Fuerzas Armadas españolas 1975–1989*. Doctoral dissertation, UNED, 2006.

Serra, *The Military Transition*, 2010.

Numerous papers presented at the five Congresos de Historia de la Defensa organized by the Instituto Universitario General Gutiérrez Mellado, 2006–2012. http://iugm.es/.

Data and plans are available at the Ministry of Defense website: http://www.defensa.gob.es/.

The quote from General Fernando Alejandre, "En el Día de los Caídos por la Patria: Lo demandó el deber," *ABC*, November 2, 2017.The quote about bubble paper is from Bernardo Navazo, "Un ejército envuelto en papel burbuja," *Política Exterior*, 156, 2013: 94–104.

A Ruling Church

9   *Catecismo y exposición breve de la Doctrina Cristiana, compuesto por el P. Jerónimo de Ripalda de la Compañía de Jesús*, 1st ed., 1616.

Catecismo de la Doctrina Cristiana, escrito por el P. Gaspar Astete, 1st ed., 1599.

El Catecismo de la Doctrina Cristina Explicado O Explicaciones del Astete que convienen igualmente al Ripalda, por Santiago Joe García Mazo, Valladolid, 1830 (annual reeditions).

Saint Augustine, *The City of God* [426 AD]. Hyde Park, NY: New City Press, 2013, quotes from Book XIV, pp. 24, 26.

From Picaresque to Corruption

10   On the picaresque:

Alonso Zamora Vicente, *Qué es la novela picaresca*. Buenos Aires: Columba, 1962.

Francisco Rico, *La novela picaresca española*. Barcelona: Planeta, 1966.

The quotes are from:

Mateo Alemán, *Guzmán de Alfarache* [1599]. Madrid: Espasa, 2013.

11   On corruption:

Huntington, *Political Order*, pp. 59–60.

Enrique Gil Calvo, *La ideología española*. Oviedo: Nobel, 2006.

Jens Chr. Andvig and Karl Ove Moene, "How corruption may corrupt," *Journal of Economic Behavior & Organization*, 13, 1, 1990: 63–76.

Manuel Villoria and Fernando Jiménez, "La corrupción en España (2004–2010): Datos, percepción y efectos," *Revista Española de Investigaciones Sociológicas*, 138, 2012: 109–34.

Carles Ramió, *La Administración pública del futuro. Horizonte 2050*. Madrid: Tecnos, 2017.

12   Estimates of black economy, tax evasion and overpricing of public contracts are based on:

Jordi Sardà, with Gestha (Technicians of the Finance Ministry), *La economía sumergida pasa factura. El avance del fraude en España durante la crisis*. Madrid, 2014, which includes a review of all previous estimates.

Comisión Nacional de los Mercados y la Competencia, *Analysis of Public Procurement in Spain: Opportunities for Improvement from the Perspective of Competition*. Madrid, 2015.

Comisión Nacional de los Mercados y la Competencia, *Guía contra el fraude en la licitación pública*. Madrid, 2017.

The quote from the president of Catalonia, Artur Mas, is from his interview in La Sexta TV, September 28, 2014.

The statement by the deputy secretary of the Popular Party, Javier Maroto, was on March 15, 2016.

The Corruption Perceptions Index is published by Transparency International: http://www.transparency.org.

Primitive Rebels

13   Félix Lope de Vega, *Fuenteovejuna* [1619]. Barcelona: Vicens-Vives, 2013.

Gerald Brenan, *The Spanish Labyrinth* [1943]. New York: Cambridge University Press, 1960.

Eric Hobsbawm, *Primitive Rebels: Banditry, Mafia, Millenarians, Anarchists, Sicilian Fasci, the City Mob, Labor Sects, Ritual, Sermons & Oaths*. Manchester: University of Manchester Press, 1959.

Pierre Vilar, *Spain: A Brief History*. Oxford and New York: Pergamon, 1967, pp. 54, 56.

14   About peasant revolts and anarchist movements:

Juan Díaz del Moral, *Historia de las agitaciones campesinas andaluzas* [1929]. Madrid: Alianza, 1967, pp. 202–5.

Murray Bookchin, *The Spanish Anarchists. The Heroic Years, 1868–1936*. New York: Free Life, 1977.

Josep Termes, *Historia del anarquismo en España, 1870–1980*. Barcelona: RBA, 2011.

Juan García Oliver, Registro del discurso del 20 de noviembre de 1937, Dir. Mateo Santos. Available at https://www.youtube.com/watch?v=SxBWAbKQfSE.

Ángel Pestaña, *Terrorismo en Barcelona (memorias inéditas)* (Javier Tusell and Genoveva García Queipo de Llano, eds.). Barcelona: Planeta, 1979.

For the communists:

Santiago Carrillo, *Hacia la libertad. Informe del Comité Central al VIII Congreso del PCE*. Paris: Editions Sociales, 1972, pp. 51–52.

15   Data about political membership and social protests:

Laura Morales Diez de Ulsurru, *Joining Political Organizations: Institutions, Mobilization and Participation in Western Democracies*. Colchester: ECPR Press, 2009.

For comparative social movements and collective action cycles:

Sidney Tarrow, *Power in Movement*. New York: Cambridge University Press, 1994.

Ruut Koopmans, "New Social Movements and Changes in Political Participation in Western Europe," *West European Politics*, 19, 1996: 28–50.

For the role of social networks in protest movements:

Helen Z. Margetts, Peter John, Scott A. Hale and Taha Yasseri, *Political Turbulence. How Social Media Shape Collective Action*. Princeton, NJ: Princeton University Press, 2016.

Sandra González-Bailón, "From Chiapas to Tahrir: Networks and the Diffusion of Protest," *World Politics Review*, April 16, 2013.

Zeynep Tufekci, *Twitter and Tear Gas. The Power and Fragility of Networked Protest*. New Haven, CT: Yale University Press, 2017.

Some data about the Indignados movement:

Carlos Taibo, *El 15-M en sesenta preguntas*. Madrid: Libros de la Catarata, 2011.

Martin Portos, "Movilización social en tiempos de recesión: Un análisis de eventos de protesta en España, 2007–2015," *Revista Española de Ciencia Política*, 41, 2016: 159–78.

Derailment from the European Track

16   The quotation from Juan Linz about the break with tradition without modernization is from:

Juan J. Linz, "Tradition and Modernity in Spain" (1972). In *Robert Michels, Political Sociology, and the Future of Democracy*, ed. H. E. Chehabi. New Brunswick, NJ, and London: Transaction, 2006, pp. 115–84.

17   There has been some controversy among historians about Primo de Rivera's motivations and performance. The quotes are from:

Raymond Carr, *Spain 1808–1975*. Oxford: Oxford University Press, 1982, p. 523.

Carolyn P. Boyd, *Praetorian Politics in Liberal Spain*. Chapel Hill: University of North Carolina Press, 1979, p. 238.

Ben-Ami, Shlomo, *Fascism from Above: The Dictatorship of Primo de Rivera in Spain, 1923–1930*. Oxford and New York: Oxford University Press, 1983, p. 22.

Ramon Villares and Javier Moreno Luzón, *Restauración y Dictadura*, in *Historia de España*, vol. 7. Barcelona and Madrid: Crítica and Marcial Pons, 2009, p. 492.

Joan Maria Thomàs, *José Antonio. Realidad y mito*. Barcelona: Debate, 2017, p. 59.

But see also, for an alternative perspective:

Teresa González Calbet, "La destrucción del sistema político de la Restauración: el golpe de septiembre de 1923." In *La crisis de la Restauración: España, entre la Primera Guerra Mundial y la Segunda República*, ed. José Luis García Delgado. Madrid: Siglo XXI, 1986, pp. 101–20.

Javier Tusell, "Los intentos reformistas de la vida política durante el reinado de Alfonso XIII," In *Democracia, elecciones y modernización en Europa. Siglos XIX y XX*, ed. Salvador Forner. Madrid: Cátedra, 1997: 295–312.

And discussion of the role of the King Alphonse XIII, especially regarding Javier Tusell's contributions:

Ignacio Olabarri Gortazar, "Problemas no resueltos en torno al pronunciamiento de Primo de Rivera," *Revista de Historia Contemporánea*, 7, 1996: 223–48.

18   The successive two countercoups during the Spanish Second Republic in the 1930s can be partly explained by the incongruous results produced by the electoral system.

The electoral rules gave overrepresentation to the larger candidacies and thus created incentives to form broad coalitions and punished the parties running separately.

As can be seen in the table, in the election of 1933, the left and the center-left parties received in total more votes (22 + 14=36 percent) than the right (34 percent), but they were more divided than the right and center-right bloc, which was allocated a large majority of seats and formed government. Likewise, in the election of 1936, the center-right and the right received in total a majority of votes (23 + 31=54 percent), but this time they were more divided in separate candidacies, while the left and center-left had formed the Popular Front that was allocated a large majority of seats (60 percent).

Table 1. Elections during the Second Spanish Republic, 1931–36

1931	Votes	Seats		1933	Votes	Seats		1936	Votes	Seats
Republican-socialists	85	89	Left		22	13	Popular Front		46	60
			Center-left		14	8				
			Center-right		30	37	Center-right		23	15
Right	15	11	Right		34	42	National Front		31	25
	—	—			—	—			—	—
	100	100			100	100			100	100

Note:

Votes and seats are given in percentages.

Left: Socialists (PSOE, USC); communists (PCE); and minor groups.

Center-left: Left-republicans (AR/IR, UR); Radical-socialists (RS); regionals (ERC, ANV, ORGA).

Center-right: Radicals (PRR); liberals (PP, PC, ASR, DLR, LD); regionals (PNV, LC); independents.

Right: Catholics (AN/CEDA); agrarians (PA); monarchists (RE, CT); fascists (FE).

Sources:

The electoral system was based on votes for individual candidates. As the voters in electoral districts of different sizes voted for different numbers of candidates, counting the numbers of votes received by the candidates may be misleading. The results of the elections here reported are based, instead, on counting the number of voters having voted for candidates of each partisan or coalitional candidacy, as presented by the following:

William J. Irwin, *The 1933 Cortes Elections. Origin of the Bienio Negro*. New York: Garland, 1991.

Josep M. Colomer, "The Spanish Pre-Civil War." In *Political Institutions*, ed. Colomer. Oxford: Oxford University Press, 2001, pp. 87–91.

And with more details in Josep M. Colomer, "Spain: From Civil War to Proportional Representation." In *Handbook of Electoral System Choice*, ed. Colomer. London and New York: Palgrave-Macmillan, 2004, pp. 253–64.

For the relation between violence and electoral campaigns with uncertain results:

Enric Ucelay Da-Cal and Susanna Tavera García, "Una revolución dentro de otra: la lógica insurreccional en la política española, 1924–1934." In *Violencia y política en España*, ed. Julio Arostegui. *Ayer* 13, 1994, pp. 115–46

Enric Ucelay Da-Cal, "*Buscando* el levantamiento plebiscitario: insurrecionalismo y elecciones." In "Política en la Segunda República," ed. Santos Juliá. *Ayer* 20, 1995, pp. 49–80.

S. P. Harish and Andrew T. Little, "The Political Violence Cycle," *American Political Science Review*, 111, 2, 2017: 237–55.

A Bubble State

19 Data sources on the size of the state:

Instituto Nacional de Estadística: http://www.ine.es/

Congreso de Diputados: http://www.congreso.es

European Statistics: http://ec.europa.eu/eurostat/data/database

Eur-Lex: http://eurlex.europa.eu/statistics/

The Ministry of Economy's updated plans for reducing public spending in "Actualización del Programa de Estabilidad. Reino de España. 2017–2020" and "Objetivos de Estabilidad Presupuestaria, Deuda Pública, Regla de Gasto y Límite de Gasto no Financiero del Estado," both available at http://www.mineco.gob.es.

Chapter 3 An Incomplete Nation

1 The idea of an "imagined community" is from:

Benedict Anderson, *Imagined Communities: Reflections on the Origin and Spread of Nationalism*. New York: Verso, 1983.

For the "constructivist" approach to ethnic politics:

Kanchan Chandra, ed., *Constructivist Theories of Ethnic Politics*. New York: Oxford University Press, 2012.

The quotes are from:

Stein Rokkan, "Nation-Building: A Review of Models and Approaches." In *Nation-Building*, eds. Stein Rokkan, Kirsti Saelen and Joan Warmbrunn. The Hague-Paris: Mouton, 1971, pp. 7–38.

Eugen Weber, *Peasants into Frenchmen: The Modernization of Rural France, 1870–1914*. Stanford, CA: Stanford University Press, 1976, p. 493.

Tullio de Mauro, *Storia linguistica dell'Italia republicana: dal 1946 ai nostrum giorni*. Milan: Laterza, 2014.

Karl Deutsch, *Nationalism and Social Communication. An Inquiry into the Foundations of Nationality*. Boston: MIT Press, 1953.

Ernest Gellner, *Nations and Nationalism*. Ithaca, NY: Cornell University Press, 1983, pp. 48–49.

Eric Hobsbawm, *Nations and Nationalism since 1780. Programme, Myth, Reality*. Cambridge: Cambridge University Press, 1990, p. 10.

James D. Fearon and David D. Laitin, "Violence and the Social Construction of Ethnic Identity," *International Organization* 54, 4, 2000: 845–77, p. 848.

David Laitin, "National Revivals and Violence," *European Journal of Sociology* 36, 1, 1995: 3–43, p. 4.

Juan J. Linz, "Early State-Building and Late Peripheral Nationalism against the State: The Case of Spain." In *Building States and Nations*, vol. II, eds. S. N. Eisenstadt and Stein Rokkan, Beverly Hills, CA: Sage, 1973, pp. 32–116, pp. 99, 102.

Juan J. Linz, "State Building and Nation Building," *European Review*, 1, 4, 1993: 355–69, p. 364.

Juan J. Linz, Alfred Stepan and Yogendra Yadav, "'Nation State' or 'State Nation'? Conceptual Reflections and Some Spanish, Belgian and Indian Data." New York: United Nations Development Program, 2004, p. 15.

Local Patriotisms

2   Josep Maria Fradera, *La nación imperial (1750–1918)*. Bellaterra: Publicacions de la Universitat Autónoma de Barcelona, 2015.

Pierre Vilar, "Patrie et nation dans le vocabulaire de la Guerre d'independence espagnole ," *Annales Historiques de la Révolution Française*, 206, 1971: 523.

Pierre Vilar, *Spain: A Brief History*. Oxford and New York: Pergamon, 1967, pp. 56–57.

Ricardo García Cárcel, "El concepto de España en 1808," *Norba. Revista de Historia*, 19, 2006:178, 185.

Ronald Fraser, *Napoleon's Cursed War. Spanish Popular Resistance in the Peninsular War, 1808–1814*. London and New York: Verso, 2008, p. 198.

Karl Baedeker, *Spain and Portugal. Handbook for Travellers*. Leipzig, London and New York: Badeker, 1908.

José Ortega y Gasset, *España invertebrada* [1921]. Madrid: Austral, 2011.

Manuel Azaña, *Diario de Sesiones de las Cortes constituyentes*, 27 de mayo de 1932.

Indalecio Prieto, "La conquista interior de España" (1936). In *Discursos fundamentales*, ed. Prieto. Madrid: Turner, 1975, p. 261.

Santos Juliá, "El fracaso de la República," *Revista de Occidente*, 7–8, 1981: 201–2.

Borja de Riquer, "Reflexions entorn a la dèbil nacionalització espanyola del segle XIX," *L'Avenç*, 170, 1993: 8 (trans. 'La debil nacionalización española del siglo XIX', *Historia Social*, 20, 1994: 97–114).

José Alvarez Junco, *Spanish Identity in the Age of Nations*. Manchester: Manchester University Press, 2011, pp. 58–59, 321.

Juan-Pablo Fusi, *España. La evolución de la identidad nacional*. Madrid: Temas de Hoy, 2000.

The Imperial Burden

3   On the generation of the 98 and the Hispanity:

Antonio Machado, "El mañana efímero." In *Campos de Castilla* [1907–17]. Madrid: Catedra, 2006.

Miguel de Unamuno, "Sobre la tumba de Costa," [1911]. In Ensayos. VII, Madrid, Publicaciones de la Residencia de Estudiantes, 1918, pp. 191–219.

Azorín, *Madrid* [1941]. Madrid: Biblioteca Nueva, 2017.

Ramiro de Maeztu, *Defensa de la Hispanidad*, 1934 (3ª ed., 1938). Buenos Aires: Poblet, 1952.

Isidro Gomá, "Apología de la Hispanidad." In *Por Dios y por España*, ed. Gomá. Barcelona: Casulleras, 1940.

Víctor Pradera, *El Estado Nuevo*. Madrid: Cultura Española, 1935.

Joan Maria Thomàs, *José Antonio. Realidad y mito*. Barcelona: Debate, 2017.

Ramiro Ledesma (pseudonym Roberto Lanzas), *¿Fascismo en España?*. Madrid: La Conquista del Estado, 1935.

On the generation of the 98 and Falange:

Ernesto Giménez Caballero, *Genio de España* [1932, 4 editions in 1938–39]. Barcelona: Planeta, 1983.

On Ortega as a "pre-Falange" thinker:

José M. Fontana Tarrats, *Los catalanes en la guerra de España*. Madrid: Samarán, 1951, pp. 22–29.

4   On Franco's books and movie:

Francisco Franco, *Marruecos. Diario de una Bandera*. Sevilla: Editorial Católica Española, 1939.

Jaime de Andrade (pseudonym), *Raza. Anecdotario para el guion de una película*. Madrid: Editorial Numancia, 1942.

José Luis Sáenz de Heredia dir., *Raza*, 1942; purged version: *Espíritu de una Raza*, 1950. Prod. Consejo de la Hispanidad.

Roman Gubern, *Raza: Un ensueño del general Franco*. Madrid: Ediciones 99, 1977.

The Damned "Mili"

5   Keith Darden and Harris Mylonas, "Threats to Territorial Integrity, National Mass Schooling, and Linguistic Commonality," *Comparative Political Studies*, 49, 1, 2016: 1455.

Borja de Riquer and Enric Ucelay Da-Cal, "An Analysis of Nationalism in Spain: A Proposal for an Integrated Historical Model." In *Nationalism in Europe: Past and Present*, eds. Justo G. Beramendi, Ramón Máiz and Xosé M. Núñez. Santiago de Compostela: Universidade de Santiago de Compostela, 1994, vol. II, p. 280.

Parochial-Catholicism

6   For revisionist histories of the Spanish Inquisition:

Edward Peters, *Inquisition*. New York: Free Press, 1988.

Henry Kamen, *The Spanish Inquisition. A Historical Revision*. New Haven, CT: Yale University Press, 1997.

For quote:

Henry Charles Lea, *A History of the Inquisition of Spain and the Inquisition in the Spanish Dependencies* (1905). London: Tauris, 2001, p. V.

7   Polls on religion issues:

International Social Survey Programme ISSP 2003, "National Identity II," ZA No. 3910.

Centro de Estudios Sociológicos CIS, Estudio no. 3175, "Barómetro de Mayo 2017," preguntas 24, 24a.

8   Manuel Perez Yruela and Thierry Desrues (dirs.), *Percepciones y actitudes hacia el Islam y los musulmanes en España*. Córdoba: Instituto de Estudios Sociales Avanzados IESA, Consejo Superior de Investigaciones Científicas CSIC, 2008.

Multiple Languages

9   Ramon Menéndez Pidal, "La lengua de Cristóbal Colón," *Bulletin Hispanique*, 42, 1, 1940: 5–28.

Montesquieu, *Lettres Persanes* (1721) (*Cartas persas*, ed. Josep M. Colomer. Madrid: Tecnos, 1986), Letter 109–10.

Eric Hobsbawm, *The Age of Capital 1848–1875*. London: Abacus, 1977, pp. 118–19.

Keith Darden, *Resisting Occupation: Mass Schooling and the Creation of Durable National Loyalties*. Cambridge: Cambridge University Press, 2013.

Keith Darden and Anna Gryzmala-Busse, "The Great Divide: Literacy, Nationalism and the Communist Collapse," *World Politics*, 59, 4, 2006: 90.

Laia Balcells, "Mass Schooling and Catalan Nationalism," *Nationalism and Ethnic Politics*, 19, 2013: 468.

Carolyn P. Boyd, *Historia Patria: Politics, History, and National Identity in Spain, 1875–1975*. Princeton, NJ: Princeton University Press, 1997, p. XIX.

Data on literacy and schooling from:

Mercè Vilanova and Xavier Moreno Julia, *Atlas de la evolución del analfabetismo en España de 1887 a 1981*. Madrid: Ministerio de Educación y Ciencia, 1992.

Clara Eugenia Núñez, "Educación." In *Estadísticas Históricas de España*, eds. Albert Carreras and Xavier Tafunell. Madrid: Fundación BBVA, 2005, vol. I.

10   Minister José-Ignacio Wert, "Españolizar a los niños catalanes," October 28, 2012.

Anne Cenmane, *La España perdida. El discurso sobre "moros y cristianos"*, Master's thesis, University of Oslo, 2014.

11   For numbers of translations and foreign films:

Ashley Beale, "From State Media to Worldwide Networks." In *Communication: From Its Origin to Internet*, ed. Miquel de Moaragas. Tarragona: Divulgare, 2012, pp. 151–72 (trans. *Comunicación: De los orígenes a Internet*. Barcelona: Gedisa, 2012).

Tribes with Flags and Chants

12   Tim Marshall, *A Flag Worth Dying for. The Power and Politics of National Symbols*. New York: Scribner, 2017.

13   Javier Moreno Luzón and Xosé M. Núñez Seixas, *Los colores de la patria. Simbolos nacionales en la España contemporánea*. Madrid: Tecnos, 2017, p. 225.

Rafael Núñez Florencio, "El litigio de los símbolos nacionales: entre la representación y la exclusión," *Revista de Libros*, June 2017.

See also:

Carlos Serrano, *El nacimiento de Carmen: Símbolos, mitos, nación*. Madrid: Taurus, 1999.

Andres Sopeña Monsalve, *El florido pensil. Memoria de la escuela nacionalcatólica*. Barcelona: Crítica, 1994.

14   The alternative lyrics for the Royal March and the Hymn of Riego of the late 1920s and early 1930s, which are somewhat different from other published versions, come from the memories of my father's family, who were living in Madrid at the time. The children's and students' versions are from personal memory.

National-Footballism

15 Karl Marx, *A Contribution to the Critique of Hegel's Philosophy of Right* [1843]. Cambridge: Cambridge University Press, 1977.
"What Is the Opium of the People?," *Economist Unwinds*, 1843, November–December 2013.

16 Alejandro Quiroga Fernández de Soto. *Goles y banderas. Fútbol e identidades nacionales en España*. Madrid: Marcial Pons, 2014.
Vic Duke and Liz Crolley, *Football, Nationality and the State*. London: Routledge, 2014.

Not Very Spanish, After All

17 Survey data are from:
Carmen González Enríquez, "El declive de la identidad nacional española," Real Instituto Elcano, *ARI* 49, 2016.
Centro de Investigaciones Sociológicas, Estudio no. 3173. Barómetro de abril, 2017.
Centre d'Estudis d'Opinió, Generalitat de Catalunya, Baròmetre d'Opinió Política, 49, 2a onada, 2017.
Euskobarómetro, Universidad del País Vasco/Euskal Herriko Unibertsitatea, May 2017.

18 On "constitutional patriotism":
Jurgen Habermas, *Identidades nacionales y postnacionales*. Madrid: Tecnos, 1989.
Juan José Laborda, "Patriotismo constitucional y Estado democrático," *Sistema*, 108, 1992: 5–14.
Josep Piqué and María San Gil, "El patriotismo constitucional del siglo XXI," ponencia política del XIV Congreso General del Partido Popular, 2002.
Gregorio Peces-Barba Martínez, "El patriotismo constitucional. Reflexiones en el vigésimo quinto aniversario de la Constitución española," *Anuario de Filosofía del Derecho*, 20, 2003.
Gregorio Peces-Barba, *Trabajos Parlamentarios de la Constitución*. Madrid: Publicaciones de las Cortes Generales, 1980, tomo I, pp. 846–51.
Xosé M. Núñez, "What Is Spanish Nationalism Today? From Legitimacy Crisis to Unfulfilled Renovation (1975–2000)," *Ethnic and Racial Studies*, 24, 5, 2001: 744.
Felipe González, "El referéndum catalán es una burla democrática," *El País*, September 27, 2017.
Jordi Muñoz Mendoza, *La construcción política de la identidad española: ¿del nacionalcatolicismo al patriotismo democrático?* Madrid: CIS, 2012, p. 7.
Mateo Ballester Rodríguez, "Auge y declive del patriotismo constitucional en España: en torno a los estados pluriétnicos," Asociación Española de Ciencia Política y de la Administración, *Foro Interno*, 14, 2014: 121–45.
On drafting the Constitution:
Soledad Gallego-Diaz and Bonifacio de la Cuadra, *Crónica secreta de la Constitución*. Madrid: Tecnos, 1989.
Josep M. Colomer, *Game Theory and the Transition to Democracy. The Spanish Model*. London: Edward Elgar, 1995, chapter 6.
Quotes from:
Gregorio Peces-Barba Martínez, "El patriotismo constitucional," 2003, p. 56.

Jordi Solé Tura, *Nacionalidades y nacionalismos en España: Autonomías, federalismo autodeterminación*. Madrid, Alianza, 1985, pp. 94–95 and ff.

Chapter 4 A Minority Democracy

1 Benjamin Constant, "The Liberty of Ancients Compared with That of Moderns," 1816. Available at https://oll.libertyfund.org.

Oligarchy and Clientelism

2 Calculations of years of democracy, dictatorship and partly free regimes are based on data from the annual series "Polity IV Project, Political Regime Characteristics and Transitions, 1800–2016," accessible at http://www.systemicpeace.org/inscrdata.html.

3 Joaquín Costa, *Oligarquía y caciquismo como la forma actual de gobierno de España: urgencia y modo de cambiarla* [1902]. Madrid: Alianza, 1993.

Raymond Carr, *Spain, 1875–1980*. Oxford: Oxford University Press, 1980, pp. 11–12.

Francesc Cambó, *Per la Concòrdia*. Barcelona: Llibreria Catalonia, 1930, p. 189.

Gaetano Mosca, *Sulla teorica dei governi e governo parlamentare*, 1884, p. 318.

Javier Tusell, *Historia de España en el siglo XX, vol. I. Del 98 a la proclamación de la Republica*. Madrid: Taurus, 1998, p. 58.

José Varela Ortega. *Los amigos políticos. Partidos, elecciones y caciquismo en la Restauración (1875–1900)*. Madrid: Alianza, 1977, p. 357.

Juan Linz, "Tradición y Modernización en España," Universidad de Granada, 1977.

Gabriele Ranzato, "Il lungo addio: La Spagna tra antico regime e liberaldemocrazia," *Quaderni Storici*, 16, 46, 1, 1981: 268.

See also:

José María Jover Zamora, "La época de la Restauración: Panorama politico-social, 1875–1902." In *Historia de España*, ed. Manuel Tuñón de Lara, vol. VIII. Barcelona: Labor, 1982, pp. 271–320.

Javier Moreno-Luzón, "Political Clientelism, Elites, and Caciquismo in Restoration Spain (1875–1923)," *European History Quarterly*, 37, 3, 2007: 417–41.

For the electoral system of the period:

Josep M. Colomer, "Spain: From Civil War to Proportional Representation." In *Handbook of Electoral System Choice*, ed. Josep Colomer. Basingstoke: Palgrave Macmillan, pp. 253–64.

Party-Cracy

4 Leopoldo Calvo Sotelo, *Memoria viva de la transición*. Madrid: Plaza y Janés, 1990, p. 57.

Alfonso Guerra, May 6, 1986.

Felipe González, October 4, 1986.

José María Aznar, *Memorias I*. Barcelona: Planeta, 2012.

Mariano Rajoy, November 3, 2009, November 6, 2015.

Jesús López-Medel, *El Mundo*, July 30, 2012.

Manuel García Pelayo, "El Estado de partidos" (1986). In *Obras Completas*, ed. García Pelayo. Madrid: Centro de Estudios Constitucionales, 1991, vol. 2, p. 2016.

Juan Rodríguez-Teruel, *Los ministros de la España democrática. Reclutamiento político y Carrera ministerial de Suárez a Zapatero (1976–2010)*. Madrid: Centro de Estudios Políticos y Constitucionales, 2011, p. 479.

Francisco Rubio Llorente, "La feria de San Miguel", *El País*, September 29, 2001.

Alejandro Nieto, *El malestar de los jueces y el modelo judicial*. Madrid: Trotta, 2010, p. 115.

Pablo Oñate and Juan Rodríguez-Teruel, "The Political Recruitment to the Spanish Constitutional Court (1980–2014)," paper presented at the ECPR Joint Sessions, University of Salamanca, April 10–15, 2014.

Group of States against Corruption, *Fourth Evaluation Round. Corruption Prevention in Respect of Members of Parliament, Judges and Prosecutors. Interim Compliance Report. Spain.* Strasbourg: Council of Europe, 2018. Available at www.coe.int/greco

5   Robert Michels, Political Parties. *A Sociological Study of the Oligarchical Tendencies of Modern Democracy*. London: Forgotten Books, 1911.

6   Antonio Robles Egea, ed., *Política en penumbra. Patronazgo y clientelismo políticos en la España contemporánea*. Madrid: Siglo XXI, 1996, p. 229.

José Cazorla Pérez, "El clientelismo de partido en la España de hoy: Una disfuncion de la democracia." In *Política en penumbra*, ed. Robles Egea. Madrid: Siglo XXI, 1996, p. 307.

José Ortega y Gasset, "El poder social" (1927). In *Obras Completas*, ed. Ortega y Gasset. Madrid: Santillana, 2005, vol. IV, pp. 89–92.

7   Bernard Manin, *The Principles of Representative Government*. New York: Cambridge University Press, 1997, p. 233.

See also:

Bonnie Field, "Transition to Democracy and Internal Party Rules: Spain in Comparative Perspective," *Comparative Politics*, 39, 1, 2006: 83–102.

Nit Atmor, Reuven Hazan and Gideon Rahat, "Candidate selection." In *Personal Representation: The Neglected Dimension of Electoral Systems*, ed. Josep M. Colomer. Essex: ECPR Press, 2011, pp. 21–36.

Javier Pradera, *Corrupción y política. Los costes de la democracia*. Barcelona: Galaxia Gutenberg, 2014.

Oscar Barberá, Juan Rodríguez-Teruel, Astrid Barrio and Montserrat Baras, "The Selection of Party Leaders in Spain." In *The Selection of Political Party Leaders in Contemporary Parliamentary Democracies. A Comparative Study*, eds. Jean-Benoit Pilet and William P. Cross. London: Routledge, 2014, pp. 108–23.

Thomas Poguntke, Susan Scarrow and Paul Webb, "Party Rules, Party Resources and the Politics of Parliamentary Democracies: How Parties Organize in the 21st Century," *Party Politics*, 22, 6, 2016: 661–78.

Minority Governments

8   For the transition to democracy in the 1970s and the further political regime:

Josep M. Colomer, *Game Theory and the Transition to Democracy: The Spanish Model*. London: Edward Elgar, 1995.

Josep M. Colomer, "Spain: A Partisan, Non-Institutional Democratic Regime." In *Spain toward the Americas*. Fundación Endesa and Georgetown University, 2010.

Bonnie Field and Kerstin, eds., *Democracy and Institutional Development: Spain in Comparative Theoretical Perspective*. New York: Palgrave Macmillan, 2008.

9   Óscar Alzaga, "I rapporti tra capo dello stato, governo e parlamento." In *Il X Anniversario della Constituzione spagnola: Bliancio, problemi, prospettive*, ed. G. Rolla. Università di Siena: Facoltà di scienze economiche e bancarie, 1989, pp. 127–28.

10 Samuel E. Finer, ed., *Adversary Politics and Electoral Reform*. London: Anthony Wigram, 1975, p. 6.

11 For the convergence of PSOE and PP on socioeconomic policy:
    Josep M. Colomer, "Development Policy-Making in Democratic Spain." In *Democracy and Development*, ed. K. A. Bagchi. London: St. Martin's, 1995.
    Josep M. Colomer, "The More Parties, the Less Policy Instability," *European Political Science*, 11, 2, 2012: 229–43.
    José Fernández-Albertos and Dulce Manzano, "The Lack of Partisan Conflict over the Welfare State in Spain," *South European Society and Politics*, 17, 3, 2012: 442.

12 For the discussion regarding a grand coalition government, see:
    Josep Colomer, "Spain, Like Europe: The Super Grand Coalition." Josep Colomer's blog, www.jcolomer.blogspot.com, December 21, 2015.

Centrifugal Autonomies

13 Josep M. Colomer, "The Spanish State of Autonomies: Non-Institutional Federalism," *West European Politics*, 21, 44, 1999: 40–52. Also in Paul Heywood, ed., *Politics and Policy in Democratic Spain: No longer different?* London and Portland: Frank Cass, 1999.

14 The surveys about the people's preferences and perceptions of the degrees of autonomy in the different communities are analyzed by José Fernández-Albertos and Ignacio Lago, "Gobiernos autonómicos e identidades regionales en España," *Política y Gobierno*, 22, 2, 2015: 23–315.
    Quotes from:
    Oriol Junqueras, September 25, 2015.
    Michael Keating and Alex Wilson, "Renegotiating the State of Autonomies: Stature Reform and Multi-Level Politics in Spain," *West European Politics*, 32, 3, 2009: 536.

The Catalan Roller Coaster

15 Some elaborations in this and the following chapter regarding size, strategies, internal divisions, conflict escalation and the international factor took some initial inspiration, respectively, from:
    Avidit Acharya, David D. Laitin and Ruxi Zhang, " 'Sons of the Soil': A Model of Assimilation and Population Control," Stanford University, Unpublished manuscript, 2017.
    Harris Mylonas. *The Politics of Nation-Building: Making Co-Nationals, Refugees, and Minorities*. New York: Cambridge University Press, 2012.
    Kathleen Gallagher Cunningham, *Inside the Politics of Self-Determination*. New York: Oxford University Press, 2014.
    Laia Balcells, *Rivalry and Revenge: The Politics of Violence during Civil War*. New York: Cambridge University Press, 2017.
    Carles Boix, *L'obertura catalana*. Barcelona: Generalitat de Catalunya, 2001.

16 José Ortega y Gasset, "Discurso sobre el Estatuto de Cataluña. Sesión de las Cortes del 13 de mayo de 1932." In *Obras Completas*, ed. Ortega y Gasset. Madrid: Taurus, 2005, vol. 5.
    Raimon, *Per destruir aquell qui l'ha desert*. Barcelona: Discophon, 1970.

Karl Marx, *The Eighteenth Brumaire of Louis Bonaparte*, 1852.

17 John Elliott, *The Revolt of the Catalans. A Study in the Decline of Spain (1598–1640)*. Cambridge, UK: Cambridge University Press, 1963, pp. 18, 532–34, 526.

Francisco de Castellví, *Narraciones históricas desde el año 1700 hasta el año 1725* (1725). Madrid: Fundación Francisco Elías de Tejada, vol. IV, 2002, p. 578.

Joaquim Albareda, *La guerra de successió i l'Onze de setembre*. Barcelona: Empúries, 2000.

18 The relations of General Prim with España Industrial are from communication by professor Jordi Nadal, who did extensive research in the company's archives.

On Wilson in 1918:

Enric Ucelay Da-Cal, "Wilson i no Lenin," *L'Avenç*, 9, 1978: 57.

David Martínez Fiol, *Els "voluntaris catalans" a la gran guerra (1914–1918)*. Barcelona: Abadia de Montserrat, 1991.

Joan Crexell, *Origen de la bandera independentista*. Barcelona: El Llamp, 1984.

On Macià's invasion plan:

Ricard Faura, *El complot de Prats de Motlló*. Barcelona: El Llamp, 1991.

For the period 1931–36, among many other works, see, for example:

Enric Ucelay Da-Cal, "El 'octubre catalán' de 1934," *Cuadernos de Alzate*, 30, 2004: 77–106.

On Civil War independence:

Josep M. Bricall, *Política económica de la Generalitat (1936–1939)*. Barcelona: Edicions, p. 62, 1970.

Pelai Pagès, *War and Revolution in Catalonia, 1936–1939*. Leiden and Boston: Brill, 2013.

19 Josep M. Colomer, *Assemblea de Catalunya*. Barcelona: Edicions L'Avenc, 1976.

Mariano Rajoy, July 31, 2006.

Javier Pérez Royo, *La reforma constitucional inviable*. Madrid: Libros de la Catarata, 2015.

Oriol Junqueras, September 25, 2015.

Jordi Pujol, September 4, 1991.

Josep M. Colomer, "The Venturous Bid for the Independence of Catalonia," *Nationalities Papers. The Journal of Nationalism and Ethnicity*, 45, 5, 2017: 950–67.

20 Jaume Vicens-Vives, *Noticia de Catalunya*. Barcelona: Destino (1954), 2nd ed., 1960, pp. 212–26.

Amadeu Hurtado, *Quaranta anys d'advocat. Història del meu temps, 1931–1936*. Barcelona: Ariel, 1967, p. 290.

Francesc Cambó, 13 de diciembre de 1934, cit. en Jesús Pabón, *Cambo 1876–1947*, Barcelona: Alpha, 1952–68, vol. 3, p. 10.

Lluís Companys, *La Humanitat*, March 3, 1936.

Ads for Jordi Pujol in *Avui*, May 29 and 31, 1984.

Carles Puigdemont, *La Vanguardia*, April 20, 2017.

Andreu Mas-Colell, Reception at Restaurant Nora, Washington, DC, USA, April 17, 2013, and *Ara*, August 6, 2017.

Anna Gabriel, October 10, 2017.

The Basque Pendulum

21 Javier Corcuera Atienza, *The Origins, Ideology, and Organization of Basque Nationalism, 1876–1903*. Reno: University of Nevada Press, 2006, p. 372.

Santiago de Pablo, Ludger Mees and José Antonio Rodríguez Ranz, *El péndulo patriótico. Historia del Partido Nacionalista Vasco. I: 1895–1936. II: 1936–1979*. Barcelona: Critica, 1999, 2001. Quote from vol. II, p. 381.

22 Gregorio Monreal Zia and Roldán Jimeno Aranguren, "El Concierto Económico: Génesis y evolución histórica," *Iura Vasconiae*, 6, 2009: 681.

José Luis de la Granja Sainz, *El oasis vasco: El nacimiento de Euskadi en la República y la Guerra Civil.* Madrid: Tecnos, 2007, chapter 13.

Ludger Mees, *Nationalism, Violence and Democracy: The Basque Clash of Identities.* London: Palgrave Macmillan, 2003, p. 20.

See also:

Coro Rubio Pobes, *Revolución y tradición. El País Vasco ante la Revolución liberal y la construcción del Estado español, 1808–1868.* Madrid: Siglo XXI, 1996.

23 On ETA:

Luigi Bruni, ETA. *Historia política de una lucha armada.* Tafalla: Txalaparta, 1987.

Francisco Letamendia, *Historia del nacionalismo vasco y de ETA.* San Sebastián: R&B, 1994.

Antonio Elorza, ed., *La historia de ETA.* Madrid: Temas de Hoy, 2000.

Ignacio Sánchez-Cuenca, *ETA contra el Estado.* Barcelona: Tusquets, 2001.

Francisco J. Llera, "Medio siglo de terrorismo y limpieza étnica en Euskadi," *Sistema*, 231, 2013: 3–46.

Diego Muro, ed., *ETA's Terrorist Campaign. From Violence to Politics.* New York: Routledge, 2017.

24 On the several forms of fiscal federalism:

Akhtar Majeed, Ronald L. Watts and Douglas M Brown, eds., *Distribution of Powers and Responsibilities in Federal Countries.* Montreal and Kingston: McGill-Queen's University Press, 2006.

Gregorio Monreal and Roldán Jimeno, "El Concierto Económico: Génesis y evolución histórica,'" *Iura Vasconiae*, 6, 2009: 686, 701.

Javier Corcuera, "Consecuencias y límites de la constitucionalización de los derechos históricos de los territorios forales," *Revista Española de Derecho Constitucional*, 23, 69, 2003: 264.

Michael Keating and Zoe Bray, "Renegotiating Sovereignty: Basque Nationalism and the Rise and Fall of the Ibarretxe Plan," *Ethnopolitics*, 5, 4, 2006: 361.

Brendan O'Leary and J. McGarry, *The Northern Ireland Conflict: Consociational Engagements.* Oxford: Oxford University Press, 2004.

Anwen Elias and Ludger Mees, "Between Accommodation and Secession: Explaining the Shifting Territorial Goals of Nationalist Parties in the Basque Country and Catalonia," *Revista d'Estudis Autonòmics i Federals*, 25, 2017: 146.

25 Ministerio de Hacienda y Función Pública, *Informe sobre la dimensión territorial de la actuación de las Administraciones Publicas. Ejercicio 2014.* Madrid, 2017, p. 13.

"Conceder un 'cupo catalán' costaría 16.000 millones más al año," *Expansión*, September 29, 2017.

A Blocked Constitution

26 On constitutional reforms:

Zachary Elkins, Tom Ginsburg and James Melton, *The Endurance of National Constitutions.* Cambridge: Cambridge University Press, 2009.

Adam Brown, "Toward a Better Understanding of Constitutional Amendment Rates," Unpublished Manuscript, 2019.

INDEX